VENEZUELA, THE PRESENT AS STRUGGLE

VENEZUELA
THE PRESENT AS STRUGGLE

Voices from the Bolivarian Revolution

CIRA PASCUAL MARQUINA AND CHRIS GILBERT

MR

MONTHLY REVIEW PRESS

New York

Copyright © 2020 by Cira Pascual Marquina and Chris Gilbert
All Rights Reserved

Library of Congress Cataloging-in-Publication Data
available from the publisher

ISBN paper: 978-1-58367-864-0
ISBN cloth: 978-1-58367-865-7

Typeset in Minion Pro and Gin

MONTHLY REVIEW PRESS, NEW YORK
monthlyreview.org

5 4 3 2 1

Contents

Preface | 9
Introduction | 13

1 COMMUNES AND THE REORGANIZATION OF SOCIETY | 29
- The Commune Is the Supreme Expression of Participatory Democracy: A Conversation with Anacaona Marín | 31
- The Commune and 21st Century Socialism: A Conversation with Robert Longa | 39
- Grapes of Wrath in Rural Venezuela: A Conversation with Angel Prado | 48
- Building Socialism from Below: A Conversation with Martha Lía Grajales | 56
- Rebuilding the Hegemony of Chavismo: A Conversation with Gerardo Rojas | 64
- The Urban Revolution: A Conversation with Hernan Vargas | 77
- Notes | 89

2 OIL, PRIVATIZATIONS, AND THE ECONOMY | 91
- The Past, Present, and Future of Venezuela's Oil Industry: A Conversation with Carlos Mendoza Pottellá | 93
- Social Inclusion Is Needed to Overcome the Crisis: A Conversation with Luis Salas | 100
- Privatizing Oil in Venezuela? A Conversation with Victor Hugo Majano | 108
- How to Get Venezuela's Economy Going Again: A Conversation with Luis Enrique Gavazut | 116
- The Orinoco Mining Arc's Impact: A Conversation with Emiliano Teran Mantovani | 125

- Heterodox and Orthodox Economics in Venezuela:
  A Conversation with Luis Salas | 135
- Notes | 148

3 CHÁVEZ, POLITICS, AND *NUESTRA AMÉRICA* | 149
- Chávez and the Continent of Politics: A Conversation with
  Chris Gilbert | 151
- Chávez, a Mirror of the People: A Conversation with
  Edgar Pérez | 158
- What's Been Learned Won't Be Easily Forgotten:
  A Conversation with Antonio González Plessman | 168
- Venezuela and Its Singularities: A Conversation with
  Reinaldo Iturriza | 177
- Chávez and the Twilight of Capitalism: A Conversation
  with Eduardo Rothe | 182
- Defending Chávez's Project Today: A Conversation with
  Elias Jaua | 188
- Everyday Life in Besieged Venezuela: A Conversation with
  Jessica Dos Santos | 197
- Notes | 201

4 CAMPESINO AND WORKING-CLASS STRUGGLES | 203
- Venezuela's *Campesino* Struggle: A Conversation with
  Kevin Rangel | 205
- Reconnecting Agriculture to Our Cultural Base:
  A Conversation with Ana Felicien | 214
- Struggling Against the "Revolutionary Bourgeoisie" in
  Rural Venezuela: A Conversation with Gerardo Sieveres and
  Arbonio Ortega | 222
- Building "Patria": A Conversation with Sergio Requena | 231
- *Campesinos* Defending Chávez's Project: A Conversation
  with Andrés Alayo | 238
- The Role of the Working Class in Venezuela's Crisis:
  A Conversation with Pedro Eusse | 249
- Notes | 255

5 IMPERIALISM, FASCISM, AND THE DEFENSE OF
   BOLIVARIAN VENEZUELA | 257
   - Venezuela's Missile Crisis: A Conversation with
     Juan Contreras | 259
   - Either Washington or Venezuela, Savage Capitalism or
     Socialism: A Conversation with Luis Britto García | 266
   - Venezuela's Constituent Assembly and the Rise of Fascism:
     A Conversation with Julio Escalona | 270
   - Venezuela in the Continental Labyrinth: A Conversation
     with Amílcar Figueroa | 279
   - The Worldwide Struggle Against Fascism and
     the Role of Marxism in the Struggle: A Conversation with
     Néstor Kohan | 285
   - Economic Downturns and State Violence: A Conversation
     with Andrés Antillano | 297
   - Solidarity Isn't a Slogan, It's a Process A Conversation with
     Vijay Prashad | 306
   - Notes | 314

6 FEMINISM, GENDER, AND RACE | 315
   - Women and the Crisis in Venezuela: A Conversation with
     Gioconda Mota | 317
   - If Socialism Isn't Feminist, It Won't Be Emancipatory:
     A Conversation with Indhira Libertad Rodríguez | 327
   - A Crisis of Social Reproduction in Venezuela:
     A Conversation with Alba Carosio | 335
   - Afro-Venezuelan Culture and Resistance: A Conversation
     with Inés Pérez-Wilke | 342
   - Notes | 351

Index | 352

Preface

Since its early days, the Bolivarian Process opened itself to the voices ("*dar la palabra*") of poor Venezuelans, the men and women of the *barrios* and the *campo* who would, in turn, become the subjects of the revolution. With Hugo Chávez, they began a creative process aimed at the reorganization of Venezuelan society.

In 1999, public squares—from agrarian Guasdualito to cosmopolitan Caracas, from commercial Maracaibo to gold mining Callao—became spaces to gather, debate, and build collective proposals for the new constitution.

In April 2002, the men and women of 23 de Enero and El Valle barrios let themselves be heard, by the tens of thousands, and their voices turned the tables on the coup against Chávez.

In 2007, the streets of Caracas were peppered with popular assemblies to build the new socialist party, later known as the Partido Socialista Unido de Venezuela (United Socialist Party of Venezuela). The debates were rich and critical of the existing state of affairs, while committed to the construction of socialism.

In 2009 and, again, in 2010, from the cold Andean town of Mucuchies to the oil refining city of Puerto Cabello and the steel mill city of Puerto Ordaz, Venezuelans gathered to build communal councils and communes. Direct democracy, as well as a sincere and open debate among equals, characterized the first steps toward the economic and political *reorganization* of society.

Today, twenty years after the beginning of the Bolivarian Process, the voices of the men and women who live, work, and struggle in Venezuela are rarely heard. Instead, they have become objects of contemplation, often portrayed as passive subjects from both the left and the right.

Venezuela, the Present as Struggle: Voices from the Bolivarian Revolution, gathers more than thirty interviews with *campesino* leaders, communards, *barrio* organizers, feminists, internationalists, and committed intellectuals produced over a one-year period. The interviews were originally developed for the independent news and analysis website Venezuelanalysis. From the initial pool of interviews, we selected the less conjunctural ones, the ones that are most useful to understand our Venezuelan reality, and we organized them thematically into six sections.

The first section, "Communes and the Reorganization of Society," brings together the reflections of the men and women who, with their daily work, are struggling to make Chávez's dream of building a communal society come true.

The second section, "Oil, Privatizations, and the Economy," brings together interviews that examine the complex multiple crises that Venezuela, a highly dependent, historically rentier economy, is facing. While acknowledging the impact of the criminal U.S. sanctions on our economy, these voices focus on the Venezuelan government's policies, both good and bad, and their impact on the society.

The third section, "Chávez, Politics, and *Nuestra América*," focuses on the political (and social) reorganization process that opens with Hugo Chávez's election as president in 1998, along with its continental impact.

The fourth section, "*Campesino* and Working-Class Struggles," brings class struggle to the forefront. The *campo* is, probably, the hottest space in the current battle against the full restoration of capitalism in the Venezuelan territory.

The fifth section, "Imperialism, Fascism, and the Defense of Bolivarian Venezuela," examines imperialist tactics and the emergence of fascist tendencies in Venezuela, while it brings about reflections on solidarity and working-class internationalism.

Finally, the sixth section, "Feminism, Gender, and Race," gathers the voices of feminists and antiracist activists. Their analysis opens yet another window into the pending tasks of the Bolivarian Revolution, which lags behind on issues such as abortion, still penalized in Venezuela.

Making *Venezuela, the Present as Struggle* possible has been a collective endeavor, since it is a patchwork that brings dozens of voices together. To the men and women who reflected with us about the Bolivarian Revolution, about the beautiful yet contradictory process of building a communal future, thank you.

We also wish to extend our thanks to Venezuelanalysis. The editorial team, and particularly Lucas Koerner, was immediately supportive of this project, which aims to amplify the voices of the men and women who—as organizers, communards, or committed intellectuals—have worked, day after day, toward the common Chavista goal of building a just, post-capitalist society.

Last but not least, we want to thank the comrades from Monthly Review Press including Martin Paddio, Intan Suwandi, and Michael Yates, for making it possible to bring these interviews together into one volume, and for their care with the edition. To them, and to everyone who has helped us to make the voices of revolutionary Venezuelans heard, we extend our gratitude.

—CIRA PASCUAL MARQUINA AND CHRIS GILBERT

INTRODUCTION

Venezuela's Revolutionary Process from the Inside

If a capitalist society tends to displace people as subjects, making capital into the real subject that determines the society's development in its broadest strokes, then it is hardly surprising that a revolutionary process in which people begin to actively transform social reality, taking charge of its direction, defies all kinds of epistemological parameters and norms, including those of historiography, to say nothing of journalism and much of what passes for social analysis.

Precisely for this reason, the enemies of a revolutionary process are not just the evidently right-wing or pro-imperialist ones. Even forces allegedly sympathetic to a revolution can do the work of undermining its bases, by framing the revolution as a *mere thing* and denying the condition of active subjects to a revolutionary people. In a widely-accepted view—one that can be seen operating now in Venezuela—a revolution becomes an abstract entelechy that is only secondarily and in a limited way something that people *do*. Or, if it is accepted that people and their actions were the *initial* motors of transformation, then at some point the revolution must shed its spontaneity to become a static idea, symbol, or slogan.

All of this should be resisted. Maintaining the centrality of human agency in a revolution may be crucial throughout its whole course, but it becomes absolutely essential when such a process of transformation enters into crisis. For if a revolution is a mere thing, or a relatively automatic occurrence that is out of the hands of the people, then how can it respond intelligently to the challenges faced in the course of its development? By contrast, if a revolution is a process in which the masses are active subjects, then correcting and finding a way forward will be the task of the very praxis-oriented agents that initiated the revolution in the first place.

That, in short, is the thesis that drives this book of interviews. The solution to Venezuela's crisis today, the revolutionary path forward, is to be found nowhere else but in the thinking and acting participants in the Bolivarian Process. Based on that hypothesis—call it the wager for the revolution as a collective praxis—the book interrogates a range of subjects actively engaged in the process. What is going on in Venezuela? What is the way forward for the Bolivarian revolution? What is most fascinating is that not only are there rich and well-thought-out answers to these questions among the interviews presented here, but there is also an enormous degree of *coincidence* in the responses given. Perhaps, we could go so far as to say that there is a *revolutionary solution to the crisis* that is collectively sketched in these pages.

An Unfortunate Convergence

Despite the diversity of their prescriptions, all mainstream positions on Venezuela systematically deny that the masses are capable of purposeful world-changing activity. That is to say, both the counterrevolution operating inside the country and the reformist pragmatism in power—insofar as they both tacitly accept the actually-existing capitalist order of things—tend to sideline the capacity of ordinary human beings to conceive and carry out self-proposed goals of importance. These political tendencies cleave to the idea of necessity, which makes the rupture with a supposedly necessary world order and the conditioned exercise of freedom that characterized the Bolivarian Process in its early years their greatest embarrassment.

Introduction

Reified forms of understanding encounter necessity under every stone. In the crisis that Venezuela faces today, the right wing contends that there is no alternative to capitalism. This is hardly surprising; it coincides with their historical mission and has been the ideological line of neoliberal capitalism since Margaret Thatcher launched the "There Is No Alternative" slogan almost forty years ago. But perhaps less obvious is that reformism and opportunism, which now dominate the government and state institutions, imposing a purely pragmatic approach to most challenges, tacitly agree and so hurry to cover up the radical measures that Hugo Chávez once promoted with a view to overcoming the actually-existing state of affairs in an emancipatory way: the commune, participatory democracy, and socialism.

Thus, from every sector, the main pillars of the current world order are affirmed—together with the path that led us there. The solution to Venezuela's problems, the government and the ministries insist today, consists of securing (capitalist) allies, private investment, increased production, and even privatization and negotiating with imperialism. Likewise, when looking back and reviewing the trajectory of the Bolivarian revolution, government spokespeople deny the existence of roads not taken; hence they also deny the possibility of alternative presents and alternative futures. In this sad but telling coincidence between the perspectives of external enemies and internally tepid sectors, the overall capitalist framework is seen as an inevitable destiny. Only the way of getting there is in dispute: shock treatment versus controlled soft-landing.

Without a doubt, both the counterrevolution and reformist pragmatism in Venezuela do not only aspire but in a large measure have succeeded in closing the window on the radically alternative future that opened up under Chávez in the early part of the century. Most especially, they are eager to cover up the sequence of reflections that led an insurgent Chávez and a revolutionary people to recognize that national liberation for Venezuela meant overcoming capitalism and constructing socialism. Evidence of the ideological capitulation that has taken place in recent years is that so many defenders of the process assert that the key issue at stake in the struggle with imperialism is simply the oil resource.[1] In their view, that is what imperialism wants to appropriate and the government defends—not the far more crucial revolutionary *socialist example* that once inspired the world!

By the same token, both sides in the confrontation implicitly agree that the key and original ideals of the revolutionary process, such as substantive democracy, popular protagonism, and new social productive relations (not just quantitatively more production), were all little more than chimeras. If the right wing disparagingly calls this original project of Chavismo "populism" (a lie told a thousand times becomes a truth!), then an overly pragmatic government for its part is eager to clear its record by downplaying the most "popular" parts of Chávez and the Bolivarian revolution's legacy.

Tertium Datur: The Commune

A horizon appears to have been closed, leaving two bleak options on the table: imperialist restoration or bureaucratic stagnation, both united in their acceptance of the capitalist world order. But is there another road forward? Does the range of possibilities exclude everything but choosing between the quick versus the slow suffocation of the socialist revolution? The interviews collected here speak clearly in this sense. What the book demonstrates, through the diverse voices it brings together, is that the socialist and radically transformative project of Chavismo—however much it is an embarrassment to constituted power in Venezuela and to the global establishment—lives on in the masses, in their thought and action.

Those interviewed here all concur that the most important thing about Chávez was his *project*: in essence a proposal that developed through time, in a dialogic relation with both Venezuelan reality and the history of really-existing socialism, to materialize itself in the project of *a communal path toward socialism*. Chávez expressed this far-from-improvised hypothesis most vividly in his *Golpe de Timón* discourse, which is often considered to be his last testament, with its "Commune or Nothing" slogan. However, the main ideas date back to at least 2009 when the commune entered into his discourse as a possible building block for socialism. What is more, the commune, when it emerged in the program of Chavismo, had an organic relationship with earlier experiments in the revolutionary process, such as cooperatives and communal councils, and also with the commitment to substantive democracy that goes back as far as Chávez's *Blue Book* of 1994.

Chávez had long been engaged with Hungarian Marxist István Mészáros's critical approach to post-capitalist regimes, and he realized by the second decade of the century that the commune, as a productive and political building block, provided a means to implement a democratic control of the production process. In effect, the commune could dismantle what Mészáros identified as the hierarchical logic of capital. Today in Venezuela the commune is rarely discussed in spheres of power, and most functionaries tacitly accept that "socialism has failed." However, the interviews collected here engage with a range of communards—from those in the rural El Maizal commune in Simón Planas township to those in the urban El Panal commune in Caracas—and they attest to how the project of the commune, which also connects with local pre-capitalist cultural patterns, survives in Venezuela as a collectively endorsed counterpoint to the pro-capitalist tendencies dominating the government.

A Crisis of a New Kind

The whole two-decade-long history of the Bolivarian Revolution is undoubtedly marked by turmoil. Yet the focus of this book is a particularly crisis-ridden moment in that always turbulent history. In the wake of the opposition's violent street actions of 2017, which involved barricades and lynchings, and the government's calling of the National Constituent Assembly, there emerged a new scenario in Venezuela. It could be described as a deadlock between opposing tendencies in which, if Nicolás Maduro's government enjoyed relative stability, then there were also increasingly aggressive U.S. sanctions, economic warfare, hyperinflation, and a bald but unsuccessful coup attempt led by Juan Guaidó in the spring of 2019.

Many episodes in this conflict, especially the more sensational, have been picked up by the world's news agencies. Yet the interviewer, Cira Pascual Marquina, a professor at the Universidad Bolivariana de Venezuela, decided in early 2018 to go beyond the mainstream news narrative—the economic statistics, body counts, and sound bites—on the assumption that Venezuelans from different walks of life were thinking and acting subjects, who would be meaningfully engaged with these developments and not as mere spectators.

The need for this kind of on-the-ground approach responds to a specific lack of information. Many people in the world are familiar with the main features of the imperialist attacks on Venezuela's sovereignty, such as the unilateral U.S. sanctions, the emptying of supermarket shelves, the invasion attempts, the sabotage of the electric system—to say nothing of the political tug of war between an always more desperate opposition and a government that showed how it was capable of defending itself during this time. However, they are not so familiar with what people did and thought in the face of these attacks and challenges.

The gaps in our knowledge about Venezuelan grassroots reality are not just a result of media biases. In fact, the widespread ignorance that this book works to correct has its roots in a recently-opened breech between the Chavista government and the Chavista bases, a failure to connect and communicate with the masses that actually defines in a great measure the period in question. It is defining because, if these years and even the whole past half-decade of Venezuela post-Chávez have been remarkable for the nation's successful defense against U.S. imperialism and the aggressions of the endogenous opposition, the period is also remarkable for what it is not. It has not involved any attempts to rally the masses, nor a radicalization of the revolution as a popular undertaking.

The Leadership-Masses Dialectic

To be sure, this breech had already begun to emerge even when Chávez was alive, if principally at the end of his political career. Contrary to popular opinion, Chávez was, for most of his trajectory, the very antithesis of the strongman figure that dominates politics today. His distinctive features as a revolutionary leader were his capacity for invention and a profound correctability within the dialogic relationship he maintained with the masses. Both Chávez's discourse and his actions belie the notion of an infallible leadership, and even during the revolution's most glorious and radical moments he made grave errors. Among the most memorable were the "third way" that he verbally espoused when taking power in 1998; his unfortunate failure to advance following the defeat of the 2002 coup attempt; and his excessive focus on the mass media in the period 2006 to 2007. Yet during most of this time, a rich exchange was taking place between the masses and Chávez, meaning that the masses *were generally there to correct him and to ensure that the revolution maintained its emancipatory horizon.*

It was only late in his career that Chávez began to err in a new context where the masses—now demobilized and converted into bystanders—were not there to correct him. For example, in 2008 Chávez became involved in highly visible initiatives that had little interest to the movement's bases, like pressuring the Revolutionary Armed Forces of Colombia's (FARC) guerrillas to make peace, or developing projects that did not have a revolutionary, self-emancipating dimension, such as Gran Misión Vivienda Venezuela—the huge housing project that drained the state's resources but has not contributed to organizing or empowering the people.

This disconnect with the masses deepened under Maduro, conditioning the whole post-2012 period. It provides the key to the current scenario, which is therefore a political crisis of a new kind. After Maduro's government lost the parliamentary elections of December 2015 (when the opposition won a powerful majority in the National Assembly), it neither turned to its own popular bases in an effort to overcome the breech that had expressed itself in this electoral result nor appealed to them for solutions. Instead, the party leadership made the extraordinary decision to *blame the masses* for the defeat (in the same way that it would go on to blame them for security and food supply problems).[2]

The current disconnect between the masses and the government, in effect, the breach between popular Chavismo and the institutional variant, may not be eternal or irreparable, but international opinion has consistently failed to take this dynamic into account. For the majority of the global Left, Maduro's government simply *is* Chavismo and the masses *do not exist politically*. This expresses itself in an ignorance of the masses' self-organized initiatives, their intellectual production, and their efforts to correct the direction of the Bolivarian Process.

All three lacunae are taken up in the pages of this book. For this reason, *Venezuela, the Present as Struggle* opposes not only the rightwing and imperialism, but the book is also critical of a global Left that has failed to adopt a class-conscious internationalism. This is the Left that has turned its back not only on the Venezuelan masses today, but also on the Greek rebellion some years ago and the more recent *gilets jaunes* movement in France. If most of the Left today fails to engage with people on a grassroots level across borders, by contrast, the approach of Cira Pascual Marquina is radically different. It is unambiguously hands-on. In this sense, it is worth remembering that "Hands off Venezuela" may be a good slogan to the degree that it affirms sovereignty and constitutes a war cry against imperialist interference, but it is a poor slogan if it leads one to ignore the internal contradictions of a political process and the aspirations of the masses!

Popular Chavismo

As with any important movement, Chavismo cannot be reduced to state politics, and even less to geopolitics or moves on the global "chessboard." Any serious account of the Chavista movement must consider the internal dynamics of the revolutionary bloc and especially the program of the bases. For that reason, the window on popular Chavismo provided by this book is invaluable. It probes deeper than the apparently monolithic Chavismo that figures in most perspectives, so we can look at a movement that remains multicolor, radically emancipatory, and most importantly, far from accommodating itself to either imperialist restoration or gradual bureaucratic retreat from socialism. It is a movement that seeks to respond to the current political crisis by pushing forward with more, rather than less, socialism. This is the Chavismo that aims to recover not so much the ingenious statesman that spectacularly confronted the Western powers, and even less the merely iconic Chávez, but rather the *popular and socialist* Chávez who embodies an incomplete project: the communal path to socialism.

The voices represented here come from diverse contexts. If there are figures from high governmental spheres such as former vice president Elías Jaua and one-time ministers such as Luis Salas and Reinaldo Iturriza, it is people from the grassroots movement that predominate. Many of those interviewed are leaders and cadres who have worked directly in the communes, including Robert Longa, Anacaona Marín, and Angel Prado. Others speak for the popular project from the standpoint of minority populations or the anti-patriarchal struggle. Further, there are intellectuals who have long accompanied the popular movement such as Andrés Antillano, Juan Contreras, Martha Lía Grajales, and Antonio González Plessman.

Despite the emphasis on the grassroots, even the most critically-minded interviewees here are not simply opposed to the state. Importantly, there is a shared understanding that popular power and the state, and by the same token communal production and the national economy, should work together. The original vision of Chavismo depended on this kind of two-pronged approach. It was a correction of Zapatismo's renunciation of state politics and sought to maintain a dialectic between popular power and the state apparatus. As González Plessman points out in these pages, popular power should not forfeit state support, and it is implicit in the interviews with Salas and Gavazut that the popular movement must be capable of developing a plan, not just on a local level, but also for promoting and controlling the vast oil resources that have figured so centrally in Venezuela's economy over the last one hundred years.

Likewise important, and differing from the globally disseminated view, is that the picture of Chavismo presented here is not as a movement made up principally of *victims* but of *agents*. The dominant discourse focuses on economic war, embargo, blockades, U.S. sanctions, fascist attacks, and imperialist coup attempts. This focus is understandable; the problem enters when the Venezuelan people are reduced to the role of passive sufferers and witnesses, while anti-imperialist politics is understood as simply asking, or at best pressuring, imperialism to stop being imperialist (as happened in social media campaigns such as *No More Trump!* and *Trump Unblock Venezuela!*). On the contrary, in these interviews the people are treated as full-blown actors and thinkers who propose solutions both on the level of discourse and concrete reality. They are people who have taken up the intellectual project of defending socialism and, at the same time, are actively committed to growing and sharing food, building communes, and organizing collectives that promote gender and racial equality.

Ongoing Class Struggle

These days it is common to acknowledge that a revolution is not a single, sudden event that might fall on this or that day of the week. Revolutions are instead *processes of rupture* that are never limited to a dramatic event such as the storming of the Bastille or the Winter Palace (though such events are often necessary parts of a revolution). Yet this kind of acknowledgment, when we encounter it among public intellectuals today, is usually offered as a mere throwaway: an apology for the vicissitudes and slowness of a revolutionary process. Almost never does the analyst take the next step and draw the necessary conclusion: that one should pay attention to and even attempt to intervene in the struggles that take place in the course of a revolution.

Tellingly, attempts to address the internal dynamics and class forces at play in the course of a revolutionary process—of the kind these interviews undertake—are few and far between. Notable exceptions are the works of Charles Bettelheim on class struggle in the USSR and Fernando Martínez Heredia on revolutionary Cuba in the 1960s, as well as the attempt of Georg Lukács and others to postulate a third (authentically socialist) way between stagnation in state socialism and restoration in the last period of actually-existing socialism. All reject the idea, dear to bureaucracies, that a revolution is separable from a struggle taking place in the present.[3] There is a philosophical position implicit here. To acknowledge that the present is traversed by struggles of an uncertain outcome is also to reject the security of a superior, god's-eye view on reality—a standpoint that, according to philosopher Marina Garcés, smooths the way for intellectuals to collude with power.[4]

In sharp contrast to the dominant idealist perspective, which turns its back on social practice, this book adopts the only meaningfully materialist approach to revolutionary analysis. That approach is based on the principle, expressed by Karl Marx and Frederick Engels as early as in the *German Ideology*, that communism is not something in our heads, in a book, or in a declaration but is rather the "*real movement that abolishes the present state of things.*" Likewise, as a materialist analysis focusing on a real movement and its complex dynamic, the book adheres to the principle expressed in Marx's eleventh thesis on Feuerbach: the task is to not merely contemplate reality but to transform it.

For the investigator who commits to this kind of project, a new world opens up! What one loses in idealism's false sense of security—whether expressed in Panglossian phrases such as "All revolutions are complicated processes" or in a progressist faith that we live in some guaranteed "change of epoch"—one recovers in the awareness of the revolution as an adventure. It is an essentially open-ended undertaking that, if always beset by the slings and arrows of outrageous fortune, for that very reason is open to the advent of the new. That sense of adventure and the uncertainty of a process still unfolding in time permeate these interviews. They speak for a present that is still pregnant with possibilities, which connects with Chavismo's original ambition of pursuing an alternative to the present state of things. For that reason, the discourse operates in a field with both greater dangers and greater opportunities than the one conceived by today's resigned advocates of conciliation and defeatist pragmatism.

The radical options set in motion during the first decade of the Latin American Pink Tide, which promised to blow the doors open on the present, not just in Venezuela but in the whole continent, come to life once again in the diverse voices of those who speak here. They demonstrate a confidence that the lifeblood of a revolution is a form of collective praxis that is always of uncertain issue, which contrasts sharply with the stability, or at least predictability, typically sought by the government.

Uncertain Outcomes

Mao Zedong famously admonished that a revolution is not a "dinner party" and is not "temperate" or "kind." Generalizations aside, it is a straightforwardly observable fact that the progressist viewpoint and the calm steady steps it envisions have nothing to do with the exceptional conditions, or even states of emergency, that have characterized the Bolivarian Revolution from its beginning. Is this tumultuousness to be regretted? The sanguine attitude of the interviewees here permits one to see how instability is simply part of a process of transformation. Moreover, it is by facing the perils—as Pascual Marquina does microphone in hand—rather than by wishing them away, that one can find the way forward, and perhaps thereby achieve that dialectical turn that for Walter Benjamin is synonymous with revolution: "the real state of exception."

The process of maintaining a revolution alive involves constant engagement with both the concrete reality of the present and the meanings of the past, interpreting both actively. This extends to Chávez's legacy. It should be faced with an agile thought attune to the shifting sands of the revolutionary present, that accepts the sudden relevance of ideas and events from the past, and seeks the possibility of leaps in the historical continuum. This may seem to be a hard bill to fill, but discursive practices of this kind are nevertheless part of ordinary people's way of thinking in a revolutionary context. The interview format captures this perfectly, and the exchange of words and thoughts in these pages testifies to the presence of a diffuse revolutionary power, a latent and possibly *emergent* force within the ongoing Venezuelan emergency.

Introduction

Consider, in this regard, the revolutionary awareness of the dialectic expressed by Anacaona Marín from the Alexis Vive Collective (El Panal Commune): "We know that tensions and contradictions remain, and we welcome them, since we do not seek a static situation. Rather we seek change, and change only happens with contradictions." Likewise, Martha Lía Grajales, who works with the Pueblo a Pueblo food distribution initiative, acknowledges the need for a battle of ideas inside the process, while she joins in a struggle to keep the movement's emancipatory dimension: "It is not merely a struggle to maintain power but also a struggle to maintain socialism as the strategic goal."

The struggle over historical meanings is taken up by Antonio González Plessman who rejects what he calls "adopting a nostalgic attitude to the past" in favor of *using* the experience of Chavismo to interpret the current situation and find a way forward. Finally, Sergio Requena of the Productive Workers Army shows how actively interpreting the recent past can fuel the popular movement: "Only the people can solve the problems of Venezuela, and from our point of view, this must be done with Chávez and with a commitment to participative and protagonistic democracy."

Projecting an Alternative

Undoubtedly the Bolivarian Revolution has entered into a new level of crisis, characterized as much by the danger of bureaucratic involution as that of succumbing to outside attack. The crisis is also an ideological one and has had a tremendous impact on collective morale. In fact, the dilemma between stagnation and imperialist capitulation can sometimes loom so large as to apparently exclude any third option. Yet this is only the case to the degree that one accepts the reified view of reality and forgets the game-changing capacity of human praxis and socially-constructed alternatives.

There is an important theoretical issue to be considered here, one thematized in Lukács's late work. The vulgar materialism that is still hegemonic in the Left often "hypercorrects" idealism by eliminating teleology, not just from superhuman abstractions like nature and history, but even from social practice itself. The possibility of choosing an alternative in pursuing a goal is nevertheless basic to the labor process (as when a "primitive" man or woman chooses a tool among a heap of stones, in Lukács's favorite example).[5] Revolutions are the most advanced expression of this kind of goal-oriented activity. Even if a social revolution is always conditioned by material reality and historical development, it is essentially a matter of posited goals and the means of getting there, which belies social and natural fatality.

Maintaining a goal-oriented revolutionary project is an ongoing effort. It requires adaptation and actualization in light of present conditions. This is as much to say that what Chávez did in the first decade of the century, which was to project a radically alternative society, should be repeated in the present, under new conditions. If the initial gesture of the Bolivarian Revolution was to reach back to Simón Bolívar's independence struggle, and reactivate it two hundred years later in the name of a new and complete independence that is socialism, something similar should be done today. In our time, it would mean reactivating *the most advanced part of Chávez's own legacy* in the name of socialism. That social project, of course, was never the work of Chávez alone but rather the work of Chávez-and-the-people together.

This book shows that, in one way or another, people from different sectors of Venezuelan society have sought to do just that in the difficult years since Chávez's death. Coming from diverse parts of society and using their own language, grassroots revolutionaries in Venezuela today coincide in the need to recover Chávez's socialist project and reactivate it in the present. They may be engaged in very different concrete struggles, but they all believe that it is in Chávez's legacy—conceived in the broad sense of a collective construction—that we can find the instruments and examples that could allow the revolution to correct its course. If, in general, this means restoring the revolution's praxis-driven and self-emancipatory character, in concrete and specific cases it can mean building the commune, organizing a food distribution network, or struggling for substantive feminism.

In the midst of difficulties of all kinds, the most conscious sectors of the Venezuelan people have worked, in a heroic and usually unacknowledged way, to correct a revolution that has slowly, even imperceptibly, become stagnated. If they have often tried to show the way forward through their examples, they have also not failed, along the way (as the following investigation shows), to articulate a vision of an alternative Venezuela, one with participative democracy, democratically-controlled production, new social relations, and gender emancipation.

Will this new way forward win out? Will it be able to influence, infiltrate, or replace the existing stagnated structures of power, causing the revolution to correct its course? It is customary to say, when reflecting on an ongoing historical process: *Only the future will tell.* But what we should really say is: *Only the struggle will decide!*

There is one positive development that weighs in the current global context. In today's world, in contrast to the 1990s "end-of-history" scenario in which Chavismo got started, there is now an emergent anti-capitalist movement in the Global North. In the imagination of people throughout the United States and Europe and even in the countries of the former Eastern bloc, there is today a searching, if sometimes visceral, rejection of the capitalist world order. The same aspiration, tempered by experience, comes from the pages of this book. Venezuela does not have to give in to the liberal economic world order, either by means of a slow restorative process driven internally or through an externally-imposed shock treatment. Nor does it have to maintain Chávez as a merely revered historical figure who is trapped in the past (which, of course, goes very well with a process of capitalist restoration). There is an alternative: which is to recover the socialist, communal, and emancipatory project that the people and Chávez conceived and fought for in the heyday of the Bolivarian Revolution. Let this book be a contribution to that effort.

—Chris Gilbert

Notes

1. It has become almost a ritual to repeat that Venezuela has the world's largest proven oil reserves. This contention should be examined critically not so much for its accuracy, since it is true, though the proven reserves of Saudi Arabia and Kuwait taken together are larger, as for what it implies: that Venezuela's revolutionary example (especially its reviving the project of socialism at a time when the project was virtually cast aside) is of less importance, and that countries like Cuba or Bolivia, which do not possess such extraordinary resources, will not be targets of imperialist aggressions.
2. The process by which the government ended up blaming the people for the electoral defeat of 2015—chalked up to their alleged ignorance and lack of political awareness—is discussed here in the interview with Andrés Antillano. In a similar way, the informal economy (*bachaqueo*) that emerged in popular sectors was blamed for the shortage of food, when in reality this grey economy was more of a consequence than a cause of the shortages.
3. Charles Bettelheim, *Class Struggles in the USSR* (Monthly Review Press, 1976); Fernando Martínez Heredia, *En el horno de los 90* (La Habana: Ciencias Sociales, 2005).
4. Marina Garcés, *Ciudad Princesa* (Barcelona: Galaxia Gutenberg, 2018), 21.
5. Georg Lukács, *Ontology of Social Being*, v.3. *Labour* (London: Merlin Press, 1978), 31.

1
COMMUNES AND THE REORGANIZATION OF SOCIETY

The Commune Is the Supreme Expression of Participatory Democracy: A Conversation with Anacaona Marín

In this interview, we talk with a member of the Alexis Vive Patriotic Force, an organization with deep roots in the 23 de Enero barrio in Caracas, which has worked to build one of Venezuela's flagship urban communes. Alexis Vive began planning for a commune years before Chávez even proposed the communal path toward socialism. Yet when Chávez announced the plan to join communal councils into a higher form of organization, Alexis Vive wholeheartedly embraced the initiative and has since then built a highly successful commune called El Panal that involves some 13,000 people.[1] We spoke with a key cadre of El Panal about this economic and political project to find out how it has coped with the economic crisis aggravated by U.S. aggressions.

The commune is usually thought of a space of construction for the political and economic reorganization of society, but it is also a space of resistance. Let's talk about the commune today, in a period where Venezuela is under attack by imperialism.

There is a confrontation of models, a clash of two paradigms not only in Venezuela and in Latin America, but also worldwide. One of the questions in the debate is: who is the historical subject? For us, that is the question of who is it that activates, who lights up the field, who pushes changes forward. And when we reflect on this issue, which means thinking about our own practice, we guide our interpretation by the proposal that developed with Comandante Chávez.

Hugo Chávez developed a hypothesis after a process of maturing, after a rigorous analysis of the Venezuelan and continental realities, and after a reflection on the revolutionary potential under our feet (based also on a commitment to justice for the poor that was there from the start). His hypothesis was: The commune is the historical subject; the commune and its people, the *comuneros*, that is where the revolution really begins. We made this proposal ours, committing to it.

We were aware that the proposal and our embracing it were going to be attacked from its onset, at its genesis. When Chávez first raised the banner of socialism in 2006, when he said that the Bolivarian Revolution must be socialist, when he said that a vote for him was a vote for socialism, he committed himself and the people to a collective project of rupture. Well, that is where we find the seed of the commune. Self-government and economic emancipation go hand-in-hand with socialism, with the people in power. So there is where we find the initial seeds for the commune: in [Chávez's 2006] proposal to build a socialist "patria."

It became clear to us then that there was going to be a new level of confrontation. We knew that the path towards socialism was going to be demonized, and that contradictions would pop up everywhere, inside and outside. Hence, we can say that the communes had not even been born yet, and we were already in resistance! But the truth is that we have been in resistance for more than five hundred years.

Today, we are not only resisting imperialism. We are also resisting old forms of production and their diverse forms of domination: from the organization of education and affective life to the organization of the formal political sphere and the economy.

Why is there a conflict? We are making a counter-hegemonic proposal to a system that is powerful, a system that seems part and parcel of what the human being is. In the face of this system, the subject stands tall and says: "Hey, this doesn't have to be so, this is not the only option." The communal subject is the one that affirms that capitalism is not a natural occurrence, it is an imposition.

The communes are counter-hegemonic spaces with a vocation for hegemony. From our commune, we aim to show that another organization of society is possible, that power must be reorganized, and that power should be in the hands of the people. That means combining new economic relations with an exercise of power in the commune's territory.

Here we are in the midst of El Panal Commune, which has a range of productive projects: from a bakery and a textile factory to cultivated land and an industrial packaging plant. How is all this organized?

El Panal Commune has some specific characteristics. We, as Alexis Vive, began to think about building a commune in 2006 and shortly after we began working on it. However, the Law of Communes wasn't promulgated until 2009. The law states that communal councils would be the embryo that would foster the formation of a commune. Here, by contrast, the forming of the commune followed its own path.

This commune came out of a practice and a set of symbols that we put on the street. In our case, the Alexis Vive Patriotic Force generated a collective practice and a discourse that pointed the way [with Chávez] towards the commune. This worked quite well: the community here, in the central part of 23 de Enero, picked up the idea and ran with it.

Here, in these territories, the "Panalitos por la Patria" [Beehives for the Homeland], which are small working and discussion groups, are the DNA of the communal body. The Panalitos are formed by people from the community with a high degree of commitment to the commune. They are the engines of the communal initiative.

Additionally, we have brigades, which is a term that Alexis Vive chose after much debate. The debate touched on the subject of the Chiliying Commune [in Hunan, China], which had various structures of participation for the people: councils, brigadists, and producers.[2] The division was based on the commitment to work and struggle. The brigades were made up of a militant group of communards with a life-commitment to the struggle. In our commune, these brigades are made up of professional cadres, and they take on the larger issues of production and distribution in the community. They are also, it almost goes without saying, highly politicized units.

Finally, we have the associated work collectives, which are the communal groups directly involved with producing goods and services. Since the commune is not an appendix of the state or the government, it must be autonomous and it must generate the resources it requires to address the community's needs. The associated work collectives are spaces for direct production, and the surplus from their production goes back to the commune and thus to the community.

All this relates to the commune's process of grassroots planning and administration of resources. Some of our resources go to sustaining a *comedor popular* [people's canteen], some to communications, some to the community's medical expenses, and some to transportation and infrastructure. We also have resources allotted for contingencies. All these resources come from the associated work collectives. After all, the commune is not just a cultural, social, and political organization, it is also an economic organization.

There is another "higher" element to the commune's organization: the patriotic assembly, the space where *comuneros* gather to decide collectively what must be done, and how, through participatory democracy.

Let's come back to the situation today: the imperialist aggression. In the past couple of months, we have witnessed a new form of war with the electrical blackout and the attacks on the electric grid. Tell us about how you have organized resistance in the commune in this context.

We are the daughters and sons of Chávez. We listened to his words and we learned. As a result of that, we understood that when you go up against capital and against imperialism, there is only one option: to prepare. If we are going to tell imperialism that we are no longer its backyard—that we have chosen the path to full independence and on top of that we are transitioning toward socialism—then we must understand that we are going to be in a war with a military superpower.

A new phase of aggression against our country has begun. They try to restrict our access to food and they have implemented a financial blockade and, more recently, an oil embargo. They also attack us culturally. They try to inspire fear in us. Most recently, they attacked our electrical system, which is fundamental for modern life.

We were aware that this was coming, so we prepared for a war economy, through organization and work. We also prepared through research and [by paying attention to] popular creativity. A contingency plan was in place. So when this new phase of the aggression began, we were ready for it with the necessary resources.

Our planning allowed us to build, in the midst of the blackout, a diesel-powered electrical grid for our collective spaces. In fact, the commune acts as a kind of state or government in everyday life, and it does so also when faced with a contingency or aggression. Obviously, that [alternative power supply] made for a less hostile environment during the blackout.

Many people do not know about the spontaneous forms of solidarity that emerged during the blackout. I witnessed beautiful gestures during those days, especially among my neighbors, both Chavistas and opposition. What happened here in 23 de Enero?

It was an all-out exercise of violence against our lives! But when faced with ugly, catastrophic situations, popular kindness, solidarity, and sisterhood blooms! This is not just some discourse: people were brave and noble. We don't believe that the human being is selfish by nature. Humans are formed in society; the human being is part of a whole, of a collective. The genesis of humanity is in the commons, in working together toward shared ends, and those collective instincts flourish when people face a warlike situation.

I can give you an example from our experience. We organize weekly fairs where fruits and vegetables are sold at very low prices through the "Pueblo a Pueblo" initiative [direct coordination with *campesinos*]. During the blackout, we sold on credit [since the electronic payment infrastructure was offline], and the neighbors came through. One by one, they came back and paid their debts when the blackout was over. One can see there that the response from the people was not selfish. People didn't take advantage of the situation, even though they could have. Instead, those days were characterized by collective consciousness.

In describing popular power I often refer to the trilogy of self-government, self-determination, and self-defense. If the commune sometimes functions as a state, as you said, that means communes generate a situation of dual power. This could lead to tensions between the existing state and the commune.

When Chávez promoted the idea of the commune, what he did was very daring. In fact, much of what was advanced in terms of the law was done via the Enabling Act [the National Assembly had given Chávez the power to legislate by presidential decree] since his proposal was sure to rub the establishment the wrong way. By doing so, Chávez broke with the logic of the state.

Álvaro García Linera talks about "creative tensions" that allow for new things to happen. When you pull away from constituted power, it opens a space for the new to bloom, and that flower springs forth from the creative tensions. We welcome contradictions. If we didn't have them, it would mean that we wouldn't have a project. Instead, we would be part and parcel with our society's hegemonic logic, which is capitalist.

On the question of dual power: we don't think of it in terms of a parallel state. . . . Instead, we consider the communes to be the crystallization of a proposal left by President Chávez. He understood that the commune, through self-government and autonomous popular economic activity, would bring about the new state, a communal state. But all that is a process under construction.

As I was saying earlier, we encounter contradictions everywhere. Although some [state] institutions may be somewhat more hostile than others, we can also say that our commune has [in general] benefited from the goodwill of people within the state, people who have cast their lot with the commune. We have received economic and technical support from the state, and that has helped us build popular power.

We know that tensions and contradictions will remain, and we welcome them since we do not seek a static situation. Rather, we seek change, and change only happens when there are contradictions.

Is it fair to say, however, that the commune is not in the forefront of the government's political discourse now?

Absolutely. Look, when Chávez became a public figure, many from the left didn't understand that they had to change course, that the only way forward was with Chávez. Likewise, many within Nicolas Maduro's government maintain the old conception of the state and don't understand that the commune is the goal.

However, that is what the Bolivarian Revolution is: a combination of very diverse currents. Within the revolution there is a latent debate about the commune. Our role is to show that the commune is indeed the historical subject. We show this through our example, and, in doing so, we hope to make a rupture with the old ways and become hegemonic.

Our contribution to this big debate is through our practice, through work. Our constructive criticism can be found in our concrete example. Building a commune brings forth a new culture, a new form of doing politics, and new economic relations. . . . Against the logic of representative democracy, we propose participatory and protagonistic democracy, and the commune is the supreme expression of the latter.

The media discourse tends to criminalize poor *barrio*-dwellers. It has been going on for a long time. Recently, there has been a great deal of focus on "*colectivos*" [a common form of grassroots organization in urban Latin America and Venezuela in particular] to make them seem as if they were merely gangs or paramilitary organizations. Has that affected your projects in the 23 de Enero *barrio*?

Indeed there is nothing new about all that. In the Fourth Republic the "*ñángaras*" or the "*tupamaros*" were the source of all evil.[3] Later the Bolivarian Circles were criminalized. Frankly, every expression of popular organization that isn't submissive has always been criminalized in history. That's because popular organizations are, indeed, a problem for the system. The mass media has always demonized the people when they organize, so it shouldn't surprise us.

Now, in this new phase of the imperialist aggression, we can see that popular action is once again being criminalized. They are in a process of rebranding *colectivos* as terrorist organizations, as the maximum expression of evil. Imagine that, poor Chavistas on the street, *barrio*-dwellers defending their territories! That should be stopped, and the most efficient way is criminalization. Why do they do this? To instill fear in the people, to keep poor people from organizing.

—April 19, 2019

The Commune and 21st Century Socialism: A Conversation with Robert Longa

Robert Longa is a key cadre of the Alexis Vive Patriotic Force, which was born during the fraught months of 2002 in which the right wing attempted to topple Hugo Chávez through a coup d'état. Based in the working-class 23 de Enero barrio, the young organization considers itself both Leninist and Guevarist. They are committed to carrying out Chávez's project of building socialism through communes and, as such, have built the El Panal Commune, which produces both basic goods and revolutionary culture. This interview with Alexis Vive's Robert Longa sheds light on that communal project and the organization's vision of the future.

As a part of the El Panal Commune, an initiative that aims to reorganize our way of living both politically and economically, could you explain to us how the commune, as a building block for socialism, relates to Chávez's legacy?

When Chávez emerged on the political scene, he connected with our [Venezuelan] roots and broke with the Eurocentric notions that the Soviet bloc imposed during the '60s and '70s: the narrow notions of development that became common on the left during the Cold War. Chávez came into the public eye talking about the Bolivarian epic and reconnecting with Latin American and Indo-American history: our history of resistance, our culture, and the legacy of our "liberators."[4]

He also broke with the model of representative democracy and began to talk about participatory and protagonist democracy. Heinz Dietrich, an author now separated from the Bolivarian Process but who at one time accompanied it, called Chávez's project of participatory and protagonist democracy "the project for new socialism." Chávez began there, from this concept of participatory and protagonist democracy, and started filling it, little by little, with content. It became a new architecture for the construction of 21st Century Socialism.

We believe that the commune, the project that brings together groups of communal councils—which to a degree are modeled on the Russian Soviets—is the most genuine organizational form that can allow popular power to take shape on a territorial level.[5] Chávez turned this form of organization into a model, the communal model. As an organization, Alexis Vive is completely in agreement with the project of communal organization, that is, bringing the communal project, which recalls the Paris Commune, into our spaces of life and work. Power resides in the people, and they must be the ones to exercise it. The people constitute power. From there, from that radical conception of power and democracy, we connect with Chávez and what he stands for . . . the concrete realization of his ideas.

This brings us to a critical encounter with some existing practices that deviate from Chávez's original concept. His project (and ours) is not one that reinstates the logic of representation under the umbrella of a new legal framework. Also, regarding the commune, it is not about renaming mere neighborhood or condominium associations. The commune is a territorial form for exercising popular power: power by and for the people. Thus, from our point of view, Chávez's commune is, if not the final model, at least the path for consolidating of 21st Century Socialism. It is the model developed to transfer power to the people, the model that Chávez outlined so that the people would assume power politically, economically, and socially. That is why we also look to the Paris Commune and other historical expressions of political revolutionary organization as we develop popular power in our territory.

You have a communal project located here in the 23 de Enero barrio: the El Panal Commune. But the influence of El Panal reaches far beyond this immediate area. Can you say something about these two levels of work?

Our collective was born here in the central zone of the 23 de Enero. This is where the first territorial exercise in communal construction happened. But a commune cannot be an island, and El Panal has since expanded to Valencia, Lara State, to form what we call "El Panal 2021 Communal Hub." Our sphere of action is not defined by imaginary lines [such as city or state borders]. Instead, it grows out of the work of the "Panalitos" [small beehives], a reference that alludes to the psycho-emotional logic of preparing and working with the people, with the masses. The *panalitos* are the immediate spaces for mass participation, to use a Marxist category, or the sphere of the multitude, to use Antonio Negri's postmodern notion, or the isthmus of the *potentia*, to use Enrique Dussel's term. The masses—the organized people— are the force that moves history. And so we come back to our earlier reflection: we understand that the El Panal Commune cannot be an isolated phenomenon in the central zone of 23 de Enero. It is necessary that this communal construction expands to the whole territory with the sole aim of bringing power back to the people ... and that is nothing more and nothing less than the Communal Confederation, which will bring the state (as it is now organized) to an end. Thus while Negri talks about abolishing the state and V. I. Lenin about toppling the bourgeois state, for our part, we say that that project [of abolishing or toppling the state] is the task of the communes.

In the Basque independentist movement, it is sometimes said that popular power should work on three levels: self-government, self-defense, and self-determination.

That is a good synthesis of what popular power is. The Bolivarian Process (and Chávez himself) changed and evolved over time. At first, the discourse focused on co-management [*cogestión*], and then there emerged a fully emancipated conception of popular power that included the commune model. In that model, some state institutions would collaborate with the popular movements following the perspective that Álvaro García Linera has theorized. García Linera said that Lenin proposed taking power by assault, but here in the Latin American experiences of 21st Century Socialism, we have come to understand that there is a new subject that comes from the popular movement and enters state institutions, and this subject must participate in the counter-hegemonic struggles within the state. It must participate in the battle against the repressive forces and against the capitalist currents within it.

The truth is that, with Chávez, there was a co-management[6] period, but communes can't stop with mere co-management; they must advance towards self-management to then move on to self-emancipation. We call this process of separation a process of "seduction," [and we also talk about] "self-determination" and "proletarization" of the *barrios*.[7] In other words, the commune must have a profoundly class-centered content to advance in the construction of 21st Century Socialism.

Thus we don't believe in halfhearted proposals. We are not dogmatic, so we understand that sometimes conversations with the enemy, conversations to reach a truce, are necessary . . . but the hegemonic core of our project (and that of Chávez) is the commune, be it urban or rural, and that cannot be negotiated. The continuation and radicalization of the revolution depends on the communal project truly becoming the connecting thread in our society. So, again, we don't deny the possibility of temporary alliances with sectors of the bourgeoisie, if it is merely tactical. Yet the only strategic alliance, if we want to remain true to Chávez, is the alliance with the people as they organize in communes.

When it comes to this issue we go to the root [in Latin, *radices*], so we are radical. We go back to Che Guevara who said that you can't build socialism with the worn-out weapons of capitalism. . . . Or, as Julio Escalona says, you cannot bring your enemy to the table to agree upon prices, if your enemy's aim is to topple you. The contradictions that we face today are long-term ones, so our strategic alliances must be made to serve the organized masses and must be subordinated to the project of the commune.

It is no secret that in the current crisis the government has chosen to pigeonhole the communal project. Some government spokespeople argue that, in the face of the crisis, the commune is not efficient in solving people's problems. However, the grassroots continue to believe in the project. So why is there this disconnect between those above and those below regarding the viability of the project?

For those involved in the commune, there are no ambiguities, no ambivalence. The contradiction may exist for those burdened with ideological inconsistencies and who do not share Chávez's strategic vision. Those who deny that the commune could be the space for building a new society are simultaneously negating Chávez's thought and action. They go against the Chavista praxis and fail to acknowledge the possibility of a human being aware of the "tactical minutes and the strategic hours," to use the words of General Pérez Arcay.[8] In effect, they deny the strategy element of the Chavista philosophy.

Here we must emphasize that, if there have been problems in the Bolivarian Process, and obviously there have, they are due to individual errors. The failures result precisely because there hasn't been enough support, because there hasn't been transfer of power [to the communes], and because some individuals haven't trusted the people. Yes, there is a kind of stagnation of communal construction, but that isn't because the model is flawed, but rather because some individuals have redirected resources away from the communes.

A case in point is the question of technology. Technology transfer is very important in the building and bolstering of communal production and [what we call] the movement toward the proletarization of the *barrios*. But the machinery imported by the state, the seeds, and other inputs . . . all of that is being channeled away from the communes. If state officials were committed to transferring power to the people, if they were able to take to heart Chávez's method of the three *R*s ("revision, rectification, relaunch"), then we would witness a blooming of the communal project. And the communal project is the only way to guarantee participatory and protagonist democracy.

It is not by chance that in Chávez's last testament he talks about the need for a change of course. In this speech he says once again that the soul of the socialist project is the commune. It is not we who say this, it is Chávez who calls on all of us to carry out the communal project, the crowning idea of his proposal. He did this as the cycle of his political life was coming to a close. His slogan "Commune or Nothing" is therefore the synthesis of his legacy.

Faced with the grave crisis in Venezuela, what does the Alexis Vive Patriotic Force propose to do? Do you strive for radicalization? A change of course in a leftward direction? Or do you think that we should take a few steps back, to later advance?

Radicalization and the deepening [of the process]. In response to a crisis that makes our world tremble, we must respond with radical changes. There's no other way forward if human integrity is the basis of our project.

Faced with the crisis, we propose "Exclusive Zones of Communal Production," and we work toward the territorialization of socialism and the proletarization of the *barrios*.[9] We aim to industrialize the *barrios* and give a class content to the Bolivarian Revolution. There can be no ambiguities in our actions or in our discourse. We now propose to deepen this revolution by following Chávez's model as synthesized in the *Strike at the Helm* speech. Beyond that last speech, there is little for us to do in terms of theorization. All we have to do is bring the proposal to life. Lenin said *without revolutionary theory there is no revolutionary practice*. Some may have forgotten it, but the path has been drawn and the theory laid out. We can say, with Silvio Rodríguez, *what can we sing if the commander did it, if he wrote the poem?* Now it is up to us to turn his poetry into action. We have to make a practice out of it. We must turn it into verb. We have to conceptualize Chávez's word through our praxis.

Chávez said to Lorenzo Mendoza once: "Don't make a mistake, Mendoza, or you'll be left with nothing" (*No te equivoques Mendoza, porque te vas a quedar sin el chivo y sin el mecate*).[10] And we say: with the Mendozas of the world, we cannot come out of the current crisis ... so we are against concessions. As *barrio* dwellers and *campesinos*, we are the insurgent subject that will make the Bolivarian Revolution flourish ... if some do not want this, if some are afraid of Chávez and his radical proposal, all we can say is that, for us, there are no two ways to go about this.

With Chávez's death we lost our guiding ideal in terms of ethics, the North Star that showed the way. Today, this whole issue of the ethical example has been widely debated in popular Chavismo. I know that preaching with the example has long been important for Alexis Vive. Do you have any reflections on this issue?

One of the main figures who set an ethical and moral example, in addition to Chávez, is Fidel Castro. He was the helmsman of Latin America and the bastion of dignity. From him and from the Cuban people we must learn resilience and endurance. But Fidel wasn't just resilient, he was also a man capable of reflection and self-criticism. Or, to go back to Chávez and his practice, we remember him as a leader who developed a rich theory, but also as a man who demanded that government cadres engage in self-criticism ... and he himself reflected on his mistakes publicly ... he taught by example and he was never arrogant with the people.

The truth is that arrogance, detachment from the people, and disconnection from territorial realities ... turning their backs on us and extending their hands to the historical enemies of the people—that cannot be the path, that won't set any kind of example!

The emergence of 21st Century Socialism comes in the midst of a crisis of paradigms, a crisis that was resolved by going back to the root of the problem, a crisis that wasn't solved by pacts or concessions. Thus, we must return to the epic struggle for socialism, to the original battlefield where there was a level ground for advancing towards our strategic goal.

As I said before, I do understand that we might have to have a dialogue with our historical enemy, but if the great love of our life is the revolution, then we cannot tip the field in favor of the enemy. The leadership must walk with the people, breathe the air that the people breathe, without forgetting that our people's emancipation is the goal, socialism is the model, and the commune is the path.

The ethical question is central to constructing the revolutionary subject and setting the example. Integrity is a key part of our love for the revolution, and it has much to do with ideological principles. We cannot accept that our ideas, ideals, principles, and dreams be negotiated.

That is, we can accept dialogue, but our principles cannot be negotiated. The contradiction is longstanding and structural, and we must commit our lives to deepening the revolution . . . which can only be done by casting one's lot with the people. The ethical and moral example that guides us will grow out of a practice that follows the commune's orientation, without manipulating Chávez's legacy. We cannot let Chávez's physical death be accompanied by the psycho-emotional death of our affection for Chávez. Remember, the Right seeks the peace of the graveyard and has given us ample evidence of this: in the *guarimbas* they burned people, they decapitated poor motorcyclists.[11] The right-wingers are the terrorists and the *guarimbas* have shown it.

We are not filled by hatred, but we disagree with the "peace moves" such as the release of Lorent Saleh.[12] We oppose the freedom of those class enemies that have killed Venezuelans because they are poor, black, or *barrio*-dwellers. This is a class struggle, and those who disregard that fact are killing the revolution's morale.

Could we say that in the practice of communal construction—in El Panal Commune, in Negro Primero Commune, in El Maizal Commune—a new ethical example is being set?

We don't have a "revolutionometer" that would say who is and who isn't a revolutionary. We cannot say who is a traitor and who is setting the example. But what I'm certain of is that, as a popular movement and as a communal movement, we are not going to leave Chávez's legacy behind. Nor are we going to turn it into a pamphlet. We are not going to make a cliché out of Chávez. We are not going to turn his words into an empty discourse that has no meaning for revolutionary practice. We are going to deepen the revolution, and if from there we come to be seen as an example, only time will tell. The fact is that we take to heart the guevarist principle of the dictatorship of the example ... [We must convince people] that the new man and the new woman are not chimeras: overcoming injustices is possible and necessary. We are committed to turn Chávez's paradigm for the construction of socialism into reality. And we will do so by way of the commune, here and now. The commune is the only path for our emancipation and for building 21st Century Socialism. We won't let Chávez down!

—November 23, 2018

Grapes of Wrath in Rural Venezuela: A Conversation with Angel Prado

Angel Prado, a key organizer of the El Maizal Commune, discusses that commune's efforts to cultivate the land under new social relations.[13] *The conversation followed hard on the heels of an attempt to jail him and two other local organizers and sheds light on the struggle of Chavista campesinos in the face of capitalist-roaders in the bureaucracy.*

Many people have heard about the El Maizal Commune, which is a well-known expression of communal popular power and because of your election in December as mayor of the Simón Planas township (position that was subsequently given to another candidate by governmental decree).[14] **Nevertheless, it would be good to open with a brief synthesis of the communal project that you are involved in.**

El Maizal is a productive commune in rural Venezuela, nested between two states in the center of the country: Lara and Portuguesa. Our commune's land, given to self-organized *campesinos* by President Hugo Chávez, is high-grade. Year after year, we have been harvesting to meet the needs of our community and the people of Venezuela. We believe that, in a global context that is marked by a profound economic crisis, we can help mitigate the impact of that crisis. We do this in (and for) our own communities, and, we hope, beyond them as well. We have a work ethic and a deep commitment to the land. The craft of agriculture—to plant and to harvest—is our human condition by birth. It is the world that we were born into.

In the last few months we faced a turbulent situation in Venezuela with deep internal and external contradictions. Then, after the May 20 electoral victory, came Nicolás Maduro's call upon the people to become active subjects in the structural transformations that our country requires. We, who have always taken seriously our roles as subjects of transformation—as Chavista *campesinos* and as working people—took the president's words seriously and decided to do our part.

So we turned the page and moved forward with an economic, territorial, and organizational plan. However, in doing so we have had clashes with powerful bureaucrats who administer the state's resources and funding. In these interactions, we have witnessed time and again the conflict between the old bourgeois state and the emerging future communal and socialist state. This clash has become tangible and material again in the last few weeks.

About a week ago, on May 26, the National Guard's National Anti-Kidnapping and Extortion Command (CONAS) arrived at the Maizal Commune. Their objective wasn't to support or encourage the collective project. Could you tell us what happened and, more importantly, why it happened?

The CONAS came to our commune supposedly following the trail of a group of illegal traffickers who sell, outside of the regular channels, supplies of Agropatria (which is the government-owned and operated supplier of seeds and other agricultural inputs).

But to understand what happened on that day, we have to go back in time . . .

On April 28, we received state financing directly from the hands of President Maduro in Carora, near the Maizal Commune. This funding was granted so that we could go ahead with the sowing of corn in May.

Most of the month of May went by and still we were unable to purchase the seeds and inputs that we needed through the regular channels. Why? Because Agropatria did not respond to the needs of small and midsize producers. Thus, we were obliged to purchase inputs outside of the regular channels, as most small producers have had to do. In effect, this is because the government is not solving the problem of the illegal trafficking of these inputs.

In any case, as *campesinos* we had no option but to produce. So toward the end of May, as the planting season was coming to a close, we were forced to purchase seeds from unofficial sellers: some 300 sacks of corn seeds (in fact, we actually needed 1500 sacks for the 1300 hectares of our land that usually were dedicated to growing corn).

The CONAS came to El Maizal on May 26. We were already "guilty" in their eyes, having committed the "crime" of purchasing inputs for the seasonal planting. This national police force came into the commune in their typical bullying style. They confiscated our phones. We were held for some six hours and taken to a National Guard jail in Portuguesa state. Eventually, we were released.

Would you say that the CONAS (and therefore the state) is criminalizing small and medium *campesinos*, instead of going after those who traffic with state-financed inputs?

Yes. Let me illustrate this by way of an example. Yesterday we learned that a *campesino* from Sanare in Lara, a coffee grower, bought ten sacks of fertilizer outside of the regular channels. When he was going back home, he was detained by a CONAS team. They presented charges against him in court, and he remained in jail [he is still behind bars at the time of publication]. His car was retained, and his mug shot appeared in the local press. . . . It seems as if the objective is to morally destroy those who are trying to produce.

But the problem with the CONAS is not a new one. When we presented an alternative Chavista candidate for mayor in our township last December [Angel Prado himself was the candidate], this state security force persecuted us for a whole day and threatened the people who were working with me, my campaign team, and myself.

In fact, we believe that there is a systematic pattern of threats and harassment against our communal project. We have denounced this, and many social movements and public figures have expressed their solidarity. Of course, the security forces will continue harassing us.

Agropatria was created by President Chávez in 2010 to replace the nationalized Agroisleña, a private corporation that sold agricultural inputs for profit. But there is more to this story. Could you give us some background to help readers who are not necessarily in Venezuela, understand the problems with this public company?

Agropatria is in charge of all the state's importing and distribution of seeds and agricultural inputs. When the company was nationalized by Chávez, he charged it with servicing all agricultural production, from the small to the large producers. But the internal logic of Agropatria makes it almost impossible for the small and medium producers to acquire the seeds and other inputs.

There were always problems, but now the situation has gotten worse. We hear people, government spokespeople, claiming that the problem is the lack of resources or other external factors. That is the explanation they give when asked why the Agropatria stores are empty. But, at the same time, we see illegal traffickers of agricultural material coming through our towns with gigantic trucks loaded with seeds and inputs that actually came from Agropatria . . . and they sell those supplies for a hundred times the official price!

So the question is who channels the seeds and inputs to the illegal market? We want to go to the root of the problem, and we are not afraid of making our accusations public.[15]

The communal project has had conflicts with the CONAS and Agropatria, but the problem that you are facing is deeper and more complex.

Right, the problems with the CONAS and Agropatria are not the main issue. Obviously, we will always denounce the harassment by the CONAS and the deep corruption that runs through Agropatria. But the problem goes beyond that.

The many politicians who don't work for the people affect us the most. Unfortunately, they are politicians associated with the PSUV [United Socialist Party of Venezuela]. Right now, many of our representatives and functionaries are in fact doing the work of the Right:

installing the logic of corruption, bureaucracy, and clientelism, which are all the same thing in the end. Thus, we witness daily moral and material degradation in the governmental sphere. A reformist logic seems to dominate that landscape.

So we have taken up a twofold task. On the one hand, we are denouncing the corrupt and anti-popular logic of the state's agricultural institutions (not just Agropatria). On the other hand, we are also making an open call—to communards, the common people, and *barrio*-dwellers—to collectively analyze the situation. Most importantly, we want these groups to make specific proposals about how to save our people in the profound economic crisis that is facing us.

We believe that, together, we can produce a methodology and a roadmap, collectively developing a plan. We are convinced that there must be a process of collective reflection and ask ourselves about the role the people should play now. In effect, we must become active so that our government isn't taken over by right-wingers disguised in red [the color associated with Chavismo], by the bloc that has usurped the state's resources. Recovering these resources and redirecting them, in part, toward agriculture and the communes would be a logical objective.

What you are pointing to is very important. It seems that, faced with the state's inefficiencies, there are power groups in the government that are hedging their bets on privatization. We have seen this occur before with some of the communally-held land and with public sector companies.

The inefficiency of state undertakings should not make the government turn to the usual capitalist solution, which is privatization. President Maduro should remember that the people who are maintaining this political process are the six million voters who, on May 20th, collectively said that they would not disappear as a political current and as a project. It's not the private sector that keeps this boat afloat!

There is also, in certain government sectors, an idea that state undertakings are always inefficient, and also that small and medium producers (or communes) are ineffective and destined to fail. But, in fact, we are the ones who work and produce in our small plots of land. We are the ones who work on the oligarchy's land and, at the end of the day, we are the ones who know how to milk a cow, drive a tractor, and heft a sack of fertilizer!

It is urgent to maintain the country's production. As the people who produce, we need to have access to seeds, fertilizers, insecticides, etc. These inputs must reach the *campesinos*, but if they get to us only through unofficial and illegal channels, that is going to impact production dramatically. Whoever allows this to happen is participating in the chaos that has set up shop in this country.

Popular, participative democracy is an aspect of Chávez's legacy, but for most city dwellers this practice seems to have become history. On the other hand, I understand the agrarian communes to be an expression of direct democracy, the beginnings of the future reorganization of society. Can you tell us a bit about communal democracy as it works in El Maizal?

Chávez always said that the popular movement should not be an appendix of any institution or current, that we must be autonomous. I think it's necessary that popular organizations understand this now. We must have our own voice. Chávez always respected and encouraged our autonomy. The idea, of course, is not to be rebels without a cause. We are not anarchists. What we must do is be politically coherent and understand our role in history.

We have a legal structure that was fostered by Chávez and the people: the Laws of Popular Power.[16] They establish a framework that is (to be somewhat redundant) popular, and thus are an expression of grassroots democracy.

In the commune, the Citizens' Assembly is the highest space for decision-making, the space where the whole community participates. Then comes the Communal Parliament, a body in which there is deliberation. The Communal Councils delegate their practical decision-making to the Communal Parliament. Again, these practical decisions follow the guidelines of the Citizens' Assembly.

Some people understand democracy as the way to get access to positions of privilege. By contrast, our participative democracy is based on an assembly that saddles you with responsibilities, and if you do as collectively decided, then you have fulfilled your role as one part of the whole.

Our democracy is the democracy of the people, and that means that, when one is elected, one must separate oneself from any personal interests.

In a nutshell, in our commune, the most important decisions are taken by the Citizens' Assembly, whereas the Communal Parliament plans and executes. Operational decisions are taken at the level of the productive unit. In other words, we don't call assemblies to solve operational problems. Then, of course, one must render accounts to the assembly.

This is democracy as it plays out in El Maizal, with its particular mechanisms. But what I can say in general is that in the new democracy that is emerging, sectarian attitudes must disappear, personal power plays must be eliminated, and no one person can impose him or herself in the decision-making process.

The spirit of full participatory democracy lives in the commune.

You mentioned earlier that El Maizal is calling people to participate in a debate that will assess the national situation and, more importantly, make specific proposals about how to overcome the crisis. How do you expect this debate to take shape? Also, is it going to be an exclusively *campesino* initiative?

There is a saying in this country: the *campesino* must fight for the land. Sometimes I take issue with this way of putting it, since it is not only the *campesinos* who need to fight for the land. The people from the city must also fight for the land. After all, what we produce in the rural areas is consumed in the city.

Sometimes, we *campesinos* wonder why people from the city do not fight with us, since they, too, struggle with bureaucracy. It is true that we have some level of support and solidarity that comes from the large cities, but we need more of it. Sometimes, as *campesinos*, we feel alone.

In the face of the many obstacles to production, the persecution, and the impositions, we are calling for an assembly—not only of *campesinos*, but also involving the sectors that don't produce. We must develop proposals together. We want to have a debate with people from the popular *barrios* of Caracas, Valencia, and Barquisimeto. We want to bring out the communes from the city and the countryside, and we want to debate with cooperatives. This kind of self-organized space is urgently needed. The class struggle that pits organized workers, on the one hand, against the bourgeoisie, the oligarchy, and the corrupt functionaries and reformists in our government, on the other, requires the participation of all humble people from all walks of life.

We believe that Chavismo is alive. Moreover, if genuine Chavismo organizes and goes out to the streets; if those of us who really believe in Chávez's legacy meet, fight, and struggle; if we develop a plan—then, whatever the obstacles, we'll be able to reestablish the dignified life that we had with Chávez.

In the upcoming days, we are going to issue a call to the nation for a debate. If the people respond to that call, which I think they will, then we will go forward together. No matter what, El Maizal is going to continue in this fight for the common good, for the communal project, for socialism. We subscribe to the "*Comuna o Nada*" (Commune or Nothing) slogan of Chávez. We will defend our land (and our production) by any means necessary. For that reason, this season's harvest, by decree of our Communal Assembly is not going to any silo, private or public. We are going to place what we produce directly in the hands of the organized communities.

We are detaching ourselves from the state's institutional mechanisms and those of the private sector. We believe that the commune has to produce for the common people, because they are the ones who need it, and because the institutions have broken the commitments they made with us. We have done our part, and from now on we are going to circumnavigate bureaucracies and the speculative market, and work with the people.

—JUNE 5, 2018

Building Socialism from Below: A Conversation with Martha Lía Grajales

Martha Lía Grajales belongs to the Surgentes Collective (a human rights organization) and is a founding member of the Unidos San Agustín Convive cooperative. She is a lawyer and holds a master's degree in human rights and democracy. In this interview, we ask Grajales questions about the dialectic between state power and popular organization, with an aim of understanding how grassroots initiatives might breathe new life into the socialist project. She argues that Chávez's socialist project lives on as an array of self-organized initiatives.

From the beginning, the Chavista movement had two ways of understanding and carrying out politics: on the one hand, there was popular protagonism, direct democracy, and grassroots organization. On the other hand, Chavismo also pursued state and institutional power. This double approach was productive for a time, and it opened the way for unforeseen expressions of popular power. Now, however, there seems to be a clear prevalence of state-level politics over popular power and grassroots organization. What's going on?

The state is a disputed territory, and [entering into it] is necessary if we want to promote popular interests, but state power is not in any way the goal. In any effort to build popular power, there must be synergy between the bottom and the top. The key issue here is that what is done "from above" must strengthen popular power from below.

We can't ignore the important role that the government has had in fostering spaces of participation and political organizing for subaltern groups. The breadth and magnitude of popular organization in Venezuela is, without a doubt, one of the Chavista government's goals, and we can count grassroots organization on a large scale as one of its big successes.

What is the problem then? First, the work that is done "from above" should not replace or appropriate that which comes "from below." That's to say that institutions shouldn't manage or instrumentalize popular power.

There are many conceptions of popular power—one conception considers such power as simply an instrument for seizing [state] power. However, once the power is in your hands, then you appeal to "historical necessity" and "national interest" to justify centralizing power. In this way, the party and the state can come to supplant popular projects and their autonomous organization of the oppressed classes.

The other conception of popular power, which is the one we believe in, assumes popular power to be both a means and an end. Popular power is about creating a new set of social relations that are outside the logic of capital, and the aim is self-government. Chávez warned that the state or the party should not institutionalize or coopt popular power. That, obviously, does not mean we should take an essentialist attitude and cut off all relations with the state for fear of losing autonomy. As I said earlier, the state is a disputed terrain that the popular movement must not ignore, but it shouldn't be considered the main objective.

Thus, the problem is not that popular power has been promoted from above. The problem is that, often, those operating in the government conceive popular power as something that is merely instrumental and which is only good for maintaining [formal or traditional] power. This conception strips popular power of all of its transformative potential. It treats the masses as passive recipients rather than as political subjects with the capacity and power to guide the revolutionary process.

But it should be said that this is not only a question about how the state does things. Popular forces also need to problematize their approach. This means that, above all, they need to develop economic autonomy, which not only politicizes their movements but also limits the possibility of state cooptation.

A popular movement that does not have its own economic muscle and depends completely on state resources is very vulnerable. If it does not behave as the state expects it to, it will lose support and its organizational work can easily collapse. Or when the government wants to support the initiative but lacks resources, that can also lead to the collapse of the movement's organizational efforts. So when popular power builds a relationship of dependence with the state, it cuts back its capacity to self-govern.

Obviously, all this doesn't mean that popular organizations should reject state support, but it does mean that when support is received, it must be oriented toward collectively developing and appropriating the means of production according to a logic that is different from capital, and which must be sustainable without the state's intervention. Otherwise, it will be impossible to advance on the path of self-government and transition to socialism.

This is a complicated business, because here the government must support the initiatives for building popular power that should gradually replace the government itself. In that process, we will naturally run into resistance from constituted power, which does not want to be replaced. However, we can advance toward socialism only if this transfer of power takes place.

The role of a popular government is to contribute to building power from below, fostering a constant modification of relations of force in favor of the people. There must be a process of permanently generating conditions for the growth of popular power. Paraphrasing [Miguel] Mazzeo: those from above should foment, not replace, popular power.

You have claimed that the Chavista popular movement needs to organize all its forces, with the aim of reorienting the Bolivarian Process. The popular movement—consisting of people organized in communes, cooperatives, worker councils, and autonomous

feminist organizations—must become something that can guide the masses. This requires a great deal of collective work but also, and very importantly, an effective communication strategy.

The crisis in Venezuela is much more than a struggle to maintain state power. It is about the struggle to maintain socialism as a strategic goal, not only in Venezuela but in the continent as a whole.

In this regard, in the midst of the brutal blockade and with internal errors having been made in the direction of the political process, there is now a strong national and international tendency claiming that Venezuela's attempt to build an alternative to capitalism was a huge failure. Moreover, it is said that problems that we are now experiencing are associated with the socialist model. It's about burying socialism as an alternative to capitalism, associating it with scarcity of food, widespread impoverishment, the restriction of political rights, corruption, etc.

So when I talk about the need for the Chavista popular movement to take a position, I'm talking about making visible all those grassroots projects that have taken shape during the emergency—all those communal projects that, in the midst of this crisis, cast their lot with building alternatives to capitalist relations, to colonialism, and to heteronormativity—and in that way point to socialism as a strategic horizon.

In the midst of this profound crisis, these grassroots efforts expand and enrich participation in politics. They also produce and guarantee food in a sustainable and sovereign way. In other words, those who are self-organized and collectively manage shared assets are more protected. These grassroots experiences are living proof that the socialist model hasn't failed. Quite the contrary, these projects go to show us that the way out of the current crisis involves placing our bets on a truly emancipatory course of action.

The numbers show this. The Pueblo a Pueblo plan is a project involving some seventy small *campesinos* (essentially farming families), and it manages to distribute food to more than 1,200 [urban] families weekly. In three years, they have produced more than 1,000 tons of fruits and vegetables on their own. They are also recovering native seeds and agroecological practices, while promoting the *campesino* organization—not only for the sake of food sovereignty, but also with a view to distribute independently. This initiative generates new fraternal relations between the people of the countryside and the city, and productive relations geared toward common welfare and toward eliminating intermediaries.

Pueblo a Pueblo's internal organizational process helped raise the small farmers' capacity to grow and distribute in an independent and autonomous manner, which in turn helped them get better pay for their labor. At the same time, the organized communities are able to purchase produce with around 60 percent savings when compared with standard market prices. All this happened in the midst of a terrible crisis, and it was made possible, first, by planning production; second, through the organizational work both in the countryside and the city; and, third, by eliminating intermediaries from the productive chain. This shows that organizing people can help us overcome the crisis, but it's also a game-changer, allowing us to avoid capitalist pragmatism, and deepening our commitment to socialism as a strategic goal.

So we have to question both the usual explanation of the causes of the harsh situation that we are currently facing, and at the same time make visible all those practices that are led by subaltern groups: projects that will allow us to find a way out of this crisis while radicalizing the process.

This, however, requires a big effort on the part of the popular movement to generate spaces of articulation. This is so because whenever these initiatives get going, pragmatists always say that one truck of produce, four kilos of potatoes, or a pair of panties [produced by a cooperative] will not solve the huge difficulties that we are living.

When faced with these arguments, I would answer in two ways. First, this is not only about the collective effort that is promoted on the local level, because without a doubt this effort taken in isolation is absolutely insufficient. The aim here is to multiply the local productive projects based on the characteristics of each territory and on what is needed for reproducing life there. The local projects should also be interlinked, allowing for the growth of what Chávez called a great spider web: a new geometry of power. This new power might well have its epicenter in the territory—that is, on the local level—but its true power consists in the capacity to connect people and communities. It is in this way that what might seem insignificant on the local level can contribute to the new practices, new policies, and new economic relations that could meet people's most serious needs.

Thus, the objective is not only to generate local productive projects but also spaces of encounter, coordination, and collective action that must reach beyond the local level in which each initiative takes place.

I would also add something in response to those who think that it's naïve to imagine solving crises from below, from the local level, and step by step: Well, we are not naïve and we do not forget about the struggle that must take place on the level of state politics. But it is precisely by accumulating force, through organizational work and forging alternative productive chains, that we can have real capacity to exert our influence on the level of state politics.

In the face of the crisis (and governmental responses that often involve reducing popular participation), new grassroots projects have been emerging. These projects are often self-managed, and they try to solve problems outside the logic of capital. We have seen people using new organizational forms that are much more democratic and horizontal. These spaces have been important for repoliticizing people during the crisis and in the face of imperialist aggression.

As a result of the multidimensional crisis that we are facing in Venezuela, many people from the popular classes no longer involve themselves in [state-sponsored] organizations. In some cases, this is due to their understandably critical view toward the government—toward both the national leadership as well as its local representatives, particularly the people assigned from above to head the CLAP and the UBCh.[17] In other cases, it's simply because solving day-to-day problems takes a lot of time and effort [due to the crisis].

However, it's a different story when we speak of the organizations that have been able to respond to the crisis with projects that operate outside the logic of capital (addressing people's material needs, such as food), and which have done this with a practice that turns people into protagonists and political subjects, as opposed to a practice that is based on the clientelistic logic promoted by the government; the projects that question the logic of privilege in the distribution of scarce resources; and the initiatives that promote relationships built on transparency and equality. These kinds of organizational initiatives have managed to maintain themselves and grow, not only from an economic standpoint, but also a political one. These organizations have not only survived, they also have been growing and getting stronger.

This shows that it's not just about solving the food problem (which is what the CLAP tries to do), but also about doing this in ways that put forward an alternative to the logic of capital, through methods that are collective and democratic. In the words of Mazzeo, *it's about government by an entire class and not by an elite.*

Those efforts seeking to build popular power from below—and which do so by developing forms that allow for a more collective and democratic way of doing politics, while also addressing people's material needs—work to repoliticize the population and raise morale. This recharges and strengthens the mass organization, while maintaining socialism as a strategic horizon. Even though they don't actually get us to socialism, they work to build the conditions for it.

Finally, I would like to ask you about the Unidos San Agustín Convive, as a concrete self-organized project. Could you explain this project so that we can understand the experience and its political reverberations? We also would like to learn how this experience repoliticizes people and raises morale, and how it belies the claim that socialism has failed and the only solution now is privatization.

San Agustín Convive is a cooperative formed mainly by women from thirteen communal councils in the San Agustín del Sur *barrio* [in Caracas]. It got going in August almost three years ago. The cooperative took shape to deal with the issue of food. When it started in 2016, there was one hub made up of five communal councils, and now there are three hubs bringing together people from 13 communal councils. Besides the distribution of food in collaboration with the Pueblo a Pueblo plan, the cooperative is also taking steps to develop textile and food production; the making of sauces, jams, and ice cream; and children's social and leadership activities—all this through a self-managed and deeply democratic process involving collective organizational forms. It is an attempt to develop revolutionary theory through practical work. Thus, it is not just an effort aiming to meet specific demands, it is also about building the conditions for socialism, beginning at a local level.

How did it repoliticize and remobilize people? Well, it repoliticized people through a practical experience demonstrating that cooperative and collective action could protect us, in the midst of Venezuela's deep crisis. Thanks to the organizational work we have done, people in the cooperative have access to food with more than 60 percent savings compared with the regular market prices (which, in turn, means that we are likely to be eating more and better). The cooperative also decreases our level of dependence, making us more autonomous and less vulnerable. Finally, the experience demonstrates, in the midst of a brutal crisis, that the only way out is through collective projects, not through capitalism.

The project remobilizes us because, for that [noncapitalist] alternative to be possible, we have had to overcome the condition of being merely dependent "recipients," and to remake ourselves as political subjects capable of critically addressing our reality and of organizing to transform it. It is not about waiting for the solutions to arrive from above, it is about building them from below. Of course, for something like this to work, everybody has to participate and get involved.

—May 31, 2019

Rebuilding the Hegemony of Chavismo: A Conversation with Gerardo Rojas

Gerardo Rojas is a Barquisimeto-based Chavista intellectual and activist. His work as an organizer began in the early 1990s, when he was in middle school. Later in that decade, Rojas participated in the occupation of a building in the barrio where he was born. That building became a community center and later, in 1998, the first community radio in Venezuela. Rojas was one of the founders of Voces Urgentes in 2002, a communications collective, and participated in the organization of one of the first urban communes, Ataroa Socialist Commune, in 2007. More recently, he was vice minister in the Ministry of Communes. Here, he talks about the contradictions that the popular movement is facing in Venezuela today, the struggle to unify grassroots resistance, and the role of international solidarity.

In recent years, your writing has focused on the issue of communal and popular organization, examining the correlation of diverse forces and bringing to the forefront a debate about the popular movement's pending tasks. One of the tasks you identify is to resurrect Hugo Chávez's core proposal, in the face of hegemonic currents in the government. The government currently proposes that the way out of the crisis is with more capitalism instead of more communes and more socialism.

For me, Chavismo is the synthesis of Comandante Chávez's thinking, which was itself rooted in the interests and experiences of the popular movement and of the working people but also grew out of the revolutions of the world, as well as the thinking, theory, and imagination of the Left.

Three elements synthesize his thinking. The first is *The Blue Book* [a short book by Chávez written in 1991, in which he presents his views on history and democracy]; the second is *Aló Presidente Teórico N° 1* [2009 speech]; and the third is the *Strike at the Helm* speech [2012]. In those three milestones, we find no more and no less than a clarion call for self-government, direct democracy, social control of the public sphere, and development at a territorial or local level. Yet we also find the outline of a national system that would bring all this together.

With those elements at hand, it is not hard to see what line we should pursue in our struggle, a path for popular action that goes hand in hand with a governance model committed to participatory and protagonist democracy, which for us is nothing other than Bolivarian socialism. That is a synthesis of Chávez's legacy.

When one reads *The Blue Book*, which precedes Chávez's electoral victory [in 1998], one is surprised to find direct, participatory democracy and self-government at its core. We are talking about the 1990s—that is when Chávez wrote it. Direct democracy and self-government were always at the core of the Bolivarian Revolution. However, with time, experience, the practice of governing, the emergence of internal contradictions, and together with advances and setbacks, the proposal gained precision and became a fully outlined integral project.

Later, in the *Aló Presidente Teórico N° 1* speech, we can see Chávez consolidating the mature proposal. The discourse touches upon various experiences of popular power, beginning with the "Mesas Técnicas de Agua" [*barrio*-level organizations for getting access to running water] and "Comités de Tierra Urbana" [Urban Land Committees, formed in the early days of the Bolivarian Process to struggle for urban land titles]. However, in that speech we find an important leap forward in the proposal regarding territorial organization and popular self-government. The new proposal comes out of historical experiences, and also from a tangible, immediate experience: the *pueblo* [common people] had already demonstrated its capacity to organize in communal councils, opening up the real possibility of efficient and transparent self-governance and collective control. The potential to go further now crystallizes in the proposal of the commune.

In addition to the *Aló Presidente Teórico N° 1* landmark speech, we also have the last political address of Chávez, the testament he left us with before he went to Cuba to address serious medical problems. That is the speech known as *Strike at the Helm*, which he delivered in the first cabinet meeting shortly after the 2012 elections and was publicly broadcast nationwide. There Chávez severely criticized his ministerial team and their administrative methods. But he didn't just question the ministers, he also made some concrete proposals, based on the collective experience so far and on his own analysis, as well as taking into account the correlation of forces at that moment.

Many who talk about *Strike at the Helm* limit its scope to the "Commune or Nothing" slogan, and that of course is key—it is one of the sentences that best synthesizes Chávez's thinking—but "Commune or Nothing" was essentially already there in *Aló Presidente Teórico N° 1*, where the communes were conceived as the base for the territorial development of socialism. However, the commune as expressed in *Strike at the Helm* transcends the earlier, merely local proposal, and its scale becomes national. Thus, Chávez now introduces mechanisms of political, administrative, and institutional coordination regarding the key issue of planning that range from the communal territory (the "commune" as expressed in the Laws of Popular Power) to the national scale.

In this speech, Chávez talks about the diverse modules, territorial units, and stages of popular development. He talks about weaving socialism into the fabric of the whole country, with the commune as the base, and the emergence of an economy based on social property. So there, in *Strike at the Helm*, Chávez acknowledges problems and makes contributions which, as I just said, take for granted the commune as a project on a national scale.... He also envisions the project growing from the communal council to the commune, then to the communal cities, and even later to the developmental districts and developmental axes all the way up to the communal state. In other words, Chávez imagines a process that goes from the local to the regional and then to the national, recognizing that planning is very important.

The coming together of the local projects of popular power (the communes) with the regional and national governments must go through a democratic debate in which there is a planning process, and where people agree on the objectives. That is why the *Homeland Plan* [2012][18] is also a key to understanding the communal proposal. It is a guide for a collective process of planning and action, where revolutionary imagination and the political project feed into a plan.

Would you say that within the government there is an excessively pragmatic and superficial use of Chávez's thinking?

Yes. Today the hegemonic sectors in the government present Chávez's thinking in a fragmented way. His ideas are not presented in a timeline that is rich and shows how his thought progressed. Instead, Chávez's thinking is presented in a sometimes even contradictory way and is deployed with particular interests in mind and in specific conjunctures. Above all, *Strike at the Helm* is cast aside because, as I was saying earlier, it is Chávez's political testament. Additionally, the *Homeland Plan* is being made invisible. In fact, a new *Homeland Plan* was developed without evaluating the original proposal. There was absolutely no public evaluation of the first *Homeland Plan*, but the government moves onto the next plan without reflection and input!

Obviously, the country's situation is radically different from the one that existed when Chávez was alive and the *Homeland Plan* came out. We are now facing a multifaceted crisis, but that is not an argument for not evaluating the first plan. On the contrary! The problem is that contextualizing and reevaluating that effort would lead back to some key ideas, from self-governance and participatory democracy to social control and political and territorial reorganization. In all that, we have a basis from which to build, and we have tangible experiences. . . . In the context of this wretched crisis, recognizing that we have very few resources and many weaknesses is tremendously important! I think this kind of reflection (and the action that would ensue) is one of our outstanding tasks. Postponing that task or sidelining it is one of the most evident shortcomings of the Bolivarian Revolution today.

We should talk about the subject of the revolution. As you mentioned, Chávez went through a theoretical-political evolution, but there was always a focus on poor people's participation in the questions that impact their daily lives. That is evident very early on, in the proposal for substantive democracy (direct or participatory democracy) envisioned in *The Blue Book*. Toward the end of Chávez's life, the same concern reemerges in the idea of a new communal society. However, today we find that the government's discourse is based on the idea that the people will be saved by private investment or the "revolutionary bourgeoisie" that Agriculture Minister Wilmar Castro Soteldo champions. This amounts to a "strike at the helm" to the right!

From *The Blue Book* forward, the *pueblo* and direct democracy became central to Chávez's thinking. With the project of a profound, substantive democracy, we have in effect a guiding principle to rebuild the hegemony of Chavismo. In this way, it would be possible to bring together more and more people, to build a collective subject with our main ideas clearly defined: the fight against corruption and the exercise of direct democracy together with the defense of the Venezuelan people as subjects that are part and parcel of a historical emancipatory struggle. Currently, the recovery of our historical memory as a fundamental base for revolutionary thinking is important, as Chávez's early writings show.

So here are three keys. First comes the reconstruction of ourselves as a collective subject, a *pueblo* with a history and a defined popular identity: Venezuelans but also Latin Americans. That was, is, and will always be fundamental to constructing hegemony, because from there we can project an identity. Second is the fight against the corrupt political system, against the Fourth Republic [the 1958 to 1999 period], which also comes early on in Chávez, and brings us to the present and a necessary critical reflection about the old mechanisms that are quite evidently [coming back] now.

Third is democracy, and when we talk about democracy, we are talking about integral democracy, that is, democracy in the economic, social, and political spheres. Obviously, there can be no real democracy if there is no economic democracy. Without it, we encounter again the farce of representative democracy, against which emerged one of the early struggles and debates where the revolution naturally favored the constituent *pueblo*.

Those are the main teachings from the early days of the revolution. There, the subject was the *pueblo*. Early on, the key was to add, not subtract, and one of the sentences that Chávez repeated most in his discourses was his call for the "defense of the *pueblo*"—the *pueblo* that has a history and a present of struggle, the *pueblo* that has an identity and gets together to transform its own reality, and that questions the historical interests of the dominant class. This class included the landowning oligarchy, against whom, in some cases, we are still struggling today, as well as the bourgeoisie, with its corporate and media interests.

Overall, it was a question of the *pueblo* combatting the powers that be, both inside and outside the state. This is tremendously urgent to think about today, because recovering it goes hand in hand with the issue of corruption. At least in his public discourse, Chávez was adamantly against corruption and was self-critical. He called for a fight against the corruption in the bureaucracy and called for the government and the people to put the breaks on this.

For us, as I was saying, the *pueblo*'s identity and the construction of hegemony are key. Initially, part of that construction was the very recognition of the *pueblo* (for the first time) in the political discursive sphere. The *pueblo* as a subject brings together *campesinos*, women (paraphrasing Chávez, "the Bolivarian Revolution will be feminist or it won't be"), and *barrio*-dwellers.

But, of course, in the process of building hegemony, the Bolivarian Revolution added sectors of society to the project with rather diverse interests. Today, an important part of the government is occupied by those other sectors, and they seek the restitution of the logic of capital. Here we should acknowledge the obvious: capitalism was never totally displaced, but we did advance toward the constitution of a social state of justice with rule of law, and they want to roll it back.

Certain sectors of our government, the hegemonic ones, aim to minimize or eliminate all the social, economic, and political advances made previously. For instance, they reject the objective of social inclusion from an economic point of view. Mind you, inclusion should not be understood in a superficial sense; we are talking about inclusion as the construction of power, of popular power, with the transfer of the means of production to the people—and this was clearly established by Chávez in *Strike at the Helm*.

Today, I would say that the main contradiction, more so than the contradiction with the opposition, is actually within [Chavismo]: this is where people have to assume positions. It is in this area where there is a dispute regarding how to proceed and how to build a social base to continue with the revolution.

In 2015, or perhaps before, the hegemonic bloc that involved the people was left behind. That was when the government began to close in more and more on itself, leaving the *pueblo* out. Today we can say that the space of power is reduced to a handful of people, and their tendency goes against the original Chavista proposal.

What can we say about those people? They have de facto power, and the people that surround them manage a lot of money that was captured through privileged access to subsidized dollars or contracting services with the state.... So we are talking about the making of a new "national" bourgeoisie that comes out of the profits produced by oil production. We must be critical about the ambiguous class character of the government, but we should also be self-critical to the degree that we weren't able to take charge of the spaces of power. That is true to the degree that we didn't call for another way of doing politics at the highest levels.

I agree with your assessment. However, you have also talked about the survival of the Chavista way of doing politics. Where do you think it is still present in Venezuelan society today?

That is important. We should recognize that there is a Chavista way of politics that is alive and well, and it expresses itself in communal work, in local organizations, and in direct popular participation to solve daily problems. These are ways of doing politics that are not supported by the government; they are either made invisible or made visible in the worst way possible. The latter is done to reduce the revolutionary potential of Chávez's way of doing politics.

Let me give you an example: recently state media did some coverage of the Altos de Lídice Commune, and they reported that a pharmacy opened there. But when you go to the commune, you discover that there is no pharmacy there. Instead there is something much larger and more important: an integral communal health system, an initiative that brings together popular canteens [solidarious lunch canteens, known as "*comedores populares*"], primary attention to the most vulnerable at home, the coordination of at least four or five Barrio Adentro [public health] ambulatories, etc. We could say that this initiative amounts to popular power recovering Chávez's Barrio Adentro initiative. What is there, in Altos de Lídice, is not a mere pharmacy, it's a system. If you go to the so-called pharmacy, you won't be able to buy anything. On the contrary, there you will be given free medication (which is received through fraternal donations mostly from Chile and Italy) if a request is made by the doctors who are integrated into the communal system.

So the state media reports that a pharmacy opened in Altos de Lídice, implying that it is the outcome of governmental policies, when what we are witnessing is really an outcome of popular, autonomous organization, which produced a lot more than a pharmacy. It is a grassroots initiative to build a communal healthcare system.

Chavismo is alive as a subject that is present everywhere, in every corner of the country. But we can say also that this subject is dispersed and facing political blackmail. In this very harsh reality, we may ask ourselves every day how to raise our voices, we may ponder if our criticisms could amount to treason or if we could be accused of treason. But Chavismo, this popular subject, is alive and well. Now the issue is how to make it visible, how to bring it together, and how to develop a collective line of action.

You talk about a "strike at the helm" to the right that is going on: a shift in governmental policy that favors the private over the popular.

Also, the government increasingly criminalizes those who struggle for their rights and it economically suffocates communal initiatives while continuing to subsidize capitalist production with the state's limited resources. However, it is also evident that a combative, popular Chavismo is reemerging and becoming more visible.

First, we should make something clear: the Bolivarian Revolution never proposed ending private enterprise. Nevertheless, since the early days of the revolution and especially in his last years, Chávez wagered on a democratic transformation of the *pueblo*'s economic rights. So there was development of the private sector, a development of state property, but also, and most importantly, there was support for social or communal property.

This becomes clear in Chávez's *Strike at the Helm* speech and in other speeches, where he said that we should move towards a society with a hegemony of social property. However, in the past few years, things have been reoriented toward private property, private entrepreneurship, and foreign investment, and the social project has been sidelined.

Interestingly, there is now a confluence of interests between powerful sectors of the government (that place their bets on the private) and the traditional Right. The discourse goes as follows: state and social property are inefficient, they are essentially corrupt, and they have caused the current economic disaster.

Of course, the managing of certain state enterprises has been flawed, but when you look closely, you can see that the problem was that the management model was undefined. It was blurry and didn't coincide with the initial proposal of participatory democracy. In our experience, state property is not necessarily inefficient whereas social property is generally efficient. It is unacceptable that the government repeats banalities about state property's inefficiency, making the Right's arguments its own, to go against what is collectively owned.

I was talking about this with some *compañeros* recently, and we were saying that the government mirrors the opposition. The discourses are close, the proposals are similar, and they both go against popular power and integral democracy, placing their bets on the private. The project of social property has passed into the background, if not eliminated outright from the government's worldview.

This situation provokes a response: the potent subject that was born with the revolution rises up. The Chavista subject is a powerful one, with clear ideas and practices that are coherent with its principles (of course, with many limitations too, such as the inability to build projects that go beyond their immediate territories). However, the Chavista subject has a common project and objectives that can bring it together for mobilization and action on a national level.

Despite our weaknesses and limitations, there is a shared political culture. It is a historical legacy that is very important. Furthermore, this Chavista grassroots subject can claim real achievements that are expressed in the *Homeland Plan* and in the proposals at the core of the revolution. It is a subject that defends the few means of production that we have, but also, more importantly, as some sectors of the government (including the so-called "revolutionary bourgeoisie") turn against the revolution, it defends the project.

Now we need to defend pure and simple Chavismo: the Chavismo that holds dear Chávez's ideas, from *The Blue Book* to *Strike at the Helm*. In that whole legacy, we can find the collectively-built Chavista project.

The hegemonic sectors of the government don't hesitate to criminalize *campesino* protests. In the meantime, they meet with the representatives of Juan Guaidó, who is truly a criminal, in Oslo and Barbados. What do you think about that?

There is an evident process of criminalization of popular struggles, at a time when there are beginning to be contradictions between grassroots Chavismo and the government. Just a few days ago, the son of President Nicolás Maduro, who is a public figure, made a clear attempt to criminalize the *campesino* struggle. He spoke in defense of the sectors of the bureaucracy that promote the thesis of the "revolutionary bourgeoisie." He criminalized *campesinos*, calling them "mafiosos." Go figure!

In this difficult conjuncture and with the negotiations that are underway with the opposition, we hope that peace will prevail and war will be avoided. An all-out war would not only be catastrophic, it would also interrupt the possibility of Chavismo coming together to defend our project from within.

This process [of defense from within] is taking shape right now, although we cannot be sure that it will come together in the end. It is happening even as we speak, driven by those of us who have real projects at a territorial level. We are all going to defend what we have. We will defend it in any way possible—one hopes without a war.

The task is enormous. It means bringing together all those who are defending the Bolivarian Revolution from the bases and with the communes. It means bringing together *campesinos*, factory workers, and women—all joining forces with organizational ambitions that go beyond territorial self-government. The coming together will demonstrate concretely that there is a way of doing politics that is different, that serves as a defense of the Bolivarian Revolution and maintains the *pueblo* at the center of its efforts.

It is not a question of choosing between one or another sector of the bourgeoisie, the new or old. They, as a class, are our historical enemies, with the new sectors of the bourgeoisie clearly carrying out accumulation by dispossession through privatizations of the public assets (which are more or less direct thefts). It is being done with opacity regarding how the transfer of assets is carried out.

We are talking about the silent transfer of means of production that has cost the Bolivarian Revolution billions of dollars to the private sphere. Much of this is now being transferred to the private sector using the justification that we are facing a difficult crisis. The hegemonic sector of the government believes this alteration of the project will make them the "saviors" of the country, although they have been at it for years and there is no evidence that we might be coming out of the crisis in the near future.

All this brings us to a complex issue: the role of international solidarity with the Bolivarian Process at the time when, on the one

hand, imperialist aggression is more intense than ever before, but on the other hand, Chavismo's internal contradictions are growing. How should people around the world undertake the double task of opposing imperialist interference, but also making popular power visible and defending Chávez's legacy?

We often say "solidarity is the kindness of the *pueblos*," and one of the things that characterizes the Bolivarian Revolution is people's diplomacy. Beyond the powerful and important state diplomacy that has been exercised during the revolution—particularly during Chávez's life, who had a clear plan to defend global multipolarity and continental integration—we should remember that this revolution provides a space for the world's peoples to meet, debate, and build true links of solidarity.

People have come here to Venezuela, and other people traveled to learn from experiences abroad. That is the basis for a true, people-to-people solidarity, a solidarity that should visibilize the Chavista subject (contradictions with the government notwithstanding). After all, this is a project that has had its limitations, advances and setbacks, but the ideas of transformation that it is based on are not particular to Venezuela but belong to the entire world.

This is a project that proposes an alternative at a time when political processes in serious crisis are compounded by ecological and social crises. The global context is marked by an obvious struggle to lead a new industrial revolution, the fourth according to some. In the face of all this, we say that there are other ways to do things.

To get people mobilized internationally, we must share our experiences with them: the communal initiatives, the popular organization to resist attacks and blockades, the internal incoherences, and the political violence coming from certain sectors of the opposition. On top of that there is the criminal interventionism of the United States, the European Union, their puppets, and the international institutions.

Here we have tangible experiences that connect us with the struggles of all the world's peoples. The crisis that we are living through here is linked with the global crisis. Just as we, as Chavistas, must get together and organize and systematize what we have learned, as well as project our tangible grassroots experiences at a national level, so we also need to have policies that apply at an international level.

It is now more than ever that the *pueblo* needs active solidarity and mobilization in favor of the idea and practice of self-government, affirming that in the face of the crisis, the only plausible goal for the people is socialism. We need solidarity to push forward the core of the Chavista project. With this in mind, we have to organize, build, and unite.

The peoples of the South, the peoples of Latin America, are experiencing enormous political setbacks, with some governments that are almost fascist and others that are neoliberal. We have to organize internationally so that these governments are not able to construct a right-wing hegemony at a continental level.

We are in a process struggling over what people take for granted, what passes for common sense. There is no doubt that we have been weakened and are in a phase of resistance, but we need to begin to advance. We have to work together to build cultural hegemony, bringing forth the key ideas and concepts that will allow the *pueblo* to rise up and go forward. That we cannot do just from Venezuela. Two-way solidarity is necessary.

Finally, we can say that solidarity expresses itself in different ways, from the medicines that get here from Chile or from Italy in the communal health system in the Altos de Lídice Commune, to the Basque Country campaign, which is collecting seeds for the El Maizal Commune as we speak. There are diverse kinds of solidarity on different scales.

All this is about solidarity with the Chavista *pueblo* and its project, and also about the solidarity with a project that works to guarantee human life. As Chávez said, what is at risk today is no more and no less than human life on earth, and that implies the need for much theoretical reflection, but also an active practice that will bring together the people of all nations in defense of life itself.

—August 4, 2019

The Urban Revolution: A Conversation with Hernan Vargas

Hernan Vargas is a spokesperson for the Movimiento de Trabajadoras Residenciales [Residential Workers Movement] and the Venezuelan Movimiento de Pobladoras y Pobladores [Settlers' Movement]. He also has an important role in the coordination of ALBA Movements. His research interests include popular economies and modes of social reproduction. For many years, Vargas has worked in popular education and organization. In this interview, we speak about one of Venezuela's most powerful social movements, which aims to reclaim urban space in the name of socialism.

Venezuela's population is highly urban, with 80 to 90 percent of Venezuelans living in cities, many in poor *barrios*. These *barrios* are spaces of informal, unplanned construction, bringing all sorts of problems, from overcrowding to the lack of access to utilities. Urban problems are aggravated by the concentration of ownership, sometimes referred to as the issue of the "urban plantation" (*latifundio urbano*). The Movimiento de Pobladoras y Pobladores [henceforth Pobladoras] operates in this contested terrain of the city and is one of the largest social movements in Venezuela. Can you explain how it works?

Pobladoras is a platform of organizations that struggle in the urban context. It is an active network that includes the Comités de Tierra Urbana [Urban Land Committees, henceforth CTU, formed in the early days of the Bolivarian Process to struggle for urban land titles], the Campamentos de Pioneros [self-constructed-housing initiative], the Movimiento de Ocupantes de Edificios Organizados [vacant building occupiers movement], the Movimiento de Inquilinos [tenants' anti-eviction movement], and the Movimiento de Trabajadoras Residenciales [residential workers movement].

Pobladoras was built over time based on some key ideas. First and foremost, we organize around a common struggle against capital's control of the city. Here, we are revising the thesis of the traditional Left that conceived the struggle exclusively from the point of view of the organized working class or proletariat. In Venezuela, this conception needed updating. Our economy is a rentier capitalist one, and here the proletarian isn't at the center of the popular struggles. In Venezuela, there wasn't even a process of import substitution! Instead, what we have are impoverished city dwellers who live by selling their labor force in the services sector, by reselling goods in informal markets, as motorcycle taxi drivers, etc.

We have developed a hypothesis based on the practice of different organizations in this platform—which in fact preceded the emergence of Pobladoras—and on the years of organization and debate within the movement. All of that led us to recognize that the subject of struggle is the urban poor. It turns out that this subject has a disposition to struggle and a horizon of aspirations that is not limited to overcoming labor exploitation: it also struggles for access to services, for the collective control of the oil resources, and for recuperating urban land. In sum, the urban poor struggles for the commons!

Pobladoras emerged in the context of the Urban Revolution. It holds dear to the project of advancing to socialism through self-governance and self-organization, [appealing to] an urban subject that is committed to popular self-rule at the local level, while building a broad, communal horizon for our society as a whole.

Pobladoras has a multiplicity of roots. An important precedent is the experience of the Asambleas de Barrio [a popular, non-traditional urban movement in Venezuela] in the 1990s. Later, there were the CTUs, which arose during the Bolivarian Process. Additionally, we can point to international influences such as the

Communes and the Reorganization of Society

Pobladores in Chile, the participatory budgeting in Porto Alegre, and the housing co-ops in Uruguay. Thus, there are various roots to the movement. How does it all come together?

Pobladoras indeed has a complex origin. To synthesize, we could say that we have three main roots that, ultimately, are really one and the same.

First, there are the historical urban movements that have, in some way or another, participated in homesteading in the outskirts of large Latin American cities. Although it's true that Venezuela, due to its rentier capitalist economy, has its own particularities regarding its mode of accumulation, the forms of urbanization here are not too different from other countries of the continent. In other words, we share the problems of urban life in the Global South.

Take Chile for instance. Once production in the factories came to a halt [first during the Allende government, as a sabotage, and later due to neoliberal policies], the urban settlers, who were formerly factory workers and lived in the poverty belts and shantytowns, began to forcefully struggle for their right to the land. So the project shifted from being a traditional working-class struggle, which was quite intense, to a very rebellious urban struggle.

The same thing happened in Argentina and elsewhere. In Uruguay, as you mentioned, there is a very active cooperative housing movement. In all of these struggles, deep patterns of cooperativism and self-management emerged, and they became key to the shaping of a political subject and a project.

As part of this whole [Latin American urban struggle], we have Venezuelan experiences such as the Asambleas de Barrio in the 1990s, which were made up of the people who built the formal city for capital, the city of the bourgeoisie and the middle classes. On weekends, through a spontaneous process of mutual help and solidarity, these people engaged in self-organized processes of housing construction and undertook mutual aid funds. . . . They built their homes together in the periphery of the city, helping each other.

The Asambleas de Barrio come, on the one hand, out of the

common struggles that the urban poor carried out against the city of capital for access to services and against police repression. On the other hand, they come out of the experience of organizing insurgent, armed movements decades before. That is the second root.

So Pobladoras comes out of a larger tendency all across Latin America of the urban poor struggling against the "city of capital" and locally it comes out of the Asambleas de Barrio experience.

What is the third root? The third root, which is really an accumulation of many struggles, is Chavismo. The people here had a powerful tradition of struggles against neoliberal logics, against the old political parties, and against the ingrained forms of doing politics. They rebelled against all forms of exclusion and mobilized around a proposal that called for a radically different national (and continental) project. That is what Chavismo was about at the beginning.

From there emerged some very interesting projects such as the Mesas Técnicas de Agua [*barrio*-level organizations for getting access to running water]. We are talking about an early period in the Bolivarian Process, the time of "councils," when communities organized to figure out how they could connect with the project of the 1999 Constitution. What I mean is that, if the Constitution promised universal access to education, then people organized to make that happen. They began to look for spaces in the *barrio* where classes could be taught with the collaboration of Cuban educators. Thus, the constitutional right combined with local efforts of organization guaranteed that millions of people attained literacy or graduated from high school or college.

The same thing happened with the issue of urban land ownership. At that time the urban poor found themselves faced with a constitution that grants the right to housing, and laws that in principle regularized the land tenancy of the plot of land for that 60 percent of the population living in the *barrios*. To say the obvious, the system isn't going to spontaneously make those rights tangible and that is when the organization came in.

Thus, the urban poor organized to do cadastral surveying [mechanism for identifying property using land registers] and to record the local histories of the *barrio*. . . . That is where Pobladoras took shape. Yet it came forward with a project that wasn't limited to regularizing land ownership for the excluded urban subject that lives in the *barrio*. Pobladoras also addressed the problems of people who face precarious rental situations, residential workers, building occupiers, etc. We all came together in a movement that extended a hand to any exploited subject struggling for these common objectives. In Chavismo, there was an urban social base that became the synthesis of all those struggles.

For a movement like Pobladoras, it's important that there is a government that is sympathetic to popular, self-managed initiatives. That is to say, there is a dialectical relation between, on the one hand, the urban subject, composed of collective and diverse forces that come from below, and, on the other hand, state power that is willing to work with the popular movement.

The Pobladoras's roots are not only those of the movement. They are, in fact, the same roots of Chavismo and of the Chavista government. Acknowledging that the government is not homogeneous (it's no secret that this government has a multiclass composition, though perhaps not as much so as the formerly progressive governments of Brazil or Argentina), we find that within the government there is a current that has a strong commitment to the people. Of course, and this goes without saying, the strength of this current has varied.

A couple of years ago, Nicolás Maduro said that the Bolivarian Process consists of different periods, and that we should study them. If we do so, we observe that not only has the government wavered, but also popular organizations have had their ups and downs.

What is unquestionably true, however, is that beginning with the coup against Chávez in 2002, we realized that the bourgeois state and status quo would not allow for universal access to education, healthcare, or the land. From then on, there was an awareness that popular organization was the only means (combined with a favorable legal framework and sympathetic constituted power) for achieving our objectives and making good on the rights embodied in the Constitution.

For instance, the United Nations recently recognized Venezuela for its policies of social inclusion regarding housing rights. In these last few years, 2.6 million houses have been built. Of those, close to one million, some 37 percent, have been built by popular power [indigenous communities, Misión Ribas (educational project), Campamentos de Pioneros, and Communal Councils].

That is an important experience, because it shows how this combination of many historical struggles has led to a new way of building housing. Those who in the past built their own houses with mutual collaboration but without state support . . . today are empowered through laws: they have the possibility of occupying land and receiving financial support and technical aid. In this way, they have achieved their objective.

It's an objective that was not the result of clientelist practices, but rather one that was attained through a long and organized struggle that entailed navigating, among other things, the diverse composition of the government. That is to say, it emerged in a context where some people at the top believe that socialism is merely a more fair distribution of the rent—more or less a rehashing of the old Venezuelan capitalist model. By contrast, we believe that socialism means social production to satisfy social needs, a focus on the people, and popular self-management in an effort to construct something new.

Regarding the goal of the Pobladoras movement, you have said that it shouldn't be merely a question of fighting for people's "right to the city" (since that could amount to merely building some low-income housing and a few parks). Instead, it should be about struggling to wrest the city from capital's control. That sounds great, but what does it really mean?

The majority of the ideas of Chavismo, and of the Pobladoras movement in particular, developed over time, in the course of the struggle. In developing the idea of the urban revolution, which is the key thesis driving our struggle, we came to reject the idea that the poor can reconcile their demands with the city as it is organized now (as if the city were a place where rich and poor could happily live alongside each other). To a great degree, the discourses based on "the democratization of the city" or "the right to the city" are about that: "democratizing" the city of capital. Needless to say, that is not possible.

More or less the same thing happens with the progressivist project, which is an attempt to extend and democratize the promise of occidental modernity. That can only happen in a very limited way in the centers of power, in the centers of capital. When you look at the configuration of global capital, you see how the central countries' elites live by dispossessing the majorities, and especially the majority populations of the Global South. Thus, that model cannot be democratized because it is based on dispossessing the other.

The "right to the city" model is not viable. We cannot democratize the model of life of the rich minority. It's not a harmonic model, extendable to everyone, but one based on structural privileges.

This is something that we discovered over time, which meant calling into question the paradigms that we took seriously a while ago. When Frederick Engels analyzed the problem of housing, he concluded that workers' housing was actually a need for capital at a certain stage of its development. However, once accumulation by dispossession begins to organize the capitalist economy, access to housing for the poor, particularly in the periphery, ceases to be a need for capital. In fact, I would even say that resolving housing problems never sat well with capitalism, but here and now, in the Global South, [Engels's] hypothesis is farther removed from reality than ever before. In our case, informal and precarious labor, with a focus on services, makes the hypothesis even more extravagant.

That means that the urban revolution has to struggle over urban space, and it must also build a new model of social reproduction. When we occupy, for instance, a vacant lot to build a new socialist community, that is not just about redistribution of the land, it's also about developing a new set of social relations in that space. As families organize to occupy a plot of land for their homes, and as they go through the process of caring for it, all that happens along with collective decisions and assemblies.

The assembly is the place where the collective decides not only how to physically construct a building, but also a space where internal social relations are debated and reconstructed. Issues such as gender violence are addressed collectively. For example, a *compañero* who is violent with his partner will be excluded from the process.

Of course, I'm not saying that these exercises of organization actually constitute forms of consolidated socialism. However, they are spaces where we struggle for control of the city, and in doing so we are struggling for another model for the city where the private is not separated from the collective. It's a new mode of producing and reproducing life in the city, a new way of building social relations, cultural relations, with new forms of interpreting reality.

So the Pobladoras movement is about building socialism at a local level, which is what Chávez proposed. That is why conceiving the commune as the space for fostering socialism is an integral part of our proposal. Here I'm not talking so much about the bureaucratic process of registering a commune, but rather about the communal project at its core, which is a collective emancipatory project. The Pobladoras, too, are contributing to the communal path. After all, that is what socialism is for us: the communes, the commons, the collective struggle for the means to satisfy collective needs.

Among the projects of Pobladoras, there is one that I find especially fascinating. It's the practice of occupying urban spaces and then building housing there, which is done by the "Pioneros" (Pioneers).

I would say that the Pioneros and their projects grow out of the whole Pobladoras movement. So, if Pobladoras is a confluence of organizations around the idea of the urban revolution, Pioneros can be seen as a kind of synthesis of all the historical currents that evolved into the Pobladoras movement.

First, the CTUs emerged because of people's need to organize to get deeds for the land where their homes were built, in the steep hills on the outskirts of the city. Then there were others who joined the movement: the people who lived in precarious housing conditions, residential workers living in quasi-slavery, tenants struggling to avoid evictions, the occupiers of vacant buildings.... Together we began to think about wresting the city from the control of capital that is growing at the expense of everything else.

All those currents come together in Pioneros camps, that aim to take over unused land which is in the hands of capital.

I'll tell you about a new socialist community, the Amatina Pioneros Encampment, which was recently inaugurated in a Gran Misión Vivienda Venezuela act [henceforth GMVV, government housing program]. This housing was built on a plot of land that we took from the Polar Corporation [a giant Venezuelan private food conglomerate]. Polar kept the lot vacant, using it to dispose waste. Under the banner of the Revolution, we were able to occupy that plot of land. A group of organized families collectively built their homes there (which, as I said before, is the immediate aim, whereas the strategic objective is to generate a new form of life). In that way, the two hundred or so "Pioneros Amatina" families generated a collective social fabric based on communality, thereby getting away from the false premise that we can individually solve our problems.

First came the housing, then the new community began to plan a socialist bakery or a vegetable garden. This process implies, of course, the distribution of work. For the community to advance, all the adult and healthy members of the family have to work, and their work has to be coordinated. That is how one new community grew. Our idea is to foster new forms of urban life based on self-organization and self-management, which is part and parcel with Chávez's project.

Inspired by [Hungarian Marxist] István Mészáros, Chávez conceived of a new kind of participation and democracy, that is, substantive democracy, which has self-management as a key element.

By the way, when we say "self-management," we aren't just talking about self-building or self-financing. No, we are talking about the people taking charge of the means to produce and reproduce their own lives. In this regard, the economic crisis has been an interesting moment for us, because it is now that society can recognize that the path of self-management is the only one that leads to real solutions.

Recently, we organized a march to the National Constitutive

Assembly, first to demand that the institution return to being really constitutive, and secondly to promote the self-management model, calling for a legal framework that would prioritize collective [ownership] over [the interests of] capital in the realm of housing.

The huge GMVV housing project is essentially a top-down initiative, since most of the homes are built by large construction companies and people don't participate in the process. That means that, between Pobladoras and GMVV, there are two very different kinds of projects, both of them vying for the state's resources (based on oil rent). One is grassroots, self-organized and based on cooperation and solidarity, whereas the other is top-down. Would you agree that there is a conflict between the top-down model that aims merely to redistribute the oil rent versus your own model which aims for grassroots control of the country's resources?

I was recently listening to an Argentinian who had done research on the Pink Tide. She pointed out that the redistributive model, whatever its limitations, was in itself the outcome of a struggle. The redistribution of resources that emerged in the progressive governments during the economic boom is not just a handout. So we could imagine that this struggle has different phases: first, there is a struggle for access (to services, to healthcare, to housing), but that struggle could morph into something else, less dependent, more autonomous, more emancipatory.

For instance, in the last few years, Pobladoras has become one of the groups carrying out the projects of the GMVV. There is a part of the GMVV that is done hand in hand with popular power, and we in Pobladoras represent a tiny percentage of that part. What's the upside of this? In these initiatives, to one degree or another, people become the subjects. As I mentioned, not all the projects related to popular power are self-managed, but they represent a first step.

When the GMVV began, we made our position clear. We said it would only be viable if it went beyond merely distributing the resources derived from the oil rent and had a basis in self-management. At that time, people considered us a bunch of crazies! Now we may still be the "crazies," but the crisis and cruel blockade has made it clear, the only way forward is popular organization and collective work.

As Chávez said in the *Homeland Plan* [2012]. Venezuela still has a rentier capitalist economy. From the beginning, Chavismo has attempted to democratize a model that is not democratizable because it's based on appropriation of wealth, on looting. . . . Within that framework, we did the best we could: millions of people graduated from high school and college, and millions of people got access to public healthcare, entertainment, housing, etc.

The problem is that the redistributive model [that maintains the rentier economy] can only go so far, and it surely cannot survive a crisis of the scale that we now are facing. For this reason, we went to the Constitutive Assembly and we said that, in the face of the crisis, the only option is self-management; the only path is to struggle for the control of the means of production. In that sense, we in Pobladoras are offering a solution.

Just as *campesinos* struggle for land and access to seeds, machinery and tools, so we struggle for plots of urban land. We also struggle for the means of production, from the building materials to the machinery needed to build our homes. In constructing our homes with our own work, we produce new communities based on solidarity.

For us, the struggle within the Revolution now is precisely that: a struggle to generate ample conditions so that the people can be the builders of their own lives. Today, I don't think that the balance of power in Venezuela is such that we can, at the moment, make our model, which is based on self-emancipation, hegemonic. Nevertheless, we must struggle to displace the old modes of rent circulation, if we don't want to lose ground.

This brings us to a very interesting debate about the Bolivarian Process. On the one hand, there are those who argue that the project is about distributing state resources more democratically and extending basic services to all, but all within the logic of rentier capitalism. On the other hand, we consider that we need to develop a new metabolism. When there was a lot of money to go around, this debate was not intense. Now, however, those who live off of the appropriation of the rent confront the popular sectors who call for a complete reorganization of the country in economic and cultural terms.

[Because this debate is coming to the forefront], we have to prepare ourselves not only for occupying urban land, but also for advancing our alternative model. For that reason, we asked for a chance to take the floor in a session at the National Constitutive Assembly. We need to make our case there and in other spaces, shaping public opinion.

Regarding public opinion, we have to acknowledge that we have had serious defeats in recent times. In the current crisis, many began to think that it was better to have well-stocked shelves in supermarkets, even if the prices are very high, than poorly-stocked shelves with accessible products. That was a battle we lost on a symbolic level.

In the historical line leading up to the present, reaching from the continent-wide movements [of the 1960s], to the struggles of the 1990s and the Chavista movement, the battle of ideas has been just as important as the struggle for the territory. There, our main programmatic points are popular control, self-management, and greater democracy from the base. All this has one objective: to guarantee the reproduction of life for working people.

—June 20, 2019

Notes to Section 1

1. "*Panal*" means beehive or honeycomb in Spanish, and it is a reference to collective construction and collective defense.
2. The Chiliying Commune was a pioneer commune in the Hunan province of China. It was the subject of a classic study by Li Chu, *Inside a People's Commune*, that Chávez encouraged people to read.
3. "*Ñángara*" is a term used to refer to communists. Initially, it had negative connotations, but Venezuelan leftists later used it to identify themselves. "*Tupamaro*" is a term used to refer to the radical urban left. It was originally used by a revolutionary Uruguayan movement of the 1960s and 70s.
4. The term "*Libertadores*" refers to the men and women who led the independence wars against the Spanish colony in the second and third decade of the 19th century.
5. In the Chavista discourse, the term "territorial" refers to a popular form of organization that has its roots in a particular area. In other words, it refers to an organization that is not sectorial, such as a union, a student organization, or a feminist organization.
6. "Co-management," as the term was used in Venezuela in the period 2005–2006, refers to the joint managing of enterprises by workers and the state or, more rarely, to the participation of workers in managing private enterprises.
7. The term "proletarization" (*proletarización*) was coined by Alexis Vive to describe developing productive forces under new social relations, bringing *barrio*-dwellers out of the precarious urban jobs available in today's Venezuela.
8. Jacinto Pérez Arcay is a high-ranking military officer (retired) and writer who was key to Chávez's education.
9. "Exclusive Zones of Communal Production," a concept developed by Alexis Vive, is the proposal for a political and legal framework that would prioritize communal development in certain areas of the Caribbean nation.
10. Lorenzo Mendoza is the biggest capitalist in Venezuela and the owner of the food production enterprise Alimentos Polar. He is an active, if sometimes low-profile, critic of the Bolivarian government.
11. "*Guarimbas*" are a form of violent street protests employed by the Venezuelan opposition. They frequently involve burning tires and the use of makeshift barricades to block roads.
12. Lorent Saleh is a Venezuelan opposition activist who was accused in 2014 of organizing paramilitary actions and plotting terrorist attacks. There was ample evidence that he conspired with international figures

to destabilize the Caribbean nation. In October 2018, Venezuelan authorities released him from jail without any explanation. It is commonly believed that his release resulted from secret negotiations.
13. El Maizal Commune is made up of 22 communal councils across Portuguesa and Lara states. Communes are the conglomeration of communal councils, and they are at the core of Chávez's proposal for a radical and democratic reorganization of society. One of Venezuela's most successful communes, El Maizal harvested some 4,000 tons of corn last year. It also produces beef, pork, and cheese as well as manages gas distribution.
14. In December 2017, Angel Prado was elected mayor of Simón Planas township. Nevertheless, Jean Ortiz of the ruling United Socialist Party of Venezuela (PSUV), with half as many votes as Prado, obtained the mayor's seat.
15. The day after this interview with Angel Prado, *campesinos* from around the country occupied a number of Agropatria stores with the aim of denouncing the problems that had emerged in the past few months. Members of El Maizal, including Angel Prado, participated in these occupations.
16. In 2010, Venezuela's National Assembly passed a series of laws including the Organic Law of Popular Power, the Organic Law of the Communes, the Organic Law for the Development and Promotion of the Communal Economy, the Organic Law of Social Auditing, and the Organic Law of Popular and Public Planning.
17. The CLAP (Local Food Production and Provision Committee) organizes the distribution of subsidized food, whereas the UBCh (Bolívar-Chávez Battle Units) are the PSUV's basic organizational units/branches at a local level.
18. The *Homeland Plan* (*Plan de la Patria*) is a five-part government program that Chávez developed in his 2012 presidential campaign. Its objectives include: constructing Bolivarian socialism, fostering a multipolar world, and preservation of the planet.

2
OIL, PRIVATIZATIONS, AND THE ECONOMY

The Past, Present, and Future of Venezuela's Oil Industry: A Conversation with Carlos Mendoza Pottellá

Carlos Mendoza Pottellá is an economist and oil expert at Venezuela's Central Bank (BCV). Here, he talks about the reasons behind Venezuela's severe drop in oil production and the future of the country's economy.

There is a discourse focused on rentierism in Venezuela that goes as follows: "We must leave behind rentierism. We must become a productive country." This is reflected today in President Nicolás Maduro's claim that "we must end our oil culture, our rentier culture." Do you believe that oil is really a curse for Venezuela?

I don't. But it is the case that the problem with oil and gas rents and the "distortion" that they create in the economy has long been an object of study and debate. The Norwegians call it the "Venezuela effect" and have tried to avoid the "distortion" by allowing only a very small percentage of the income generated by their oil industry to enter the economy. Others call it the "Dutch disease."

The truth is that Venezuela is the owner of enormous profits that are not the result of human labor carried out in Venezuela but rather an international monopolistic structure. Our wealth has a very specific origin: we are owners of something that is finite, a scarce resource that is universally necessary. . . . This has a great potential to foster a diversification of the economy. But it can also have a negative effect on the productive apparatus.

It is true that when you introduce an overwhelmingly rentier component [profits not derived from labor carried out in the nation itself] into a developed capitalist economy, as would be the case in Norway, it tends to create distortions. But that is not the Venezuelan case. When oil exploration began here, this was not a developed country. We had nothing to protect. We were the poorest nation in the continent, a country that had passed through two savage wars (the Independence War and the Federal War), a country with stilted population growth, illiteracy, and malaria. It was a country without a notion of "nation," without frontiers, a no man's land. Venezuela was the most abandoned territory on the continent.

In other words, when oil exploration and exploiting begins, Venezuela's productive apparatus could not be destroyed by the rent, since the country was severely underdeveloped and peripheral.

Right. When the oil industry began in Venezuela, capitalism was implanted here like a cancer, but it did not displace "productive" capitalism. With the oil industry, there came a reorganization of the society and the territory. The oil profits were (and are) managed from Caracas. Caracas was where the money was, everything else was a backwater. Thus, the country began to be reshaped, with the Caracas-Maracay-Valencia-Maracaibo corridor containing the vast majority of the population.

Back in the 1930s, Alberto Adriani, our first economist, described how our wealth was not the result of our own labor, but rather due to particular circumstances: we are owners of a finite resource that is internationally required, causing large sums of money to flow into the economy. From there—and based on the Ricardian perspective—comes the moralistic perspective that interprets rent as "sinful."

Leaving behind the moralistic attitude, what Venezuela really must do is look for ways to distribute the rent rationally. And yes, it makes sense to invest in healthcare, education, infrastructure, and national defense. There is nothing sinful there. Also, investment in culture and science is important, and Venezuela has made great advances in those fields.

Now, it is true that the economy's rentier character leads to limited development in other areas. What has happened in Venezuela, and what tends to happen in rentier economies, is that the state facilitates the buying of hard currencies by subsidizing exchange rates. This, in turn, implies that the local currency is overvalued, making foreign production cheap, and everything that is produced locally expensive. As a consequence, everything is imported and national production dies out.

The first to describe this situation, as I mentioned earlier, was Adriani. He predicted that Venezuela would become an enclave and buy everything abroad. He reflected on how the oil income would disappear in trips to Paris and the purchase of fine silks. Later, in the '70s and '80s, we witnessed the trips to Miami and the "Está barato, dame dos" ("It's cheap, give me two") phenomenon.

From Adriani's reflection comes Arturo Uslar Pietri's hypothesis about "sowing petroleum" as a way to develop a more diversified economy.

Going back to the Manichean interpretation of Venezuela's future, it is common to assume that Venezuela has one of two possible destinies: a productive future which is good, and a rentier one that is bad.

Yes, we must firmly reject the discourse that goes as follows: the rentier destiny, the "bad" one, involves using the rent for social investment, thus promoting parasitism. The productive and good destiny, according to this interpretation, is about investing in private businesses, with investment in schools, hospitals, and housing being "bad" rentierism.

In fact, what we must decide then is what we will do with the resource we collectively own as Venezuelans: should the destiny of the rent be social or private?

You have claimed elsewhere that a part of the surplus must be reinvested in oil production, another part must be directed at social programs, and a percentage must go toward diversifying the economy. But how should the latter be done, given the economic and historical processes that you have described?

Obviously this is hard, but since the income coming from oil has been drastically reduced, we are forced to diversify. The oil industry will continue to generate an income for the nation, which has to be administered to satisfy social needs, but it's never going to be what it once was. So economic diversification must take place, and it has to happen with resources from the diminished oil profits, with planning and good management.

Ninety-six percent of Venezuela's economy is based on international oil sales, but oil production has been falling dramatically. In 2012, Venezuela received USD$97 billion from oil sales. Three years later, in 2016, Venezuela got only $39 billion, and in 2017, a mere $28 billion! Part of the explanation for this drop in income is the falling oil prices (the external factor), but there is also an internal factor, the collapse of oil production, which has dropped by half in a decade, to about 1.5 million barrels a day, and the loss of well over half a million barrels a day in the last year alone.

Let's first focus on what I consider to be the main problem. For the last decade and a half, or even longer, the focus of oil exploration and exploitation has been the Orinoco Belt.

It was a flawed plan, because it went hand in hand with the expectation that oil prices would stay well above $100 a barrel. Everyone got roped into this idea: that Venezuela had the largest oil reserves without taking into account the real nature of the oil in the Orinoco fields.

It is correct that we are the owners of 15 to 20 percent of the oil on the planet, but the truth is that a lot of that oil cannot be exploited today. When we think about the extra-heavy oil in the Orinoco Oil Belt, it is indeed an enormous reserve that can last for many hundreds of years (some say it will last 500 years), but these projections are absurd. They have absolutely no economic meaning today! To give an example, big corporations project a maximum of 15 years into the future.

So Venezuela cannot say that it has 600 million barrels in its reserve, for it is impossible to exploit that in the foreseeable future. There may be an enormous accumulation in the Orinoco Belt, but only a small part is actually exploitable, and exploiting it is very expensive. In truth, Venezuela has a 15.000 to 20.000 million barrel reserve. That is what can be tapped in the foreseeable future.

For that reason, Venezuela should shift production to the northwest oil fields in Zulia.

Yes. The exceptionally high oil prices ten years ago led us to neglect our limited but real and important production capacity. We forgot that our conventional fields produce 30, 24, and 20 API[1] oil that goes directly to the refinery, and that we should focus on stimulating that kind of light oil exploitation. The fields in the Maracaibo Lake and elsewhere [conventional wells with lighter oil] are indeed declining. Perhaps they will last for only another 50 years, but five decades of profitable production is very good!

The temptation of investing in the Orinoco Oil Belt—of developing the largest exploitation project that could potentially yield six million barrels a day—was based on the projection that the price of oil would permanently remain well above $100.

So instead of updating existing wells (there are some 30,000 perforated conventional wells, half of them not in use), which could increase production by 25,000 BPD per well, all the investment went to the Orinoco Belt.

Since I don't believe in magical solutions, I hold that what we should focus on now is updating these conventional wells. In other words, a cost-benefit analysis indicates that we must shift our investment away from the Orinoco Belt and back to the conventional wells. That alone would help stabilize production.

Some analysts are coming to the conclusion that the decision-makers of the oil industry in Venezuela are pushing toward privatization. Do you believe that to be the case?

When you have a plan that requires $60 billion in investment and your income is $5 billion per year, what are you implying? That you are looking for someone to come and invest. That is the logic of privatization and anyone can read it between the lines.

So the conditions for privatization are here. The Venezuelan state seems incapable of managing oil production now. On the other hand, I would not say that the tendency toward privatization is planned. I think it is involuntary. I think it is the result of a perfect storm. The collapse of production opens the door to "outside saviors" who will take on operations.

With regard to this, we must understand that if private companies run the operations piecemeal [exploration, servicing, exploitation, distribution], and this is likely to happen, then PDVSA [Petróleos de Venezuela] as such is not literally privatized, which would be unconstitutional. What is likely to happen then is that subsidiaries [de facto private undertakings] run the operations.

Through the subsidiaries [*filiales*] there would be an indirect privatization, which is permitted by a loophole in the Constitution of the Bolivarian Republic of Venezuela: Article 303 states that PDVSA and the wells are non-transferable and are the property of the Republic, but that subsidiaries can assume operations.

We understand that one of the factors pushing toward privatization is the plummeting production. Thus, I think it is important to understand why Venezuela's oil production has gone from 3 to 1.4 million BPD (barrels per day). What are the main factors that have led to the current production crisis?

In addition to my assessment, which is that we shouldn't have focused our strategic planning on the Orinoco Belt because pumping oil there is only sustainable with very high oil prices, the main issue is that there has been a snowballing of management and operational problems. Combine these with serious corruption—which the government is perhaps trying to address—lack of control, a massive exodus of qualified workers in the last year, and the lack of resources and daily maintenance, we come to the current catastrophic situation.

Lack of maintenance is accelerating the closing down of conventional wells, and production in the Orinoco wells is not profitable, so it is also being reduced. All this leads to a possible standstill.

But there is a way out, and I repeat myself here: fomenting conventional oil production.

Hugo Chávez bequeathed us, as a tangible legacy, the state control of the oil profits. As Chavistas, how should we fight against the privatization of the oil industry?

Well, it has to be talked about, it has to be discussed, we have to explain, and we have to push for a campaign. The problem is that this discussion and campaign are not happening, because we are in a political context in which, when a critical voice emerges, then that person is categorized as opposition, as the enemy. There is no capacity to reflect scientifically from above, and those with critical perspectives within do not want to get involved in the game, as it may have negative political consequences.

—May 1, 2018

Social Inclusion Is Needed to Overcome the Crisis: A Conversation with Luis Salas

Luis Salas is former Venezuelan vice president for productive economy. He now teaches political economy at the Bolivarian University while writing prolifically about Venezuela's economic and political scene.

In this interview, Salas responds to our questions about the economic measures that the government implemented in August 2018, which include a reconversion of the Bolívar currency and an anchoring of this reconverted currency, the Sovereign Bolívar, to the Petro cryptocurrency, as well as a minimum wage hike. We asked him to explain and evaluate these measures, and their likely effect on the country's future.

What are the causes of Venezuela's current crisis, and to what degree can the government's recent measures solve the problem?

We can't say that the crisis has only one cause. There are structural causes that have to do with historical conditions and the structure of the Venezuelan economy, but I think our situation today is in a large measure attributable to attacks on Venezuela's exchange rate that began in 2013 in the context of Hugo Chávez's worsening health and then his death. The arrival of President Nicolás Maduro to power led to a very aggressive monetary attack, and what has happened since then has much to do with the immediate and medium-term effects of that.

Later on, other elements entered the picture. In my view, a large part of the responsibility lies with the inefficacy of the government's measures to offset and reverse the effects of these [monetary] attacks. Moreover, many policies even contributed to making things worse, as for example, in the areas of prices and currency exchange.

Also, we have to consider the sanctions, even if they are more recent (beginning in mid-2015), and the falling oil price. These are factors that come in to complicate the situation, but I don't think they are the fundamental causes of what is happening now.

Additionally, the handling of the debt has not been very apt. First, the practice has been to simply pay the debt without asking for any kind of renegotiation or restructuring. We only asked for restructuring when it was already very late, when the sanctions were already there, and moreover when we had paid a very large amount: more than $70 billion. That meant that we sacrificed a large part of the imports to pay for that debt without reducing the country's risk and without abating the atmosphere of conflict.

Because of the financial blockade, Venezuela has difficulty accessing international financial markets, and can only access them if it pays very high interest. The last attempt to break out of the blockade, which was the Petro, was itself blocked. I think that all this has contributed to the crisis. Later on, there are other factors that make the situation worse, such as what is happening in the state oil company, PDVSA, and new practices that have been introduced in the society such as the illegal economy, etc.[2] The hyperinflation that we are seeing has to do with all those things brought together over the long term.

There are many uncertainties about these new economic measures. One concern is the anchoring of the Sovereign Bolívars to the Petro, and in turn the Petro to the price of the Venezuelan oil barrel. That really only makes sense if one could exchange Bolívar for Petros and Petros for oil barrels or the equivalent in hard currency. Is that the case? It's clear that in a market economy, the value of a currency can't be a matter of mere decree. In effect, how are we to understand the idea of "anchoring" the currency?

As you yourself indicate, I think the anchoring of the Sovereign Bolívar to the Petro is essentially a matter of decree. There are many things that continue to be unclear here. There is a formula that was established in which the value of the Petro corresponds to the current price of an oil barrel. From there the government set up an exchange rate with different currencies, such as the dollar and the Sovereign Bolívar. Those are the basics.

They say the Petro will function as a unit of account as was the case with the Real in the context of Brazil's "Plan Real." However, they also continue to claim it is a cryptocurrency, even though we don't know exactly how it can be used, nor how it will be used. The President said there will be a surprise announcement about it in October or November, but similar announcements have been made on earlier occasions. A pre-sale and a sale were done, in which supposedly we got $3 billion, but we don't know what happened with that. Nor do we know if it will be a currency or a cryptocurrency for external commerce, or if it is for internal commerce too. Based on some decisions the government took before the Petro came out, we can suppose it is also for internal circulation. That raises the issue of how it will coexist with the Sovereign Bolívar. Possibly Venezuela will have a system with two currencies, as in Cuba, with the peso and the CUC (Cuban Convertible Peso), which have different values and cause a set of distortions.

So, for now, the anchoring of the Sovereign Bolívar to the Petro functions as a governmental decree, but whose economic base and future functioning is still to be seen.

With regard to socialism—which was Chávez's strategic objective—do you think that the recent measures amount to a step forward or a step backward? Or perhaps they are a step backward to later go forward.

I have said on other occasions that if there is one weakness in the current economic policy, it is that it lacks definition. In the time of Chávez, one understood that there was an economy that, although it was operating in a capitalist context, there was still an implicit process of transition toward a goal—that was, socialism (even if we didn't know exactly what kind of socialism beyond some statements).

Now, even though socialism continues to be part of the discourse, in practice the general tendency is toward policies that wager on a kind of neo-industrialization, counting on the Venezuelan private sector.

It seems to be along the lines of the classic discourse in Venezuela of substituting so-called "rentier capitalism" for industrial capitalism, with a nationalist bourgeoisie, etc. At the same time, there has been support for the communes, but with time the communal project has lost more and more importance. The same goes for the EPSs.³

So the announced measures, assuming that they work, seem to be part of a stabilization plan in the conventional sense, even if they contain elements that are heterodox and nonconventional. They seem to be the result of a pact with the most concentrated private sector regarding prices, and there is talk about the reduction of the fiscal deficit.

Whether all this amounts to a step forward or a step backward is still to be seen. Most elements point to it being a heterodox plan in an overall framework of capitalism that is trying to develop industry and attract foreign investment. In that sense, of course, it doesn't seem to escape the logic of the traditional plans of that kind.

There seem to be cycles in the Venezuelan economy: a kind of pendulum swing that goes from oil booms to profound crises, which are followed by adjustments, belt-tightening, and liberalization (such as the hike in the sales tax and the freeing of the exchange rate that is going on now). In that sense, the government's new measures seem to be proof that we have not gotten out of the old labyrinth of dependent capitalism. How can we break with the inertia of this ongoing cycle?

How to break with the inertia and stop the pendulum swings? I think that historically in Venezuela there has been a mistaken interpretation of rentism and oil dependence: the mono-producing, mono-exporting nature of the Venezuelan economy. Oil is seen as the problem. The tendency is to treat oil dependence as if having oil were the root of the problem. In fact, I think that oil is a comparative advantage that the Venezuelan economy has and we have not known how to take full advantage of it.

Instead, I think that the problem of the Venezuelan economy is that it has a structural duality, as the old Latin American theorists called it, in which there is a primary economic sector that is very developed, with a level of productivity comparable to the first world (I am speaking of the petroleum industry, leaving aside its current problems). On the other hand, there is the second sector of the economy, industry and manufacturing, which is very dependent on importation for its inputs, and is also technologically backward.

In effect, I think the problem is not petroleum. The problem is that the second sector, which was weak even before oil entered the picture (in fact, the little that it has developed has been due to support, leveraging with oil profits). So the challenge of a country like Venezuela is in regard to how we develop sector two. Now, that brings us to another problem: With whom should it be developed? With the existing industrial group? With a new emergent group? Or with some other group?

In Venezuela, there is an old slogan: "sowing petroleum" [*sembrar petróleo*]. The intellectual Arturo Uslar Pietri invented the slogan, and it was put into action by the government of Isías Medina Angarita. The proposal was to transform Venezuelan capitalism, which was essentially commercial and financial, not very productive and even "parasitic" (as it was called at that time), toward developing the national bourgeoisie. But it was the national bourgeoisie itself who opposed that project and brought down Medina Angarita in 1945. In fact, the principal resistance to the project of industrialization comes from the national bourgeoisie, for whom it is inconvenient.

In that sense, the most important steps taken have been under Chávez, especially later on, when it was understood that it didn't make much sense to develop an industrial capitalism in Venezuela with private sector capitalists, though one didn't have to deny them participation. Instead, one needs to industrialize, thinking not only about productivity but also including new productive actors, based on diverse kinds of productive relations. That is where the EPSs come into play, and also the cooperatives and communes. There were a bunch of non-private economic projects, in which new kinds of producers emerged.

I think it's always rhetorical or cliché to say that in Venezuela we have to produce more. Yes, we have to produce more, but also we have to produce with other actors and agents. At least that is what history has shown and even the present points to: the private sector in Venezuela does not have the vocation to carry out a process of industrialization. It has to be a process leveraged by the state's forces (the main economic agent in the country) that will reach out to other sectors that can include the private sector, but essentially it must involve economic actors in relations of social property and other forms of organization, alternative ones.

Since one cannot separate the economy from a range of social, cultural, and historical factors, I would say that no macroeconomic measure (or even a battery of such measures) could solve the current crisis. If that is the case, what transformations are needed in our society so that ordinary people can begin to live better?

In effect, this is a multifactorial situation, and it also requires multifactorial solutions, not just macroeconomic measures. The solution would have to involve elements of a cultural order, etc. Now, I think that the first big step in the solution to the Venezuelan structural crisis would be a greater inclusion of the population into national life. That was achieved with Chávez between 2003 and 2012. But the medium-term problem has to do with the sustainability of that inclusion, which is exactly what was lost from 2013 to the present.

In principle, no national policy makes any sense without that inclusion. It is not only a matter of social justice and people living well, but also a matter of economic effectiveness. Importantly, the process of social inclusion between 2003 and 2012 led to people having more access to education. They became more educated and trained, and thus prepared to participate in a process of economic transformation.

An example of that is all the brain drain that has happened in the last few months to a year, in which people here were given free education (of a kind that would be impossible for many people in other parts of the world to access), and now they are leaving to become cheap wage labor in other parts of the world. In economic terms, it is as if we were exporting multipliers in the sense that all the investment that we made in education and technology is going to benefit other countries.

People got education and training, but simultaneously something took shape that hadn't existed before in Venezuela: the emergence of an internal market sufficiently robust to sustain an industrialization process. In Venezuela, there has always been a tendency to consumerism, but in the framework of an economy that was highly exclusive. Although consumerism did not go away, in Chávez's epoch (in fact, we saw much evidence of it), that should not hide the fact that there was a widening of the economic sphere and of the salary, leading to increased buying power. That, in turn, led to an effective demand that made the Venezuelan economy work for a long time. So I think that there are important elements that we need to consider, that should not be overlooked: social inclusion is fundamental, but also economic and political sustainability.

Is there anything else you would like to add?

If today's private sector, without a push in the petroleum industry, is going to return to the level of production similar to that of 2012, it would need to grow annually for a decade at about four or five percent. Moreover, it would have to surpass its current productive capacity by 350 times to supply the local market and generate exports, if we are talking about profits from other sectors substituting for the petroleum profits! That would involve an effort that from my point of view is simply impossible.

There is another element that is not usually mentioned: that big push in petroleum production will need to go hand in hand with an equally giant injection of electrical energy. Everyone knows about the problems that the Venezuelan economy confronts with regard to the supply of electricity. Our capacity to generate electricity is very run down. Some say that it is operating at about 50 percent of its capacity. To recover the other part, a great deal of investment is necessary.

As long as that is not done, there cannot be any alternative industrial development, because the businesses simply need electricity to function and they can't take it away from the residential sector, because that would lead to people being without electricity. In summary, to begin recuperation, it's necessary to get the petroleum industry going and update the electrical system, because the other option amounts to putting the cart before the horse. It doesn't make sense and the goal wouldn't be achievable.

—August 29, 2018

Privatizing Oil in Venezuela?
A Conversation with Victor Hugo Majano

Victor Hugo Majano is a blogger whose La Tabla website has been a reference for critical-but-committed Chavismo, since its founding in 2012. In an epoch in which serious investigative journalism has virtually disappeared, Majano has doggedly sought out hard-to-get information about Venezuela's politics and economy. In this interview, we asked him about the taboo subject of the privatizations taking place in Venezuela's cherished oil sector. It is an extremely sensitive issue, because oil constitutes the backbone of the nation's economy and also the basis of its population's well being for the foreseeable future.

There is a profound crisis in the Venezuelan oil industry, and the government has chosen the "orthodox solution," by creating favorable conditions for foreign investors (such as implementing the Law of Foreign Investment and lifting taxes).[4] Recently, the government has promoted "Joint Services Agreements," which seem to resemble the Open Oilfield policy ("Apertura Petrolera") of the 1990s.[5] What are the similarities and differences between the privatizations taking place today and those of that decade?

We can see similarities, for example, in the very words used to frame the contracts. The term "Operating Agreements" used in the 1990s can seem a lot like the current "Joint Services Agreements." There are also similarities in the sense that both aim to avoid legislative and constitutional control over private investment in the oil sector.

Articles 302 and 303 of the Bolivarian Constitution prevent the oil industry from being privatized. For that reason, the oil sector's

Oil, Privatizations, and the Economy   109

operation has generally been transparent, especially during the last decade. It has been based fundamentally on the concept of "Full Oil Sovereignty" that was laid out in 2008, leading to the practice of shifting all the "Joint Agreements" or similar contracts in the oil industry to "Joint Ventures." Joint Ventures are simply a scheme in which the Venezuelan state takes over 60 percent of the company's stock, whereas 40 percent is in the hands of private investors.

Obviously, the current scheme changes things completely, and for this reason, it resonates with the 1990s' Open Oilfield policy. The big difference is that it is not so public and transparent as the agreements signed during that decade. It's more furtive and complex from a legal standpoint, while the financial and contractual schemes that are being employed increase the level of opacity.[6]

The original formula for joint ventures under Chávez targeted the Orinoco Oil Belt, where there is a lot of dependence on foreign assistance, especially in the area of technology. The oil there is an extra-heavy crude that needs improvement processes to make it suitable for exporting to foreign refineries. Those processes require many imported inputs, diluents, and other chemicals, including naphtha. So the kind of oil exploitation that happens in the Oil Belt generates a big dependence on foreign actors, both in a logistical and financial sense.

Evidently, the logistical and financial problems have become more serious in the recent economic war years. This is one of the reasons for the large fall off in production in that zone [Orinoco Belt]. And in a way, this fall-off begins to justify (perhaps even deliberately) agreements with foreign investors addressing the problems associated with the improvement of extra-heavy crude oil.

Who has participated in these privatizations? Are we talking mostly about foreign companies or national ones, big players or small ones?

In this last phase, one has to look at two issues. One is the emergence of a new set of Joint Ventures. There is a very interesting joint venture that was established last year in the midst of the political and legislative turmoil, which is PetroSur. It's a mixed enterprise for the Orinoco Oil Belt involving stockholders of the Derwick group: they are shady investors of Venezuelan origin who have close relations with a set of Spanish counterparts. The process of founding PetroSur was carried out with a high degree of opacity, mostly because the Supreme Court's Constitutional Chamber issued Sentence No. 31, with which they took away the opposition-controlled National Assembly's power to control mixed enterprises.

That step led to the institutional crisis and the violent conflicts that took place in April, May, and June of 2017. The conflict lasted until July when the National Constituent Assembly was launched. The Supreme Court's decision to take away that power from the National Assembly was the main motive for the conflict, since the decision seemed to be designed just for the purpose of making such joint ventures. For that reason, it raised suspicion. That is to say, it appeared that the decision was specifically aimed at allowing the entry of such business groups into the oil sector, which is certainly one of the main historical ambitions of Venezuela's traditional bourgeoisie.

In effect, the Venezuelan bourgeoisie has always wanted to put its hands on the oil industry. Eighty years ago Arturo Uslar Pietri, the famous editor of the newspaper *Ahora*, coined the phrase "sembrar petróleo" ("sow petroleum"), which means simply passing resources from the oil industry to the traditional agricultural and livestock sector—the main sector of the Venezuelan bourgeoisie at that time. So it seems as if we are going back to that old scheme, except that we have some new players too.

The second set of issues associated with the privatizations is a lot more recent. It has to do with the current orientation of the oil industry and the forming of Joint Service Agreements. Except for the Chinese corporation Shandong Kerui Petroleum and [Brazil's] Petrobras—both of them are participating in Petrokariña—these agreements involve relatively unknown actors. A large number of business groups have popped up, outfits that we have never heard of, new players on the field.

In August of this year, Energy Minister Manuel Quevedo presented a list of seven businesses involved in Joint Services Agreements. He stated that private participation aims to recoup oil production mostly in the west of the country, which is where the oil is easiest to exploit because it is light oil. However, of those seven companies, only two, the earlier mentioned Kerui and Petrobras, are well-known ones!

So we are talking about businesses that are mostly unknown or, to the degree that they are known, are linked to sectors that historically have had nothing to do with the oil industry. One of them, for instance, is connected to shipping and has ties to Conferry, a Venezuelan ferry company. In turn, it has ties to Venezuelan navy officers. It would seem that this is simply a process in which the contractors that have operated in the shadow of the state by offering services and supplies for public projects are now trying to gain direct access to the oil industry.

The privatizing tendency goes hand in hand with a discourse, within Chavismo, that aims to justify it, by alleging the inefficiency of public enterprises. That way of thinking, however, overlooks the fact that the private sector's "efficiency" relies in a great measure on subsidies from the Venezuelan state. If privatizing means transferring the state's and the citizens' property to private hands, what does it tell us about the government's current direction?

First, let's look at the justification for the privatization processes that has been picking up speed recently. The verbal disparaging of the public sphere has been going on for a while from within [the Bolivarian Process]. It seems as if this libretto crept in over the years precisely to prepare the way, that is, to reach the point where basically nobody can say no to privatizations since many state enterprises are in a profound crisis or have simply come to a halt.

In other words, the process of privatization is not only accompanied by a discourse that justifies the shifting away from the public sphere, but the truth is that there are now material conditions that justify the privatizations underway. That is what we are seeing in most publicly-owned companies: a disregard for production that has generated a crisis. This includes the oil industry, where the collapse of production is extraordinary, having gone from three million barrels per day to one million in six years.

So, in addition to the discourse, there has been a purposeful neglect of the most basic oil operations in Venezuela's west, both in Lake Maracaibo in Zulia State, and in the western plains region (Barinas and Apure States). It's there that the problematic alliances with shady firms, such as those with Derwick Associates, are taking shape.

The light oil there [in the west] is very easily extracted, but production is lagging. Yet it is also an area where we had recent positive experiences with [joint venture] Petrozamora involving PDVSA in a coherent partnership with Rosneft. The results have been very good, especially after the elimination of some criminal behavior that was associated with the earlier drop in production. In other words, we are not destined to fail! There are options! Looking at the big picture, it would seem that falling production in those areas is the result of deliberate steps that justify the entrance of the private sector in altogether new conditions.

I think it's important to point out that, from the oil industry to other public enterprises, there has been a process that hasn't only happened in the discourse but also, and especially, in material reality. The current situation is not only characterized by the oil price drop and the whole issue regarding financial instability due to the sanctions imposed last year by the United States. There is also ample evidence that points to a deliberate effort to generate the collapse of public enterprises.

Obviously, if we recognize the complexity and purposefulness of all this, the alarms should sound. We must ask who the actors are behind all these maneuvers. For instance, if we look closely at the food sector, then we have to inquire: who are the actors deciding to privatize, and who had managed the enterprises until recently? Is there a direct relationship between these two parties? Yes, in some cases it's even the same people! The same person who acted deliberately so that the production would fall and is now recommending privatization. There is hard evidence for this. There are many people who were directors of public enterprises and now are managing their transference to the private sphere.

How are privatizations being carried out? Under what legal framework and corporate model?

In the oil industry, the decisions are made at the national level. They are somewhat more transparent because it is open to public scrutiny, and there is a need to attract foreign investment. But we must also consider that some of the agreements may fall outside of the established legal framework. We should really take a look at the Joint Services Agreements and Strategic Associations that are partnering with existing Joint Ventures.

In other words, an enterprise that is supposedly a state business but has external participation enters into an agreement with another private enterprise. In this way, private participation in the endeavor goes beyond what is established by law, and you have a Trojan horse inside. That is to say, existing Joint Ventures are bringing in new partners, and nobody knows on what terms.

There are several enterprises in the oil sector that have entered in this way. One would be Southern Procurement Services (SPS), which is operating in the Maracaibo Lake area and in Venezuela's eastern region, in the lighter petroleum wells. SPS is a very new company formed precisely to operate in this new context, and it is not alone: there are several "new players" made-to-order for the current situation.

In other areas, the privatization processes are even more opaque and far more sordid. A while ago, many state enterprises that were centrally-managed were decentralized. They began to be transferred to governorships and townships. Following that, processes of privatization were initiated at local levels without any kind of supervision or public bidding and notice. Thus, "perfect" alliances between the local authorities and the local bourgeoisie begin to take shape in ways that cannot be audited or even made public. When you move around the country, you find out that this plant or that enterprise, which used to be state-owned and operated, now belongs to a local businessperson.

Lácteos Los Andes [dairy company], which the state expropriated from its owners in 2008 with a very generous indemnification, is being handed over in an agreement where there is likely to be no payment to the state. Thus the private sector enters the picture as a kind of "savior" to recover production levels and to "help" the state, which has been incapable of managing the plants.

The Bolivarian Process has been highly democratic. Substantive democracy, however, depends on access to information about governments' and states' decisions in the economic arena. Yet there has been a great deal of opacity with the recent privatizations. How should we understand this, and what is to be done?

That's the biggest threat that we face. Given the situation, some concessions must be made, but in a transparent way and within the legal framework. I'm not sure why the debate is not out there, but it needs to happen! It seems as if, from the left, since we are supposed to be in a socialist revolution, we cannot talk about privatizations. Clearly, however, if we have decided to make alliances with the private sector, they must be transparent.

This is important so that "crony capitalism" doesn't take over: the logic of friends dividing up the pie. That cannot be! When there is no other option, privatizations must be done publicly and through a process that indemnifies the state for the infrastructure, the share of the market, etc. Otherwise, the private sector enters freely and, like birds of prey, seizes the little that is left. They privately appropriate the nation's resources, and the nation gets nothing in return.

Moreover, in the oil industry, the new players are obtaining concessions such as access to subsidized dollars, use of state infrastructure, special concessions to import, and privileged control of the market. This sort of thing doesn't usually result in a sound productive scenario, even within the logic of capitalism. It is an opaque system where deals are made behind closed doors, and there are no limits nor pursuit of efficiency in the most basic capitalist terms! It is not going to work. It's not going to help increase production, which is absolutely necessary now.

This brings us to Agriculture Minister Wilmar Castro Soteldo's recent comments [about the need for a "revolutionary bourgeoisie" in Venezuela]. We must have a frank debate about the bourgeoisie now. What is the bourgeoisie that has emerged in the last twenty years? What sectors of the bourgeoisie have grown with Chavismo's economic policies? Who had (and has) access to subsidized dollars and made fortunes through different mechanisms?

Thus we come back full circle to the issue of privatizations. Who are they benefiting? Who are the players? Obviously, these privatizations respond to the interests of a certain part of the emerging bourgeoisie, aiming to get fresh assets and revitalize themselves financially and technologically. Many of the privatizations underway don't make sense from a productive point of view. Often, the only argument has been labor issues, but in those cases, the best solution would have been retraining programs for the workers.

So the question that we should be asking is, what kind of bourgeoisie do we have, and if we are to establish alliances, how and with whom should we do so?

—OCTOBER 19, 2018

How to Get Venezuela's Economy Going Again: A Conversation with Luis Enrique Gavazut

Independent researcher Luis Enrique Gavazut, who was a member of the Presidential Economic Observatory, shares with us his thoughts about the roots of the country's economic crisis and outlines a series of policies to combat it.

In your view, as a researcher and lecturer, what are the circumstances and causes that have led to Venezuela's current economic crisis?

The situation in Venezuela over the last few years has been one of frank deterioration, due in part to the falling oil prices. That, in turn, contributed to a drop in the state's hard currency revenues, which is key to satisfying the population's needs.

To understand the Venezuelan economy, you must recognize that access to hard currency ultimately derives from one source only: the state. Historically, 95 percent of the hard currency revenues in Venezuela come from PDVSA, which is our country's flagship corporation. The private sector does not generate hard currency, because the privately-owned part of the productive apparatus, at least the sector that is not based on oil or mining, is not oriented toward exports.

When we look at the economic sectors that are geared to the immediate satisfaction of the society's needs, we see that there are huge difficulties. Levels of production, already small before the crisis, are dropping very rapidly. Right now, the national economy is operating

Oil, Privatizations, and the Economy

at 22 percent of its installed production capacity and imports have fallen by 80 percent in recent years, which explains the shortages that we are facing today.

This means that there is a terrible recession.

But things haven't always been this way. A few years ago, in 2013, when Nicolás Maduro took over as president right after the death of Hugo Chávez, things weren't as they are today. What happened then is that the private sector, especially foreign and large national capital, took the decision as a bloc to begin an economic war against the country. What was their objective? Toppling the government.

In other words, the most powerful economic actors in our country began to operate according to a political logic rather than an economic one. Evidence of that was their decision to slow down production and the decision to divest. In other words, since 2013 they began to take steps that affected the supply of goods in Venezuela, which we have come to call "induced shortages." This is a real phenomenon that has happened here in Venezuela, and it is an important factor in the crisis.

In the face of this, the Bolivarian government attempted to sustain people's purchasing power by increasing salaries and maintaining the social programs. That propped up a robust demand for goods and services for a while, but the private sector had already decided to cut off supply. Of course, a robust demand and reduced supply leads to serious disequilibrium, and prices begin to climb very rapidly.

What you have said so far focuses on the politically-driven causes of the crisis. However, there are other factors. Venezuela has large debts and in recent years the burden of payments has become quite heavy. Additionally, the country finds itself less and less able to borrow money and the oil prices have been notably unstable. This reduces the supply of hard currency for imports or social programs, unless the government were to default on the debt in a systematic way, as Argentina and Ecuador did very successfully earlier in the century. How do you evaluate these factors?

The scarcity of hard currency is key to understanding Venezuela's current situation. When the state cannot offer foreign currency in the local exchange market, the whole economy gets out of whack, since this is an economy that was shaped by the oil rent for decades. It is so not only in the public sector, but also in the private sector. It affects imports of consumer products, means of production, and intermediate goods. State imports that are directed at non-private distribution systems have shrunk too.

At the same time, we are witnessing a precipitous drop in PDVSA production, which is the consequence of a series of bad decisions in the industry: policy makers imagined that the oil bonanza was going to last many more years, and thus enormous investments were made in the Orinoco Oil Belt, where Venezuela has giant long-term potential for heavy oil production.

What happened? All those investments went only halfway and still require enormous volumes of capital. On top of that, while these investments were being made, there was a flagrant disregard for the maintenance of light and medium wells in Zulia and Anzoátegui. That is where our production should be focused now, since lighter oil is more easily extracted and sold on the international market.

The fall in oil prices and the drop in production have left PDVSA—which had acquired a huge debt precisely to make investments in the Orinoco Oil Belt—in a precarious condition. In the face of that situation, the company began to have problems meeting the terms of the debt. This put us in an emergency situation, where we need financing to recover the economically-viable wells, the ones that produce light and medium grade oil. But most of the doors that extend credit are closed. It is this vicious circle in which the oil industry currently finds itself.

You have criticized the Economic Recovery Plan that President Maduro launched in August. Can you explain your main arguments?

The Economic Recovery Plan is based on a series of theoretical premises that, from my point of view, are false. That is why it hasn't worked and won't work. The first problem is that the monetarist theory of inflation on which it is based simply does not apply here.

Basically, what we have here is a severe contraction of the economy, a very profound recession. The premise of the monetarist theory is that if demand is reduced by decreasing liquidity, then consumers won't have money to pay for goods and services, and that, in turn, will bring prices down.

But in the Venezuelan case, all that policy will do is close the stores, which means even more recession! Factories, stores, supply centers—much of what was still in business—have been shutting their doors at a rapid pace since August 20, when the Economic Recovery Plan was announced.

To maintain what there is of economic activity in Venezuela and to preserve the enterprises that are still operating, it is imperative that there be some demand. That means that the minimum salary must go up periodically, and social programs and direct support to the working class through bonuses must be maintained (direct and indirect subsidies must stay!). It is the government's role to continue doing this.

In other words, proposing a recovery plan with the main objective of zero fiscal deficit and the contraction of monetary liquidity by limiting the emission of so-called "inorganic" or unbacked money is a solution that won't work here and now.

In fact, when faced with this situation, the state was obliged to adjust its own policies through a salary hike, just ninety days after the plan was announced!

There is another aspect to the Economic Recovery Plan that was announced last year, which is the incentive to private investment. Is it working?

From my point of view, that part of the plan is also quite problematic. Those who designed the plan seem to think that giving incentives to the private sector will generate a favorable reaction from businesspeople. Having received these incentives, the private sector will (so their thinking goes) invest and increase production. Private investment, in turn, will lead to economic stability.

The theory behind giving incentives to the private sector doesn't work here as it might work in other economies. Here we have the most favorable exchange rate in the world and the cheapest labor in the world. Now labor is actually free because, since August 20, the state has been paying the wages of private sector workers! In other words, if you come here and you set up a business, the state will pay the salaries of the workers. This is something that has never happened before. With this we pass into the annals of economic history! To top it all off, the economic recovery package eliminated import tariffs.

So the country offers all this, which, in principle, should attract a great deal of private investment. But it's not only that: here taxes are very low and they aren't progressive (leaving aside the fact that there is a huge tax evasion, which has been the case for a long time). Venezuela also has the cheapest energy, the cheapest gas, the cheapest electricity, and the cheapest running water in the world. Then, on top of that, you can add all the comparative advantages that Venezuela has, from climate to location (proximity to the U.S.).

In other words, Venezuela is a paradise for private investments if we follow the incentives theory and the theory of comparative advantage. And yet the private sector hasn't invested here!

How do orthodox economists explain this situation? They say that there is no legal security. That is the classical argument. But it turns out that in Maduro's presidency there hasn't been one single expropriation [of private assets]! The politics of expropriation and nationalization ended with President Chávez. For six consecutive years, there hasn't been one single expropriation, and this government has no intention of doing it ever again. In fact, a year ago the National Constitutive Assembly passed the Foreign Investment Law, one of the most servile and "deterritorialized" laws in the world. Additionally, Venezuela has special economic zones that offer incentives of all sorts to private investors, including guarantees of legal security.

So, obviously, the problem isn't legal insecurity, nor does the solution lie in giving more and more incentives to the private sector. Recently, a Chinese functionary spoke to top government leaders on public television here, and he declared that they have a robust private sector [in China] because the Chinese government gives incentives to that sector. Maybe that has worked in China, but in Venezuela the theory doesn't apply.

The only way to stimulate the Venezuelan economy is [increasing] the oil rent. It is the only thing that works. We can look at this historically, and we will see an exact correlation: to the degree that the oil rent grows—and thus the supply of hard currency in our exchange market rises—then we see increased installed production capacity and some investment taking place, both national and foreign. But this happens only during an economically expansive period!

In the recessive period of the cycle, when oil revenues shrink, the state cannot offer subsidized dollars. Then we immediately see divestment, closing of factories and other enterprises—not only private ones but also public enterprises. This is what is happening now.

By the way, here we come to an issue that is often misinterpreted. Common sense says that an enterprise, because it is public, will be less efficient than its private counterpart. That is totally false! For instance, in Venezuela today both public and private enterprises are inefficient, on the border of collapsing if they haven't done so already. That is happening [to both] because there is no oil rent.

Yet the moment that hard currency comes into the state's coffers, then the economy will come back to life.

Let's look at the case of Lácteos Los Andes, which is a state dairy enterprise that has come to a halt. You can be sure that, if the revenue from the oil profits go up again, then we will see its production get back in gear, and their products will reappear on the market. It's just the same with a private, international corporation such as Goodyear, which recently closed operations in Venezuela. Goodyear stated that it pulled out of Venezuela because it could not operate here. But if the oil rent goes up again tomorrow, then you will see Goodyear reopening its plants!

Think of it this way: the biggest inefficiency possible in an enterprise is for it to cease operations. If we see it that way, then both Goodyear, a private corporation, and Lácteos Los Andes, a state-owned industry, are equally inefficient.

Can you explain Venezuela's role in the global economy, as an oil producer, and the problems that this sometimes leads to?

Venezuela is a rentier economy. We don't develop our own science and technology. Obviously, this situation makes us economically dependent on hard currencies [to get access to foreign technology].

Why does the private sector not invest in Venezuela when the revenues from the oil rent shrink? Because investment here happens in hard currencies. In other words, a private investor expects to get his earnings in U.S. dollars, because he earlier purchased technology, machinery, and other inputs also using U.S. dollars (although generally subsidized by the state). Thus he expects to recover the investment in dollars. . . .

For this reason, the investor says, well, if in this economy the access to dollars becomes very limited, then I'm just not going to invest in Venezuela. That is why, when the oil rent recovers, when we are in the expansive phase of the economy, when the oil boom happens, the investors come back since they know that dollars will be made available by the state.

Why is it that private investors don't generate dollars, as is the case in other countries? Because when the design of globalization took shape, Venezuela was not planned as a base for exporting. Procter & Gamble, for instance, made export platforms in Mexico, Brazil, and Argentina, and smaller platforms in Colombia and Panama, but that didn't happen in Venezuela. Venezuela is not considered a base for exports with the exception, of course, being oil exports. So Procter & Gamble is not going to set up a plant to produce here, as it would be competing with itself. Some countries are bases for exploitation of workers employed in export industries, whereas others are simply sites for extracting rent. In this case, Venezuela is a country whose role is to generate rent.

What solutions do you propose for Venezuela's quandary?

There are three steps that must be taken. First, the state must make productive investments. The Venezuelan state cannot avoid taking on this role. That means, like it or not, Venezuela's economy must be socialist. Given our conditions, if Venezuela is to come out of the current crisis, it will only happen by taking the path to socialism. President Chávez reached that conclusion when he said that the only possible path for the Venezuelan economy is socialism.

What is socialism? Well, the state must invest in means of production instead of stimulating private investment. Instead of offering subsidized dollars, the state needs to establish state manufacturing plants in association with organized communities, with the communes. This is key: joint projects in which the state and organized communities work together.

The other option would be to continue limping along with the bourgeoisie, courting private investors with incentives that are totally inefficient. To continue insisting on that course would be demented! It would be like traveling a well-known path once again and expecting to arrive at a totally different destination!

The second step is in the area of macroeconomic measures. We need to stabilize the exchange rate in Venezuela. To do this, from my perspective, there must be two strategies.

The first one is to totally liberalize the currency exchange market in Venezuela. The point of doing that is to attract the legal sale of hard currencies that are now arriving to the country through remittances, or of the dollars in the hands of small exporters of goods and services. Those dollar revenues, which are under ten billion a year, could be very important for our economy. Drawing off the dollars that now enter into the parallel market and allowing those transactions to happen in a legal, formal, public, transparent market would be a step forward. That is only going to happen by eliminating the exchange controls.

Now we have an exchange market that is legal but is totally useless: the DICOM market. Arguably, it's a market that is fake, because it doesn't attract dollars, and it doesn't offer them either. In other words, [my proposal is to] convert the current parallel market, which is the real benchmark for transactions carried out in Venezuela, and turn it into a transparent market. That would be a way to stabilize the exchange rates.

The other [important strategy] is to generate conditions for the correct functioning of the Petro, as a financial asset that is fungible in the market, in other words, an asset that can be easily exchanged for other currencies and with competitive transaction costs. Unfortunately, the Petro does not obey this logic. That is why the Bolívar-Petro anchoring failed as evidenced by the recent 150 percent devaluation. The anchoring didn't work because the Petro has no [real] life as a financial asset right now. If this were to happen, and it can happen if the correct decisions are taken, then the Petro could become an important tool [for recovery].

In the realm of macroeconomics you suggest liberalizing exchange rates plus a Petro that functions as an exchangeable asset. You also argue for state investment in productive projects in collaboration with organized communities. Those are the first two steps that you recommend. What is the third?

It's urgent to rescue PDVSA. I believe that all the state's efforts, all of its resources, must be channeled towards PDVSA. The recovery of the oil company's production levels must be the focus of our economic policy now. With every dollar that comes in, we must evaluate the effect if it is invested in PDVSA versus another kind of use in the economy. The state should channel all available resources in dollars into human potential, etc., to raise the production levels of PDVSA.

In other words, there shouldn't be a dispersion in other "Productive Motors" that in this moment are totally useless since they aren't going to bring dollars into the economy. Our primary focus should be PDVSA, and also perhaps include the mining sector as part of our main concerns. That sector may be necessary in our crisis despite being really a disaster, because of the environmental impact, the loss of sovereignty that comes with it, and the destruction that it brings to indigenous communities.

In other words, we need a new monetary policy, we need a state committed to developing productive forces with the participation of organized communities, and we need to recover PDVSA's production.

—JANUARY 3, 2019

The Orinoco Mining Arc's Impact: A Conversation with Emiliano Teran Mantovani

Environmental activist Emiliano Teran Mantovani, a member the Venezuelan Political Ecology Observatory, has closely followed the emergence of the Orinoco Mining Arc. He sees the new series of megaprojects as disastrously accelerating an uncritically accepted extractivist logic. In this interview, Teran argues that there are alternatives to an economy based on extraction that, aside from the environmental and social damage it produces, has failed to deliver results in terms of capital accumulation and development.

There is a tragic lack of knowledge about the Mining Arc in Venezuela. Can you, very briefly, tell us something about when it got started, its scale, scope, and environmental impact?

The Mining Arc was proposed not too long ago, in 2011, by Hugo Chávez. . . . But I would like to add the following: in reality, the Mining Arc emerged as a project during Rafael Caldera's second presidency. Debates about the environment entered the public sphere in the mid to late 90s, when Caldera put forth a decree deregulating the forest reserve Imataca to introduce mining there. That is the very area where the most important mines of today's Mining Arc are located. The mobilization [against it] was such that that decree remained in some way neutralized. It wasn't taken down, but it was neutralized. They couldn't bring it to completion. It was under Chávez that this decree was finally formalized . . . and the permit to carry out mining in that forest reserve was issued.

That story is important to tell, because it comes from a whole logic of recolonizing the South, a logic that has been part of development projects in Venezuela for a long time. Actually, all the contemporary developmental, progressive projects (like the Bolivarian Process) followed that logic.

In 2011, under Chávez, the Guyanese Mining Arc or Orinoco Mining Arc was announced. Then there was even a discussion of a two-pronged project together with the Orinoco Oil Belt, with mining projects over the whole extension of the territory. We are talking about an extension of 111,800 square km, 12 percent of the national territory—which is about the size of Cuba, to get a sense of the scale. Mining of gold and diamonds, coltan, bauxite, and iron are the proposed projects.

This involves reopening and giving a new push to already existing mines. It's not as if all the mines are new ones. There are already-existing mines that will be given a new push, but it also involves opening up new mines. For example, coltan mining is totally new in Venezuela, and it means penetrating the Parguaza forest and opening coltan mines there. It also means opening new mines in Imataca, formalizing diamond minds in the west of the country, and expanding the mining of bauxite and iron, which is old in Venezuela.

The Orinoco Mining Arc involves new legislation that, in effect, puts the zone outside of normal law and the Constitution [that is, as a special economic zone]. One could even talk about a regime of exceptionality, deterritorialization, and loss of sovereignty. Can you say something about the conflict between popular sovereignty and the needs of global capitalist accumulation?

That is very important. At first, for Chávez's government, the Orinoco

Oil Belt and what we now know as the Orinoco Mining Arc were initiatives aimed at overcoming the exhaustion of the model of accumulation via oil exploitation. Before Chávez, the focus was the extraction of light and medium crudes from [the western border state of] Zulia, but those wells were drying up. So, within the [extractivist] model, there is a shift to extracting non-conventional oil from the Oil Belt region [in the east of the country]. This, of course, has a much greater environmental impact and greater cost. Hence, the Mining Arc follows the same logic, bringing new life to a model in crisis.

I say this because, if during Chávez's government the Mining Arc had a character of expansive developmentalism—a kind of reformulation of the extractivist model—under the Maduro government the focus on mining takes on the nature of an adjustment policy. It's a radical adjustment, even though it isn't the typical macroeconomic adjustment (which would be about redistributing surpluses upward).

This adjustment has to do directly with territorialization and radical penetration [of national sovereignty] based on a few instruments.[7] First, since 2016, Venezuela has been under a formal and declared state of exception. That state of exception is within the context of an economic emergency.

Then, there is another instrument: the Special Economic Zones. These follow the format of Chinese neoliberalism, a form of radical deregulation of territories, in which any obstacle for capital's rapid development is eliminated: taxes, customs, permits, labor laws, environmental restrictions, you name it. This state of exception even means assigning a sort of ad hoc governor to the territory in question.

The Orinoco Mining Arc was finally formalized, in its current incarnation, in February 2016 with Presidential Decree 2248. It was declared a special economic zone. As such, it is constituted as a territory of complete deregulation, so that capital can develop freely at whatever price. That presupposes eliminating rights of all sorts: democratic consultation, the right to work, the right to life, the right to a clean and healthy environment, etc.

The regime of exception was put in place hand in hand with a special military zone. So the Mining Arc is both a special mining zone and a special military zone. This has the characteristics of a military regime. Why? Well, Decree 2248 states that groups who oppose it are opposing national interests, and in opposing national interests they enter into a kind of crime against the state itself. That is said very clearly in the decree.

Now, when you look at this from the point of view of democratic consultation—which, in a project of this magnitude, must be done not only because it is stated in Venezuela's Constitution, but also in adherence to international law—the process has been carried out in very irregular ways, with a lot of manipulation and co-optation. To give one example, indigenous people have complained about television appearances of co-opted chiefs who don't represent them, and these co-opted chiefs were backing up the project.

Additionally, environmental impact studies are conspicuously absent. They have been announced, but nobody knows where they are. Nobody knows anything about them. Add to that that citizens have the right to be informed about the character and scope of the agreements that have been made, but they remain a total mystery. All the information that we have is based on promises of ecosocialism, but we know, based on scientific studies and Latin America's accumulated experience, that megamining is one of the most devastating industrial activities. So clearly the Mining Arc represents a regime of exception following a policy of adjustments of the most radical kind, a neoliberal path that is very radical.

Clearly, as you mentioned above, megaprojects with this kind of impact need to be submitted to participative processes and democratic ratification. Yet, many of the peoples who live in the Mining Arc are those least able to make themselves heard in the centers of power. This seems all the more tragic since such peoples often have cultures and sustainable forms of life that might be important in forming and shaping a viable postcapitalist society.

The people who live in the Mining Arc are diverse. They are not only indigenous people. We should remember that there are cities like El Callao, which has a mining tradition since the 19th century.

Regarding indigenous people, what you have said is key. The indigenous peoples are not a subject that is separate from us. True, geographically that has generally been the case, but politically indigenous peoples are constitutive of our identity as the Venezuelan identity is pluricultural. Venezuela is in reality a republic constituted by very diverse cultures, not only *campesino* cultures but also indigenous cultures that shape us as far as our traditions and habits go, as well as our way of viewing life, our way of eating, dressing, etc. All that is part of our identity. They are not subjects that we have to thank, but rather they are a part of us.

In their forms of life, their cosmovision, we find hints or clues to conceive other ways of living, an alternative to the model that exists in the present moment. These aren't things that are in a far future or remote past, but instead have to do with practices existing right now. These include practices of the Yekuana people, for instance, who have their own conception of "living well" (*buen vivir*), but also ways of working the land, medicinal practices, social practices.

I don't think it's good to romanticize the indigenous peoples, since they have been culturally penetrated and many now have become involved with mining. It's simply a fact. They have been subjected to a long process of colonization, although it is also true that in the Bolivarian Revolution their rights were constitutionally recognized. But, with the co-optation of leaders and the creation of indigenous bureaucracies, their constitutional rights were bypassed.

When we talk about a rehashing of colonization and territorialization, we can point to two grave factors. First is the issue of health. The state of health of some indigenous peoples in the area points to the danger that some of the tribes could disappear soon, because they are dying of measles, malaria, and other diseases that have spread rapidly due to deforestation and rechanneling water.

There is an idea circulating in the public sphere that the solution to the problem of illegal mining is large-scale mining. It is true that since the middle of the last decade illegal mining grew exponentially. Chávez first responded to that by developing programs and projects so that people would have other alternatives. Today, with the excuse of organizing mining, those programs were abandoned and, with the territorial expansion of mining, well, naturally indigenous groups lose sources of income such as tourism. This is the case with the Pemon people, who have seen tourism fall off dramatically and are thus obliged to mine.

And so it becomes true that big corporate mining is the only option. Or is it? Really, instrumentalizing the environmental devastation that industrial megamining causes cannot be the only option.

The other problem with illegal mining, which is alive and well, is that it is not outside the state, because part of the state collaborates with the process. It's not possible that ten or twelve tons of gold could be smuggled out of the country every year, which is what public functionaries say, and that nothing can be done about it. For instance, in El Caura the only way people have to get gasoline for the pumps (to get the gold out) is through military posts. So we are talking about a participation of the state in a process that is bleeding dry the country.

Also, illegal mining, among other things, leaves giant pools in the process. They use spouts of high-pressure water to make landslides to access the gold. Pools are left behind where mosquitos reproduce, and we see that now Venezuela has the worst index of malaria in Latin America, according to the World Health Organization. The situation is affecting miners and the local population first, with devastating consequences, but the phenomenon is spreading north throughout the country.

Who are the main actors involved in the Mining Arc?

In the Mining Arc, full-scale operations haven't yet begun. We are, basically, in the first stage of a large-scale initiative: attracting investors. To state the obvious, the Venezuelan situation is one of high political vulnerability—it is considered volatile—and this makes large investors leery of making investments that might be followed by losses.

What has been happening is that the state has initiated a sort of process of auction, offering better and better deals, better and better concessions to corporations. Hence the creation of the special economic zone, and more recently the lifting of all tax payments [Economic Recovery Plan], as well as the granting of other advantages for large corporate interests.

The government spoke initially about some 150 companies from more than 30 countries being involved. Many of the deals have been verbal negotiations, others have been memorandums of understanding, which is when two parties sign a document stating that the parties sat together to negotiate but it's not an actual agreement.

Mining has begun by companies such as Canada's Gold Reserve, a company that Chávez's government kicked out of the country in 2009, due to the environmental impact of its projects in the Imataca Forest Reserve. Further, there have been some real agreements with Chinese corporations. This has occurred in the following way: when Venezuela asks for a rescheduling of its debt payments with China, then, as a payback, . . . China asks for broad concessions. This is how things took shape for the projects of Chinese companies such as Yankuang Group (which has been mining gold since 2015).

The corporations that have initiated exploitation are junior mining companies. A junior mining company is like a chess pawn. . . . They basically initiate negotiations, opening a path so that, once the situation is stabilized and the agreement consolidated, then the large corporations such as Barrick Gold can come in. Gold Reserve and the other corporations that have come in are, basically, junior companies.

Other key and highly problematic actors in the Mining Arc are the military companies. These are made by military people who form companies that enter into joint businesses (with the Venezuelan state). CAMIMPEG is one such enterprise, but there are many others. This is, in fact, a rebirth of the sort of concessions that Juan Vicente Gómez gave out in the early 20th century: small coteries of friends that divided up the pie of state offerings.

A radically anti-extractivist position seems unfair. How are nations of the Global South to advance when, in the short and medium run, their only chances to develop seem to be via extraction of raw materials? Many countries of the Global North transitioned

from extractive economies to industrial ones in modern times. So, wouldn't it be unfair to deny that possibility to nations of the Global South? Isn't it unjust to make the nations of the Global South bear the burden of the planet's environmental crisis?

I'm not sure that I agree with some of those claims. First, the past fifteen years of progressive governments in Latin America have been characterized by an extractivist logic. These weren't decisions made by the people; the decision came from above. We saw them playing that card, as if there were no other options.

Let's go over one of the typical arguments given: "We need to open this new mine, we need to open a new oil well, we need to initiate new projects of soy monoculture." And why do we need to do this? Because we need hard currency for development.

One of the issues here is that there is no discussion about how to distribute the surplus. The reasons for opening our territory to mining is the same: hard currency is needed. But if we look at the ten years prior to 2014 (when the price of raw materials dropped), in those ten boom years some 500 billion dollars came into the coffers of the Venezuelan state. So, before opening a new mine, the question we should ask is, what happened with all that money?

To understand Venezuela's rentier capitalism one must understand the country's architecture for the distribution of the oil profits. That architecture shapes the whole national domestic economy. The distribution of oil profits shapes power relations and diverse forms of consumption. In other words, if the state has an eternal subsidy to gasoline, as is the case in Venezuela, that is going to foster a specific kind of consumption. It's going to determine the way people go from one place to another, and promote the widespread practice of importing vehicles.

Further, when we talk about distributing oil profits, we also have to talk about taxation. According to CEPAL data, Venezuela and Chile are the countries in the continent where the rich have to pay the least income tax. [In Venezuela] the sales tax, a regressive tax, has increased, and it falls on the shoulders of the poor.

Oil, Privatizations, and the Economy

How can we connect this with extractivism? I'm going to give you an example. One of the largest debates concerning extractivism in Latin America was regarding the Yasuni National Park in Ecuador. If you increased by 1.6 percent the taxation on the 200 largest corporations and wealthiest families, that would bring into the state's coffers the same amount of money as would be brought in by 25 years of oil extraction in the Yasuni reserve.

This is the case with any Latin American country. Instead of opening the debate on the issue of unequal distribution, the only solution that enters the discourse is exploiting natural resources: opening new fields, new mines, etc. Then, when the prices of commodities drop, the discourse gets ramped up: more extractivist initiatives have to be pursued because there is a crisis and, of course, the only solution then is mining or drilling more wells. However, it turns out that we got into the current crisis because the extractivist logic was on steroids during the last decade and a half.

Additionally, mining has an impact on other kinds of industry, since it affects electrical production. In Venezuela most of the electricity comes from hydroelectric plants. But the kind of mining that happens in the Arc will affect riverbeds and reduce the flow of the Caroni River, which is the river that feeds the Guri Dam, the main source of electricity in the country. Thus the generation of electricity will fall off. That is going to have an adverse effect on the economy, even on the existing oil refineries and other sectors of the oil industry.

Unfortunately, debates about mining and extractivism are silenced. So it turns out that the Mining Arc is going to end up adversely affecting productivity and life in Venezuela, and that includes oil production, which is actually effective in generating income for the nation.

What can people do who want to monitor, protest, or simply stay informed about the Mining Arc?

It is necessary to get people mobilized again, and that mobilization must be autonomous and independent. We are facing a government that has deviated from its path and has little to do with the initial project of Chavismo's popular bases, which had an emancipatory orientation and proposed an alternative transition. That bloc must recover its social agenda that involved demands regarding labor and salary, together with claims related to gender, indigenous rights, and the land.

There is a very serious environmental crisis in Venezuela and the environmental agenda must be taken up by all, focusing particularly on a struggle against this new form of "adjustment extractivism." There are alternatives, and the popular movement has to forge a project: a path away from the current devastation that we are witnessing in Venezuela. That, in turn, requires a process of autonomous construction and debate, allowing us to overcome the current logic of environmental devastation.

—October 10, 2018

Heterodox and Orthodox Economics in Venezuela: A Conversation with Luis Salas

This is our second interview with Luis Salas, former Venezuelan vice president for productive economy who now teaches political economy at the Bolivarian University. Six months after the first interview, Salas continues his analysis of the economic measures that the government has implemented since August 2018, describing how they have morphed into an orthodox adjustment package. He also addresses the options that can be taken to come out of the current crisis.

You are part of 15 y Ultimo, a website and research collective that investigates the Venezuelan situation from a left-wing Chavista perspective, with economic issues as the main focus. The Venezuelan economy is a rather complex subject due to the multiplicity of contradictory agents and actors, the government's restriction of information, and the mainstream media's persistent misrepresentation of Venezuela's problems. In light of this complexity, how do you go about analyzing the country's economic life? What is your methodology?

In *15 y Ultimo*, we decided a while ago that to analyze the situation in Venezuela, especially with regard to economic policy, several particularities had to be taken into account.

Traditionally, an economic policy is examined with one eye on its objectives and another on its results. In Venezuela's case, the relationship between objectives and results is often very tenuous—it is true that this happens elsewhere, but it is more exaggerated here. And the failure to meet the objectives can have its roots in both internal and external phenomena.

So I believe that the traditional method for analysis is not viable for us, at least not in our circumstances.

The question is, then, what is the most objective method to analyze our economy and the policies implemented by the Bolivarian government? We go about our analysis not so much by looking at the stated objectives, but by examining the instruments that are put in place, how they work as a whole, how they interact with each other (or counteract each other), etc.

In other words, economic policies have goals and instruments. Here we propose to examine the relationship between the instrument and the goal, because it may be stated that the objective is to finish off hyperinflation, or fight speculation in the foreign exchange market. But objectives and results are mediated by the instruments. So we have opted for analyzing the instruments.

On August 2018, the government launched, with great fanfare, the Economic Recovery Plan, which involved anchoring the Bolívar to the Petro and incentives to foreign investment. That plan didn't produce the expected results. What was the relationship between instruments and objectives there?

The Economic Recovery Plan announced by President Nicolás Maduro had some clear objectives: to prevent the dollarization of the economy, to put an end to hyperinflation, and all that came with the larger objective of initiating an economic recovery after a period of some five years during which there was a severe contraction of the Venezuelan economy.

But the truth is that, when you analyze the August proposal—and I said this in an interview last year with Tatuy TV—one can see that there are at least two different plans within it, and the plans are frankly contradictory. They undo each other.

One part of the plan had to do with monetary reconversion [eliminating five zeros from the nominal value of the currency], anchoring the Bolívar to the Petro [with the Petro's value tied to the value of one barrel of petroleum]. Although the plan was poorly defined, it reminded us of the Real Plan [in 1994 Brazil issued a second currency, the Real, to stabilize its economy and curtail inflation]. Thus, it seemed as if the Petro would operate as the Real operated in Brazil, although not in exactly the same way, since in Brazil the Real ended up replacing the Cruzeiro. But, in any case, there were elements that made us think that there was an attempt at constructing a heterodox economic policy.

Another important component of the Economic Recovery Plan, which wasn't orthodox either, was the concerted prices policy [prices of basic products would be set by negotiation between the capitalist class and the government].

At the same time, however, policies were announced that were more conventional and orthodox from an economic standpoint. This is the other aspect of the plan. First, they announced a strict fiscal deficit reduction policy, which is a highly problematic orthodox (or liberal) measure. So as the Petro project was being put in place, a new and unorthodox policy, we saw the application of instruments to reduce fiscal deficit being applied and also, as you mentioned in your question, an orthodox foreign investment stimulus plan.

How do you evaluate the announcements made by President Maduro last November?

Some one hundred days after the Economic Recovery Plan was made public, Maduro gave a televised address informing that, to meet the [original] objectives, some "correcting factors" would have to be set in place. At that point inflation was even higher than in August, which meant that there had been a progressive devaluation of the Bolívar and the policy of agreed prices had had no impact in what things really cost in the supermarkets.

As I mentioned before, the Economic Recovery Plan's key feature, in its first phase, was the Bolívar-Petro anchoring; it was an attempt to stabilize the Bolívar and curb hyperinflation. What began to happen in late November is that the Petro—which was initially conceived as a cryptocurrency—was operating on two levels: on the one hand, it was a cryptocurrency in the discourse [of government officials], and, on the other hand, it became a unit of account (meaning that part of the nation's budget would be calculated in Petros, as would tax units, etc.).

The Petro had by now two different public roles, and it would soon have two different values! Furthermore, the November announcement broke the Bolívar-Petro anchoring, since the value of the minimum wage, which was to be [as per the August announcements] half the value of the Petro, dropped in relation to the Petro.

The Petro didn't operate as a cryptocurrency, but rather became a savings mechanism. It was similar to a bond. It resembled the bonds issued by countries when the goal is to reduce monetary liquidity.

What happened is that the Petro, which had already become some sort of "crypto-asset," was now attached to the DICOM [state-run foreign currency auction]. This meant that with any variation in the DICOM (at that time the auctions were held on Mondays, Wednesdays, and Fridays) the value of the Petro changed: as the dollar went up in relation to the Bolívar, the Petro also went up.

Whatever the DICOM dollar exchange rate was, it was multiplied by sixty [the approximate value of the oil barrel in USD]. That is how the value of the Petro was calculated, and thus the Bolívar-Petro anchoring—the key element in the initial Economic Recovery Plan (and the policy that was to stabilize the value of the Bolívar)—was overridden.

All this meant that there was a continuous and orchestrated devaluation of the Bolívar, which happened until the end of the year. In the last auction of 2018, on December 28, the gap between the official DICOM marker and the parallel market [the black market for trading foreign currencies] practically disappeared. In those days, everything seemed to be pointing to a unification of the exchange rates [via liberalization of the official exchange rates], but that didn't happen. By the beginning of January, the parallel market began to climb once again. [On April 22, four days after this interview with Salas, there was a new Bolívar devaluation to 5200 Bolivars per USD, meaning that the official exchange rate again approximated very closely the parallel market; a few days earlier the Bolívar was officially devalued from 3300 to 4000.]

At that point, Venezuela's Central Bank [BCV] and, most likely, the Finance Ministry, accelerated the policies aimed at forcing a unification. What did they do? They restricted monetary liquidity dramatically, reduced the legal banking reserve, and froze salaries . . . but prices continued to rise. . . . Then came January 28, which is when the exchange-rate shock therapy was implemented in full force.

On the night of the 28th, some tweets from the BCV and a brief press release announced that there was going to be a shift to a new monetary anchor, and that the official exchange rate would be around 3300 Bolivars to the dollar [in early September, the official exchange rate was about 60 to the dollar]. Additionally, we were told that the BCV would implement the economic policies needed to maintain the exchange rate at about that level.

They implemented a monetary anchor, which should not be confused with an exchange anchor—an exchange anchor is what would have happened if the BCV had injected dollars into the economy to stabilize the exchange rate, but that didn't happen. Instead of injecting dollars into the exchange system, what they did was a radical restriction of monetary liquidity in Bolivars. I call this a "monetary lobotomy."

They did a kind of shock therapy in the foreign exchange market. In other words, the official exchange rate was brought very close to the parallel market, while there was a restriction on the issuing of Bolivars.

The BCV stated that its aim was to stabilize the exchange rate, put a cap on hyperinflation, and recover purchasing power. This is a typical case of an economic trilemma. You can do the first two things but not the third at the same time, since you need to reduce purchasing power to reach the first two objectives. In this regard, there are almost no differences between what [former Venezuelan president Rafael] Caldera did in 1996 or what [Mauricio] Macri is doing in Argentina now with the "Doble Cero" plan, and the policies that the Bolivarian government is implementing.

Immediately after the late January announcement, I said that these policies might stabilize the exchange rate for a while and could slow down inflation. However, this would no doubt come with enormous social costs.

And it happened. . . . People's purchasing power dropped even more. In a way that resembles Ricardo's Iron Law [salaries tending to the minimum wage necessary to sustain life], people began to live at the level of bare subsistence. That, of course, went hand-in-hand with underconsumption. In other words, a drastic fall in consumption came about, which meant that the country's economy contracted even further.

You call this a process of "monetary lobotomy." Can you explain what you mean by the term?

Sure. To curb hyperinflation, they decided to paralyze economic activity, bringing material existence to a bare minimum. That is why I call it a monetary lobotomy.

It's like a psychiatric lobotomy, formerly used for patients with schizophrenia: the most severe symptoms of the pathology won't express themselves after the treatment, but the consequence is that the patient is left in a catatonic state. Here the "inflationary schizophrenia" was controlled briefly, but the tradeoff was that the economy was left in a catatonic state.

Now this orthodox anti-inflationary policy—applying monetarist policies—is problematic and questionable under any circumstances, since it necessarily raises poverty and produces economic contraction. However, in our case, it is much worse! First, the Venezuelan economy has been in an economic free fall for five years now. We are talking about a situation in which, prior to the application of these monetary measures, the economy had contracted 50 percent since 2012. Implementing these policies generated further contraction, which in turn led to much larger problems!

Furthermore, when we consider that these [monetarist] policies were applied to an economy faced with sanctions for more than a year now, then we can see how the policies would end up unintentionally

Oil, Privatizations, and the Economy

reinforcing the purposeful smothering of our economy from outside. In other words, we are facing an internal smothering in addition to the external one!

For many years, the government's economic policies seemed to be merely reactive, but now there appears to have been a shift toward a more active stance with the government actually having a strategy, although it is not public. Let's talk about this shift in relation to the current process of dollarization.

Indeed, as you say, the government's policies went from reactive—an ambulance chaser—to being more proactive with the "monetary lobotomy" and other adjustments put in place over the past few months.

For many years, the government's policy came *ex post facto*. Basically, they established new frameworks legalizing [extra-legal] activity. For example, the government's response to widespread violations of price controls was to liberate prices. And to solve the parallel, illegal dollar market problem, the exchange rate was liberalized [to be equal to the parallel, black market rate]. They chose to turn legal infractions into the law.

More recently, we have seen that the government flexibilized the exchange market and, in doing so, it also loosened-up on monetary sovereignty. Why? When you flexibilize the exchange market, which comes with the free convertibility of currencies, you open the door so that other currencies, which aren't the Bolívar, will begin to circulate more freely in the national economy. (By the way, in constitutional terms, the Bolívar is declared to be the "one and only currency" that can circulate in Venezuela.)

Other currencies first began to circulate in the tourist sector, where the government legalized payment with foreign currencies, and later with the cryptocurrencies, with the Petro taking the lead.

At first, the Petro was presented as a cryptocurrency for international transactions, but later President Maduro began to talk about budgets in Petros, payments in Petros, savings in Petros, etc. So really what happened is that the Petro opened the door for other cryptocurrencies. The cryptocurrencies, in turn, opened the door to normalizing the circulation of other currencies.

At around the same time, in mid-2018, the National Constituent Assembly eliminated the Illicit Exchange Law. Later in the year, the Supreme Court handed down [two different] sentences legalizing payments for services and labor contracts in U.S. dollars. Additionally, on December 28, the SENIAT [Venezuelan tax agency] issued a resolution that allows tax payments in dollars and other foreign currencies.

Here we can see a coordinated institutional change in policy, affecting the National Constituent Assembly, Venezuela's Supreme Court, and the state's tax office.

It's very important to point out that—in addition to allowing other currencies to circulate in the economy—the government has been simultaneously restricting the circulation of Bolívars through its new monetary policy. All this in an economy where the Bolívar is more and more depreciated every day!

If you take, as a starting point, the value of the Sovereign Bolívar on August 20, 2018 [the day that the Economic Recovery Plan was announced] and you compare it to the Sovereign Bolívar on April 12 of this year, you can see that the devaluation has been about 99.5 percent! This is a variation in terms of real value. (In nominal terms, the devaluation is about 5000 percent.)

We are facing a strange situation in which, due to the monetarist policy that the government has recently adopted in the effort to reduce inflation, there are far fewer Bolívars than needed circulating in the economy, but on top of that, those Bolívars are now worth far less.

To put this in numbers, when you take the total economic liquidity in Bolívars, from bills and coins to all the money in banks, etc., and you divide that by the official DICOM [state-run foreign currency market] exchange rate, then the monetary mass comes to 1.3 billion dollars. In other words, if the government wanted to exchange all the circulating Bolívars to USD, all it would have to have would be 1.3 billion dollars. (I make this calculation based on reports issued by the BCV on April 5, which was the last report issued.) On the other hand, if we consider only the Bolívar bills and coins that circulate in our economy, that yields somewhere between 60 and 70 million dollars.

All this means that if the government were to come out today and announce that it was going to formally dollarize the economy (which I don't think will happen), all it would need would be 1.3 billion USD to do the currency shift. That represents just 11 percent of the country's reserves, which are already seriously depleted.

If you add to this that Venezuela, given the massive migration triggered by the current crisis, is one of the main countries receiving family remittances in the region, that will give you a general panorama that shows how polarized things are getting.

Conservative estimates say that last year some two billion dollars entered the country as remittances in 2018. Now it must be taken into account that, even though that may be a good estimate of what was sent, not all of it arrived in the country as greenbacks; often there is banking triangulation, and in the exchange process some dollars stay in accounts abroad. So a super-conservative estimate would be that half of that initial two billion arrived to Venezuela. If you add to that the fact that in many businesses you can now pay with international credit cards, we can then safely assume that in our economy there are more U.S. dollars than Bolívars circulating. (And that is if we are only talking about U.S. dollars. To that one should add euros, cryptocurrencies, etc.)

So I would say that we are not in a process of dollarization in the strict sense of the word. We are in a process of de-Bolívarization. The Bolívar, due to policies and spontaneous phenomena, is being expelled out of the economy. Obviously this could rapidly open the path to full dollarization, or it could open to a period similar to the one in Zimbabwe where there was a sort of monetary chaos, with a multiplicity of hard currencies and cryptocurrencies circulating in the economy. A consequence [of that chaos] is that it is impossible for the Zimbabwean government to apply economic policies.

In a word, we are in a process of de-Bolívarization that can take us to dollarization after the current economic chaos, or we could sink more deeply into chaos.

Now what is paradoxical about this situation? The fact is that the government's economic policy is contributing to dollarization, even if that's not the aim. In other words, if dollarization hasn't advanced more, that is because the sanctions, especially the financial ones, prevent more dollars from coming into the economy.

We have a situation in which, on the one hand, the government's economic policy (most likely unintentionally) pushes our economy toward dollarization while U.S. sanctions put a break on it. Interestingly, however, Director of the National Economic Council Larry Kudlow, who advises the White House on U.S. and global economy policy, said recently that in a context where Maduro wasn't president, there is a plan to inject dollars into the Venezuelan economy through smartphones, in a general plan to dollarize the economy.

The issue here, however, is that the conditions for dollarization are being created, and they are in part generated by the government's own economic policy!

What economic policy should the government implement given the current situation?

One of the most troubling things about the current situation is that the government seems to have no unified criteria regarding the objectives of its economic policy. On top of that, whatever objectives there are, are very vague. A concept such as "prosperity" is not a clear objective, it's more like a desire. In an economic plan, prosperity cannot be the aim. A plan must define aims clearly, through strategies and policies.

The first thing that the government should do now is to clarify its objectives. Once the objectives are there, then comes a process of prioritizing, organizing, and planning.

I'm telling you this for the following reason: Venezuela has a lot of potential, but anybody who knows something about planning knows that when you have limited economic resources immediately available, you must direct them toward the areas where they can yield a better performance.

To give you an example, I think that developing tourism has

potential in Venezuela, but for that to happen, large investments in infrastructure are required.

From my point of view, a prejudice about the rentier character of Venezuela's economy took root here, and it's highly problematic. Being a rentier country is bad, some will say, or it is sinful, so Venezuela has to overcome this stain by becoming a productive country.

Of course, I don't believe that Venezuela should continue to depend exclusively on oil. However, the problem is not that we receive resources that come from oil sales, but rather that we depend exclusively on those sales. If we have oil revenues, that is obviously not a problem in itself; it is not a sin.

In the current situation, if this is a country that has enormous oil reserves, a country that has been exploiting oil for more than one hundred years, a country with the "know-how," a country that has secured markets. . . . Then, it's quite obvious that, in productive terms, all efforts should focus on recovering oil production. Further, we should keep in mind that oil generates hard currency immediately, which is what is needed to boost other sectors of the economy.

In November 2018 you published a report in *15 y Ultimo* stating that there was a crisis situation in Venezuela's electrical system, and that any economic recovery plan had to prioritize fixing that problem.

That's true. Last year we released a report stating that economic recovery in Venezuela will depend on rapidly addressing the problems in the National Electrical System. We did so well before the sabotage of the Guri [hydroelectric dam where over 70 percent of Venezuela's electricity is generated]. We said that electricity production had to be stabilized [many regions of the country have been undergoing widespread blackouts for years now] and increased if the country is to recover from the current crisis. This is a proven fact: increasing the GDP of a country by one percentage point would require an increase in electrical consumption.

We have been calling attention to the dire situation of the electrical system for more than half a year now. However, we began investigating the issue even earlier: ever since the government started to focus on the cryptocurrency solution [December 2017], which came with much talk about currency mining farms, etc. It seemed pretty absurd to us that the government would be encouraging cryptocurrency mining—which comes with an enormous use of electricity—in a context where the electric system was showing clear signs of wear and tear. In fact, outside of Caracas, blackouts have been a problem for years now.

In a presidential address last year, in which Maduro was talking about regional development, there was a blackout right in the middle of the broadcast. We then published a report that we had been working on, bringing attention to the problem with the National Electrical System. In essence what we pointed out was that with current electrical capacity, development is not possible, because it would tax the system so much that it would end up collapsing (or else widespread electrical rationing would have to be applied).

With the attack in March of this year, this problem has become even bigger!

After examining the National Electrical System, we came to the conclusion that the problem isn't an issue of investment. Enormous investments were done around 2010. The problem isn't that there isn't a plan. In 2014 there was a plan developed. The root of the problem is management of the system and its resources.

[Because of the attacks] there is now infrastructure damage that must be repaired, and that will require investment. So given the circumstances, instead of renovating sidewalks in Caracas, what should really be done is recover the electrical system. To repeat: the renovation is necessary not only to keep life going, but also because it is an economic project that has the potential to increase other economic activities.

Summarizing your ideas, then, you propose that the recovery plan should focus on fixing the oil industry and electric system.

Yes. That could open the way for development in other areas. We are talking about taking seriously the activity that will allow us to move forward in other sectors of our economy.

You have to provide a clear orientation to the economic policy, and you have to make a plan with the resources you have. That's the problem of the Fifteen Motors Plan [a 2016 plan to recover the Venezuelan economy involving fifteen areas, from agro to banking to oil to tourism]. The government's economic policy was so dispersed then that it had no coherence or direction.

So we must anchor our economy to something, and it stands to reason that oil and electricity are that thing. It doesn't matter if we like it or not; it's frankly our only option. Also, it makes no sense that we go around saying that we have the biggest oil reserves in the world if we are incapable of exploiting them. Oil must be the spinal column that is used to get us out of the current crisis.

— April 26, 2019

Notes to Section 2

1. API gravity measures the weight of oil in relation to water: less than 10 API means that it is heavier than water and will sink.
2. Salas refers to practices such as smuggling, hoarding, and engaging in speculation with subsidized goods that became widespread in Venezuela from 2013 to the present.
3. EPS initially stood for Empresas de Producción Social (Social Production Enterprises). The initiative began in 2006 as an attempt to provide an alternative model for businesses in which production would be community-based and there would be a more humanized workplace. A couple of years later, due to an awareness that only enterprises based on social property instead of private property could produce a significant transformation, people began to speak instead of Empresas de Propiedad Social (Social Property Enterprises), changing the meaning of the "P" in the acronym.
4. The National Constitutional Assembly passed, on December 28, 2017, a law that gives the executive the power to exonerate foreign investors from paying taxes as well as from territorial and environmental regulations. The objective is to create favorable conditions for foreign investment.
5. Between 1994 and 1999, Venezuela underwent a shift toward privatization of the oil industry both upstream and downstream. This process was triggered by a drop in production and prices, which legitimated the process in the public eye. PDVSA, the state company, entered into unfavorable partnerships, as a minority partner, with foreign transnational companies such as ExxonMobil, Royal Dutch Shell, ConocoPhillips, Chevron, and Total.
6. An example of this would be a Joint Venture (60 percent state, 40 percent private), entering into another Joint Venture with a foreign corporation. Through this kind of iterative process, the actual share of PDVSA in the enterprise could drop well below 50 percent.
7. "Territorialization" with regard to neoliberalism refers to a process that involves the state passing authority over to non-state entities, which expand their control of a territory.

3
CHÁVEZ, POLITICS, AND *NUESTRA AMÉRICA*

Chávez and the Continent of Politics: A Conversation with Chris Gilbert

Creator and co-host of the Marxist educational television program Escuela de Cuadros, *Chris Gilbert has written about the Bolivarian Process's revolutionary approach to the past in* Walter Benjamin in Venezuela, *and about Hugo Chávez's strategic vision in* The Chávez Hypothesis. *In this brief interview, Gilbert touches upon the importance of recovering a political discourse in Marxism, the battle over historical meanings, and how to confront the emerging fascist threat—all in relation to the crisis that Venezuela is facing today.*

You have claimed that there is an important historical dimension to socialist projects that many analysts overlook. In Venezuela, that historical component is obviously present because of Chávez's references to Simón Bolívar, Ezequiel Zamora, and other figures from Venezuela's revolutionary past. Yet that dimension often falls by the wayside when people tell the story of the Venezuelan revolutionary process, especially in the more "scientific" accounts.

Yes, that's right. First of all, backing up a bit, I should say that I am struck these days by how, in the ideological crisis that has followed on Venezuela's economic and political crisis, people tend to go back to very crude simplifications. In effect, they often fall back to thinking that what they have always believed was right (as if nothing were to be learned from the Venezuelan experience over the past 15 years).

For example, some people are quick to say that Chávez should have just advanced toward socialism, taken the means of production, etc. It may well be true. But what we must attend to is the nature of this discourse: it is always framed in terms of "should have," "needed to" ... Yet, in politics, the most important question is often what mediates between the "is" and the "ought." Otherwise, making socialism would just boil down to laying out a series of categorical imperatives and following them.

Then there are people who say that the problem was that the Bolivarian Revolution only went halfway. That criticism could mean one of two things. On the one hand, it could mean that the revolution failed because it wasn't completed, which is more or less tautological (like saying it failed because it failed). On the other hand, it could mean something about timing, i.e., that the revolutionary process was too slow, that it paused too long at one point.

The latter would be a reasonable argument, but what is problematic is an outright rejection of mediations, as I fear is often the case when people criticize revolutions for only going "halfway." It's obvious that to go the whole way you have to go halfway first, so the problem is not that you go halfway before going all the way—which is a logical necessity—but how long you can stay halfway and which mediations between the present situation and the final goal are beneficial and which aren't.

The general error that I see is people disregarding and throwing out mediations altogether. In politics, sometimes the main problem is not so much the ultimate goal but rather how to get there—in brief, strategy and tactics, and Chávez had a genius for both.

In this sense, it's important to point out that political activity and class struggle do not take place in some kind of Newtonian ether. Instead, both happen in history. So what I argue is that Chávez activated a historical possibility, a latent revolutionary tendency in Venezuela, which drew on Bolívar, Simón Rodríguez, and Zamora, and also the popular movements behind them. It's a rich tradition, but perhaps we can summarize it with a shorthand, as Chávez did, using the proper name "Bolívar."

That was the historical legacy that Chávez pulled out of the past, dusted off, and put into action. It is interesting to me that when most people give an account of the Bolivarian Process today, they have nothing to say about Bolívar. How different that is from Chávez, who couldn't stop talking about Bolívar! Was he crazy? Ninety-five percent of the existing political analyses—whether critical or affirmative—implicitly assume that this part of Chávez's discourse was just madness or populism on his part.

In summary, you think that class struggle in Venezuela has an irreducible historical component.

That is a good way of putting it. In effect, class struggle always takes place in history. That much is clear. But the important thing to realize is that a social class is not part of some universal *dramatis personae* that enters into different historical scenarios. No, in fact a social class, whether proletarian or bourgeois, takes shape in history and even forms itself in the drama of history, through struggle. This, of course, is not to deny the role of the productive apparatus in determining social classes, but rather to recognize that the formation of a mode of production is itself a historical process.

For example, in Venezuela the formation of the working class—as a class dispossessed of the means of production—has everything to do with the failure of Bolívar's project, which involved land reform and the construction of a sovereign continental bloc that could face down the colonial metropoli and the emerging British Empire. For that reason, the oppressed class in our context, insofar as it is conscious of its situation and insofar as it has its own project, is Bolivarian. Its revolutionary project is Bolivarianism.

The problem with a lot of sociological (ahistorical) perspectives on class is that they strip the class of its self-assigned projects. In effect, the members of a social class are transformed into a kind of naked, bare life. Or they become mere placeholders in a static social stratification.

In your view, the Left has often overlooked politics and done so to its own disadvantage. Politics has been its weak suit.

Yes, that is absolutely right. The reasons are complex. First of all, capitalism is the first social formation in which the economic and political spheres achieve significant autonomy. This happens to such a degree that the economic sphere can be studied apart, for the first time in human history, as governed by a set of economic laws. By the same token, the first scientific analyses of capitalism had to focus on its economic dimension.

In this new form of society, the most important expressions of power are not part of what is called politics. A worker is exploited by the boss, dominated by the boss, or more exactly by capital itself, but the boss has no special political power, nor apparently does capital either. That is what is novel in capitalism. Meanwhile, what passes for politics increasingly becomes an empty show or fairy tale (Karl Marx talks about the "idealism" of the state and contrasts it with the "materialism" of civil society) that has apparently nothing to do with the world of suffering where people struggle for their daily bread.

But it is one thing to realize this and it is another to let politics fall by the wayside. In fact, capitalism wants that to happen. It wants us to think that its forms are eternal and history has ended. (Francis Fukuyama said this a few decades ago, following G. W. F. Hegel, but he was really just articulating something that's implicit in every capitalist theory.) Yet at some point, the workers, the oppressed, have to wake up from their slumber and formulate, from their own position, a political question. They will have to launch a political project (admittedly, changing the nature of politics and changing its rules) aimed at bringing down both the capitalist state and the special kind of semi-political power that is incarnated in private property.

That is why I think Chávez is important for relaunching the Left into the political sphere. Remember that the dominant leftist model when he started in the 1990s was Zapatismo with its apparent rejection of state politics, its political abstentionism. Well, Chávez jumped with both feet into politics, donning the tricolor sash, becoming President of the Republic, etc. Of course, in so doing he landed into a den of vipers. But he was pretty good at doing battle with those animals (in no small measure because he maintained an open, dialectical relationship with the masses).

But most of the Left isn't like that. Precisely because the revolutionary

Left has a certain faith that political projects will spontaneously emerge in reaction to exploitation, it has a weak grammar of politics. There are some notable exceptions, including V. I. Lenin, who pointed out the fallacy of spontaneity. Antonio Gramsci, too, developed an interesting discourse on politics, as did Leon Trotsky. In fact, there were fascinating debates about political strategy and tactics in the Third International during its first decade. Since then, however, the Left has often shown a chronic lack of creativity. Take state power! Organize an independent party! I agree. But how to do so? Remember that Lenin once thought of working with the eccentric Orthodox priest Georgy Gapon. He quickly abandoned the idea, which is fortunate. But the important thing to remember is that creativity and invention are important and inevitable parts of politics.

This situation has created a kind of void in our discourse, an impoverishment of the Left's political repertoire. As a result, it's simply the case that you might learn more about political power by watching an episode of *Game of Thrones* or paying attention to Chávez-in-action than by consulting some leftist manual.

Mind you, Lenin himself is not the spare, schematic figure—offering readymade answers to everything—that sometimes figures in the popular imagination. Lars T. Lih has shown how Lenin articulated his project with a set of weighted terms such as *narod* (≈people), *vozhd* (≈hegemon), and *vlast* (≈power), which were all deeply rooted in Russian history and culture. They formed an important part of Lenin's political grammar. Well, I think Chávez did the same thing, using the rich resources of Venezuelan and Latin American history to construct a powerful political discourse.

If there is a danger in overlooking the creative political discourse that emerged in Venezuela's recent history, there must also be a price to pay for similar errors on a global scale. When the Left attempts to face the current worldwide crisis, does it fall into similar errors?

Globally, the dangers are all too evident. In a word, if the Left forgets about historical meanings and politics as fields of struggle, it leaves those spaces open to the Right, to fascism. Perhaps with some exaggeration, I have compared Chávez's reactivation of politics to his discovering "the continent of politics." Well, the problem is as simple as this: If the Left doesn't occupy that continent, then the Right will not lose time in doing so.

It's happening right now. Look at how the extreme Right in the United States reaches into the country's history to develop its symbols and codes, its horrible iconography of white supremacism. Now it has an ally in the presidency! Faced with that situation, the Left in the United States shouldn't be ahistorical—that's simply suicide. Instead, it should jump into the historical fray and declare itself to be abolitionist. It should be defending the incomplete projects of Nat Turner and John Brown.

In the Spanish state, the fascistoid party Vox, which has suddenly reared its head in Andalusia, is also deploying a retrograde historicism. Should we face them down imagining that history begins just yesterday, with the so-called "transition to democracy?"[1] Of course not, although that is the mainstream response. In fact, the Left should go back much further and declare that it's going to defend Durruti, Nin, etc., pointing out how there's some unfinished business in history that goes back to the *Guerra Civil* and beyond.

In Venezuela, it's terrible to see how the right wing has begun to appeal to the Bolivarian legacy, and they also just called for a *cabildo abierto*, which is an idea that has profound historical resonances. But we on the left should be doing that! We should have anticipated it and headed them off!

What's become clear in the crisis is that politics is an open terrain of struggle. In part, it's a struggle over historical meanings. Politics is a territory that is rife with danger—it presents an ample array of deviations and abuses of power—but the most dangerous thing is to abandon that territory to the enemy!

Here a certain kind of historical revisionism has played an especially insidious role in disarming the Left. It tells us that the problem with twentieth-century fascism was its "voluntarist" politics. No, the problem with fascism is that it was genocidal, racist, anti-Semitic, anti-communist, and anti-democratic. But historical revisionism tries to deprive the Left of "voluntarist" (i.e., interventionist) politics altogether by putting Jacobinism and fascism in the same basket. Yet now, more than ever, the left needs to be very Jacobin—that is, it needs to be democratically wielding state power, history, creativity and force—precisely to win the battle against fascism!

— January 22, 2019

Chávez, a Mirror of the People:
A Conversation with Edgar Pérez

Organizer and intellectual Edgar Pérez, better known as "Gordo Edgar," participated in the most important events in recent Venezuelan history, from the Caracazo to the 4F insurrection and the anti-coup mobilization that brought Chávez back to office in April 2002. A well-known personality in the popular movement, Edgar grew up in the 23 de Enero barrio in Caracas, but most of his activism took place in La Vega, a very poor barrio that, like 23 de Enero, takes pride in its history of rebellion and grassroots organization. Growing up in the 1960s and 1970s, Edgar calls La Vega, where we interviewed him, "a school for revolutionaries." In this conversation, "Gordo Edgar" reflects on the vicissitudes of the popular movement while analyzing the role of Hugo Chávez in the Venezuelan revolution.

It would seem, in some mainstream narratives, that prior to Chávez emerging, there were no struggles. You yourself had a rich experience of activism, joining the urban resistance, working with insurgent movements, participating in counter-hegemonic cultural production, and you were active during the insurrections of 1989 [Caracazo] and 1992 [4F insurrection]. What can you tell us about the popular movement before Chávez?

First, I should say that the popular movement, with its struggles, has periods of peaks—moments when society has come to the boiling point—and periods when it recedes somewhat.

Let's take a look at our history. In the '60s and '70s, during the [guerrilla] insurgency, the popular movement in the city, in Caracas, and particularly in La Vega, was very active. Here, in La Vega, Bandera Roja [a revolutionary party at that time] developed a legal front, the CLP [Popular Struggle Committees], whereas the PRV [Party of the Venezuelan Revolution] had a mass front here as well, which was Ruptura. Finally, there was another organization which was the OR [Revolutionary Organization party] with the Socialist League as its legal front. By the '70s in La Vega, in addition to these organizations and a widespread environment of rebelliousness in the barrio, we had the grassroots Christian movement in its most radical and popular form, doing work in the community based on the premises of liberation theology.

One key figure here was Francisco Wuytack, a Belgian priest who arrived around 1965, was expelled from the country during the first term of Rafael Caldera's presidency [1969–1974], and came back in clandestinely a few years later only to be expelled once again during Carlos Andrés Pérez's presidency [1974–1979]. He truly shook our community because he brought in sectors that were lukewarm to the struggle, by linking their beliefs with the struggle.

So the '60s and '70s were impressive decades, decades of mobilization and action, when the barrio was boiling, and when the popular movement was the epicenter of daily life—a very rebellious popular movement!

Then the '80s came, and there was a falling off of popular organization. The '80s were not as effervescent as the '70s, but the general stupor was broken by the events of February 1989, or what is known as the "Caracazo," but should really be called the "Guarenazo" to do justice to the people who sparked the popular insurrection, which began in Guarenas.

So the Caracazo breaks with a sleepy decade Basically, the dam broke on February 27, just weeks after Carlos Andrés Pérez entered his second presidency [1989–1993]. The economic situation then was tremendously difficult. It was extreme.

Pérez had been elected by an ample majority of people who held the memory of the economic boom of the '70s. The basis of his victory was the prior bonanza. It was a false promise because his government implemented neoliberal adjustment policies just days after taking power. That, on top of the deteriorated economic situation, was the trigger for a popular uprising that began in Guarenas and shook Caracas.

During those days, people, humble people, took over the streets—we made them our own. We affirmed our existence in a process of expropriation of the expropriators. It was a totally spontaneous insurrection. There was no party or vanguard leading it . . . the vanguard was the people. It was us, the people from the *barrios*, doing justice, taking what should be ours. The old organizations, the parties associated with the Left, they were immobilized by the rush of events.

We are talking about two or three days when the people were center stage, and they corralled the political class and the rich. Those days were followed, of course, by a brutal repression that left us angry, having lost four to five thousand people, but it didn't leave us numb, whereas it left the rich quaking in their boots.

Thirty years later, when we reflect on that rebellious outburst, we may ask ourselves about the conditions for insurrection today. The fact is that, for a variety of reasons and policies, both internal and foreign, our material conditions are worse than those in 1989. . . . But the truth is that, with all the suffering and all the contradictions that we are facing today, we haven't lost hope. We have a collective project that may be nebulous when it comes to the policies that are implemented from above, but we have a project that maintains our hope.

When we, the people, flooded the streets on February 27, 1989, and the days after, that was an expression of our rejection of neoliberal policies, but it was also a move to access the promised land, the land of goods and merchandise, an attempt to access what hegemonic society held as good and desirable. So first we went for the food—we were hungry—but then came the shoes, the refrigerators, the TVs. Today, under grueling circumstances imposed from within and from without, many of us hold on to a larger project.

Chávez, the memory of Chávez—and we should be wary and not turn him into a god—is what keeps the dam from breaking now. . . . He is the only dead man who wins elections but, more importantly, he is the only dead man who guarantees unity and hope, and reminds us that there is a path toward emancipation: the commune. Chávez was eliminated physically, but his ideas are ours now. Now he is integrated into the people because he was one with the people: he was one of us.

What happened in the 1990s in the *barrios* of Caracas?

In the '90s, the *Asambleas de Barrio* [Barrio Assemblies] began to grow as spaces of organization at a territorial level. They were permeated by libertarian [in Spanish, libertarian refers to anarchist] ideals, and new connections among people began to emerge there.

In these Asambleas de Barrio, debates were driven from below. People talked about their problems among their peers, and we looked for collective solutions. It wasn't the old parties, it was the people from the *barrios* who took center stage, and the movement grew very rapidly, precisely because the restrictions imposed by the parties were broken by a new kind of practice that made each participant into an equal. This experience was very important in the early days of the revolution when the CTUs [local committees for allotting land titles to barrio dwellers] and the Mesas Técnicas de Agua [local committees organized for water access] emerged.

Around that time, we began to hear that in the military barracks an insurrectional movement was brewing. This wasn't too much of a surprise since we had news of [revolutionary] work being done inside the barracks since the mid-'70s and we had expected a popular military insurrection for a while.

Douglas Bravo [commander of the FALN, Venezuela's guerrilla movement from the early '60s through the '70s] had talked about this possibility. Alfredo Maneiro [politician and theorist who participated in the insurgency in the 1960s] did so too, and Kléber Ramírez [a university professor who organized the PRV's penetration into the military] had also predicted it. Kléber, in fact, was the founder of the Bolivarian movement that would eventually be led by Chávez. He and his people had infiltrated the barracks, which meant the movement wasn't simply built by Chávez. Instead, Chávez worked with something that was already there.

So in 1992, at the peak of the Asambleas de Barrio movement, when once again the popular movement was heating up, Chávez entered the stage. The truth is that when the insurrection happened some of us took part in it [as civilians], but much of the society had doubts since the 1989 [Caracazo] massacre was carried out by the military.

However, when Chávez and his people were defeated and he was given two minutes on television to surrender, what the people saw was a man like us, "a man of the people." Obviously, his *"por ahora"* ["for now" refers to the two minutes on TV after the insurrection in which Chávez recognized his failure but hinted that the struggle would continue] moved us. It shook us. There was a process of identification with the man, and his message became part of the popular discourse while Chávez was behind bars.

Two years later, when Chávez came out of prison, the terrain was ripe for constructing something new.

Look, as you know, I'm a libertarian anarchist, a Caribe [the rebellious indigenous group that had settled much of the Venezuelan territory at the arrival of the Spanish colonists] libertarian, so I don't believe that a man can single-handedly reorient the course of history. However, it is true that Chávez was a catalyst for the coming together of multiple popular initiatives and proposals. His role was important for the popular movement's rapid process of maturing.

A few years later, when Chávez opted for the electoral path and the possibility of "storming the fortress" of Miraflores [Presidential Palace], the popular movement cast its lot even more with him. In this regard, I would like to say something here. I think it's wrong to say that Chávez understood the people. Chávez did not simply understand the people and their project. Chávez *was* the people. Through him, the people saw themselves in a mirror.

Often, Chávez is seen as having created the revolution: Chávez as a messianic figure whose calling was to transform Venezuela. That reading, of course, erases the collective effort. In fact, between Chávez and the people there was a rich and fluid relationship. The people interpellated Chávez; they corrected him along the way and

Chávez, Politics, and Nuestra América

even rescued him after the 2002 coup! How do you understand the relationship between Chávez and the people?

I agree. The *pueblo* became the main actor—they took on the leading role—when Chávez became president. But let's go back a bit. Throughout the '90s the discourse of "the end of history" was widespread in politics, in the academy, and in the media. That was also the time of the hegemony of *pensée unique*.

Chávez emerged in that apparent desert—which, as I said, was boiling underneath—and stood up for Bolivarian thought. In so doing, he cast aside the end of history hypothesis, making history part of the present. So really what we found was Chávez as an actor, but the people too were becoming a visible political subject and political actor. Of course, there were contradictions. The people interpellated Chávez, the people corrected Chávez. All that is to be expected in a process where there was a common objective shared by the people and the man in Miraflores Palace.

Let me give you an example. Chávez put the idea of the commune at the core of our project. The commune is a proposal that comes from the anarchist worldview—it is not top-down, it is a grassroots, from below proposal—and has a basis in our pre-colonial history as well. As the great communicator, and from the privileged space of influence that he held, Chávez called on people to build the communes in an exercise of self-emancipation. Then, the commune took on its own life in the popular imaginary . . . and real communal experiences began to emerge. In a contradictory way, however, Chávez also strengthened an institutional framework that was at odds with the commune.

In the USSR, in 1920, Pyotr Kropotkin wrote a famous letter to V. I. Lenin (a letter which, by the way, Chávez quoted in a public address). He told Lenin that if the project wasn't in the hands of the people, in the hands of the councils or the soviets, the revolution would be lost. Chávez himself understood the contradiction between the commune and constituted power, and he vacillated between one and the other. . . . However, I would say that he ended up siding with the commune and with the people.

But look, while Chávez, a man of the people, embodied this contradiction, the people also fell prey to the hegemonic conception of power: interpreting power as residing in Miraflores.

Dogmatic Marxism-Leninism also assumes that the key issue is controlling the presidential palace (or the state). In this regard, it should be made clear that the people haven't taken control of the state apparatus. ... Perhaps that's because they are not interested, perhaps because the people understand that power doesn't reside in one building.

So the spirit of our collective project resides in the slogan "Commune or Nothing," in an experiential process, a process of building from below. Here we can count on the laws of popular power that can sometimes help, but are sometimes a hindrance. Most importantly, however, we stand by the proposal [of the commune] that breaks with hegemonic power relations, both capitalist and statist.

We should understand another thing when we reflect on our revolution. Communal councils and communes cannot be imposed by decree, as we have witnessed on several occasions. Ours is a project of self-liberation. They cannot come to tell us what we should do, how we must organize ourselves.

As a project of self-liberation, we will also run into problems ... because the revolution embodies a massive problem: a cultural problem first and foremost. It is not mainly an economic problem, as certain dogmatic theorists claim. Of course, current economic relations must be ended, but the revolution is a cultural problem that can only be solved by the people when they become agents, when they become the center of their own lives.

Clearly, the popular movement can experience ups and downs, as you have been pointing out with regard to Venezuelan history. What do you think has happened to the Left and the popular movement in this country right now?

Well, first we have to acknowledge one important fact: this revolution took shape under the auspices of an economic boom. This is a revolution that was done with money! Remember that Venezuela is a country that is very rich in natural resources, and because the state is the owner and the manager of the oil wealth, it profoundly shapes politics here.

In Venezuela, a clientelist political practice developed early on. It had an important role in the governments of the populist *Adeco* [Acción Democrática] party prior to Chávez's election in 1998.

The Bolivarian Revolution empowered people early on—there is no denying that—but it simultaneously reinforced the old clientelist practices, which came to penetrate the popular movement. As a result, the popular movement became more dependent, less autonomous.

Really, the only revolution that has been done with money is this one, and that makes things very difficult! At the end of the day, everybody expects the state to provide the resources to do anything. That limits people's creativity and weakens the popular movement from within. Dependence on the state was a hindrance to autonomous organization. We are paying the price for all that now!

There is another problem, and that is not particular to Venezuela. That problem is institutions. When I talk about institutions, I'm referring to parties, governmental offices, and ministries. Institutions operate under a logic that is cautious by nature and deaf to the people's demands.

Basically, the predominant tendency in institutions hasn't been a revolutionary one but a reformist one. Conversely, the people look to the institutions [for salvation]; they have become passive, waiting for institutions to direct the revolution. That creates a greater level of dependence that hinders people's creativity and damages the organic character of the movement. This has happened here in Venezuela, and we have to stop it.

Most people in institutions are not committed to making the revolution more radical, which is necessary. Those people are committed to a mere reform, which is absurd in a country with our conditions. Reformist change actually is not possible here. They are only interested in maintaining their posts, they are wedded to the status quo. What is more, in the institutions there is a right-wing—a Chavista right wing!—which is hegemonic. From those spaces of power, the Left and popular tendencies are interpreted as problematic.

The [institutional] problem has much to do with the colonization that is still alive here. I'm one of those people who shares with Enrique Dussel the idea that decolonization is important. What the Left has done once and again is to repeat models that have nothing to do with us.

The commune is, however, something different. The commune is our project. It is not a "colonized" proposal, since it comes out of historical experiments such as the Paris Commune and, more importantly, has deep roots in the communal forms of organization that existed here prior to the arrival of the Spanish. We can also draw links with the Black *cumbes* [Maroon settlements in Venezuela]. We are always looking to the outside, beyond our frontiers.

Would you say that a process of decolonization is important if we want to come out of the current crisis?

Yes, that is the key. We have to recognize ourselves. We must stop looking at ourselves in the mirror of the West. . . . Eduardo Galeano talks about this, about the discovery that wasn't and the discovery that is still pending. Our memories have been erased. That is so much the case that people don't know anything about the history of the *cimarrones* [runaway slaves] or of indigenous people and what they brought to our culture. When we finally learn about our culture and learn about our roots, that will bring about something new.

We have been in an induced amnesia for the past 500 years, and it turns out that the occidental form of politics still organizes our political sphere. Simón Rodríguez [Venezuelan philosopher and Simón Bolívar's teacher] said that we must create a new utopia on this continent, new institutions; he said that we shouldn't let ourselves age prematurely by adopting the institutions of the old continent. Europe is very worn out, the United States is what it is. We have to create our own institutions.

Rodríguez also talks about *toparquia* [power organized at a local level]. He meant power operating on the territorial level, which goes hand in hand with self-government.

The government is penetrated by a top-down vision and in it the

Right, as I said, is quite present. Still, we will defend that government whenever faced by an imperialist aggression. However, beyond this kind of defense, our main focus should be to find forms of organization that are ours. We have to overcome 500 years of colonialism. That isn't easy, but it is our most urgent task now.

— June 14, 2019

What's Been Learned Won't Be Easily Forgotten: A Conversation with Antonio González Plessman

Antonio González Plessmann, who holds degrees from Venezuelan and Ecuadorian universities, has been a human rights activist and militant leftist since the 1980s. A former vice rector of the National Experimental Security University, he took part in the process of police reform initiated in 2006. Today González Plessmann is part of the SurGentes collective and is working with the Pueblo a Pueblo project in San Agustin barrio in Caracas. In this interview, he offers important insights into the revolutionary potential that Chavismo unleashed early in the Bolivarian Process. It's a potential that, he contends, could be set rolling again.

Hugo Chávez's taking power went hand in hand with a huge wave of popular participation. For example, the Venezuelan people mobilized for and participated in the Constituent Assembly in 1999 (with its sessions appearing on national television), and they got involved with the literacy campaigns, the Urban Land Committees, and the Communal Councils. In effect, people became active subjects of change. Today, by contrast, there is a logic that is much more "top down," as is seen clearly in non-participative projects like Gran Misión Vivienda Venezuela and a Constituent Assembly that takes place behind closed doors. Can you explain this historical trajectory?

Beginning in 1999, popular protagonism—together with a more equal distribution of wealth and greater autonomy vis-à-vis the world's hegemonic powers—was a pillar of the political process. Poor people came on stage as political agents. It was the essence of the revolution, its vitality!

Between 2009 and 2012, Chávez upped the ante on that project, which he summarized in 2012 with the slogan "Commune or Nothing." Picking up on previous experiences of popular organization, Chávez assumed that the [Bolivarian] Revolution's success depended on expanding spaces of territorial self-government: spaces where people were creating new kinds of sociality from below, based on more democratic economic and political practices.

All this was part of a process of building what Chávez said was a "spider web" of territorial organizations, aimed at a new socialist democracy of a special Venezuelan kind. It was a great experiment in promoting popular power from the state, and it succeeded in mobilizing and raising the morale of a large swath of the country's poor people. All that was expressed in a programmatic way in *Alo Presidente Teorico N° 1* [2009], the *2013–2019 Homeland Plan* [2012], and in the *Strike at the Helm* speech [2012].

In 2013, however, several crises came together, which explain why the government changed course on many issues, including popular power. On the one hand, Chávez's death brought the end of the charismatic and strategic leadership that had unified diverse sectors around a popular program. On the other hand, there was a drastic fall in oil prices (lasting from 2014 to 2016), which hindered our capacity to import the intermediate and final goods that the country needs.

It's important to recall that, despite all that was done in terms of social inclusion, the [Venezuelan Revolution] had not significantly modified the country's productive apparatus during the previous 15 years. That's to say, the rentier economy was not transformed along the lines of a new leftist model. On the contrary, we became even more dependent on oil exports, which made up 77 percent of total exports in 1997 and 94 percent in 2014!

Another structural problem that has become very evident today—now that the state has fewer resources—is the widespread corruption of politicians, with most of the corruption involving the use of privileged access to foreign currency to make real or fake imports.

Yet beyond these structural problems, we also have to look at how badly the government managed the economy between 2013 and 2017, mostly through doing nothing or taking only short-term measures. Additionally, we saw a more radical onslaught on part of the local and international Right, who understood the country's economic and political crisis as an opportunity not only to achieve regime change, but, above all, to teach a lesson to the Venezuelan people. Their idea was to "show" the revolution's failure and prove the impossibility of any effort to overcome capitalism by democratic means.

With the ebbing of progressive forces of the region, we see the Right staging violent protests in 2014 and 2017, rejecting election results in 2013, and sabotaging the economy. Then comes a covert blockade and then later an open one together with interference by the United States and other right-wing governments. All this has made [Maduro's] government very weak since its coming into being in 2013. The government manages to stay in power, but it fails to overcome the crisis—to say nothing about maintaining the program of a democratic transition to socialism.

A part of the Chávez leadership took control of the state apparatus and the PSUV. It closed ranks and carried out purges, opting for a strategy that implies the progressive elimination of democratic spaces. That group legitimizes its actions by pointing to the economic war and the conspiracy of the right, which are very real, and then its proceeds to limit various forms of expression of the popular will.

This takes place in relation to the questions of the state. Examples include cancelling the recall referendum promoted by the opposition, delaying by one year the elections for governors, deciding not to do a popular referendum to convene the constituent assembly. But it also takes place in popular organizational spaces. In 2016, they suspended the elections of the Communal Councils throughout the country, and, in 2017, the new line was that only PSUV members could head up these institutions.

In parallel, the bulk of the government's social action focused on CLAPs and on bonuses [direct subsidies to individuals]. The Communal Councils fell by the wayside in the popular spaces, because the CLAPs generated a capillary organizational structure based on what is most important for the people: access to food. Unlike the Communal Councils, where the community chooses its speakers and representatives, CLAP spokespeople are designated by the state and the party.

In practice, that amounts to a state-led sabotage of the Communal Councils, weakening them as spaces of popular power. It took away their role as interlocutors dealing with both the community and institutions, and instead turns militants into people who work mainly with the state. In 2017, Nicolás [Maduro] himself declared that CLAPs were "the greatest expression of popular power."

In summary, the government's survival strategy amounts to opting for organizational forms that are controlled from above, that have no autonomy, and that are traversed throughout by depoliticizing systems of patronage. They are abandoning the project of constructing socialism from the grassroots. That [dynamic], of course, collides with many defiant Chavista projects that exist throughout the country, which are now aware that "only the people can save the people."

Although participation seems to be waning in Chavismo, there still are wonderful demonstrations of popular power and self-organization—expressions of what Chávez called "territorial socialism." These range from flagship communes such as El Maizal and El Panal to self-managed initiatives such as the Movimiento de Pobladores or the Productive Workers' Army. How can we reactivate the latent revolutionary potential of the Chavista project, which is surely part of our collective memory?

In the midst of the many crises that affect us as a country, and as leftists and Chavistas, it is important that we stand up proudly to defend our Chavista identity. We should remember that, as poor people and leftists who led the Bolivarian Revolution, we achieved important things: we became political subjects, with class consciousness and an awareness of justice, we distributed the national wealth more fairly; we substantially improved our lives; we achieved an autonomous foreign policy; and we broke with the myth that there are no alternatives to liberal democracy and capitalism.

But this is not about adopting a nostalgic attitude toward the past. Instead, based on what we have experienced in Chavismo, we should interpret the current situation and think of ways out. For example, we can contrast Chávez's sovereign oil policy with the de facto privatizations that are taking place now in PDVSA. Likewise, Chávez's questioning the racist and class character of the Fourth Republic's security operations can be juxtaposed to the extrajudicial executions that the National Bolivarian Police's FAES groups and other [state security] forces carry out in popular neighborhoods today.

In this way, standing up proudly as Chavistas, we can call into question political deviations from the project that we signed on to, that belongs to us as a people and that allowed us to improve our lives. From that same position, we can also go out to meet the popular sectors that are in the streets today claiming their rights: for example, workers demanding their labor rights, popular communities insisting on public services, sick people claiming their right to health, peasants demanding their right to land to produce food and their right to security for their lives and physical integrity, etc.

Today the Chavista program of popular power no longer can count on the state as an ally, as it was in the past. Recognizing that is the first step. It's up to the Chavista bases themselves to promote that project and do so from below. To build popular power you do not have to ask anyone's permission, nor is it a requirement that you have the support of the institutions or their legitimacy. In fact, in a global context, Venezuela was an exception, because popular power is [usually] something that is built outside of the state or in opposition to it.

One thing that is key to reviving participation today is that our programmatic ideas be connected to material results. Organizational projects and collective endeavors should always be associated with the material solution to daily problems. They should demonstrate that it is possible to enforce one's rights as a result of self-organization, solidarity, direct and plural participation, mobilizing, and insisting that the state and other powers that be fulfill their duties.

At this point in time, there is no room for an abstract political discourse based merely on global proposals, aimed at the society or political situation, if they don't go hand in hand with solving our immediate problems. Political power and credibility turn around resolving concrete problems through self-organization and accompanied by democratic teaching processes. In all of this, it's important that popular organizations achieve an economic capacity that enhances their autonomy.

The projects that you mention, along with a few others, are deservedly in the limelight, because they are based on real concrete practice—not platforms or short-term results that derive from transitory financing. These projects have broad social support because they are about people themselves making profound changes in their day-to-day reality.

Finally, I believe that it is necessary to build horizontal links across the broad spectrum of projects that are all expressions of popular power; because if they remain isolated, they will be defeated. Linking them requires humility, political maturity, and a pluralist logic that permits us to democratically address our differences. We must build trust among the diverse sectors of popular, leftist Chavismo, and we must build it on the basis of doing things together, beginning with small things and later turning to bigger ones.

This popular leftist sector, although it does not currently constitute a nationwide political force, nevertheless has an incredible moral authority. That means that it could be the basis of a Chavista regeneration that would relaunch the socialist program, the program of popular power.

You are an active participant in a self-organized, popular initiative in San Agustín, a working-class barrio of Caracas. Can you tell us about this experience?

I am part of the SurGentes collective, which for the last four years has been working with popular organizations in San Agustín del Sur. It's a group of women in the collective who do the direct work in the barrio, and they do it with a lot of passion and revolutionary spirit. Together with people (mostly women) from eleven neighborhoods in San Agustín they built the cooperative Unidos San Agustín Convive, which distributes vegetables twice a month, at more than 70 percent below the market prices. This is possible through an alliance with associated producers of the Pueblo a Pueblo network. In this way, we get around the distribution mafias and other intermediaries, bringing together people from the rural areas and the city.

The cooperative is very careful with its internal processes, which are based on democracy, pluralism, transparency, rendering accounts, and politicizing militants. We have seen that many Chavistas (and non-Chavistas) have lost interest in popular organization, when they see that there are privileges in the distribution of resources. That is to say, the community's "representatives" enjoy preferential access to the state and they impose decisions, thereby squashing popular protagonism.

The fact that our collective's members have been very careful to respect [democratic] process is what has allowed the cooperative to grow and take root in the community. People realize that politics here is being done in another way. We are demonstrating, sometimes clashing with the bureaucracy, that in the midst of the crisis it is possible to grow and accumulate forces. In addition to improving people's diet, we are raising their political awareness through democratic practices that are part and parcel with the Chavista and socialist project. All this without excluding anybody.

Now we have gotten a truck, donated by the ONA [National Antidrug Office], and resources to repair it, and we have started a fabric workshop that is generating an income for the cooperative and its workers. Also, we have self-financed daycare three times a week in addition to running a small agroecological farm. Finally, we are in permanent communication with other movements and collectives that promote popular power both in urban and rural areas.

Now people are beginning to take a critical look at the whole progressive cycle (sometimes called the "Pink Tide") that took shape at the beginning of this century in Latin America. Some analysts and groups are concluding that it was an error to have tasted the forbidden fruit of state power. As I understand it, you disagree with that point of view.

Chávez, Politics, and Nuestra América

At present there is a section of the Latin American intellectual Left that, in taking stock of the region's so-called "progressive" processes, concludes that "it was not worth it," because today we are more dependent, more extractivist, and less democratic than before. That analysis goes hand in hand with a kind of turn away from the state. Instead, we are supposed to commit to the community and to projects that arise from social movements.

My aim here is not to present these arguments in a reductive way, since I believe they are important and necessary for the left's internal discussions. The arguments are much more complex than those I mention here. I only summarize the position briefly to explain my disagreement with the idea of turning away from the state. That's because, despite it being clear today that seizing power is not the same as controlling the state—which is the key thing in a revolution—still, in my opinion, merely accumulating forces from below cannot secure sustainable and structural changes.

The right wing has never renounced state power, because the state continues to be the locus of a dense network of power relations that crisscross society. To turn away from the state is to lose the game by forfeit. Processes of societal change must be carried out both "from above" and "from below," without turning our backs on these contested spaces.

Nor, in spite of the enormous complexities that it meant for the Venezuelan process, should we be ashamed that the state itself promoted organization (that is, "from above"). This inevitably led to a tendency toward taming and controlling [the popular movement], often through patronage, but we also need to be clear that it was due to this state support—a political decision on the part of the Bolivarian Revolution—that the country's largest experience of popular organization and participation could take place.

What people have learned in this process of politicization—even in that mix of autonomy, rebellion, patronage, and docility that has developed these days around the state—is a great thing and a very important one. The same goes for the "political" use of oil (administered by the Venezuelan state) to distribute wealth internally and promote spaces of autonomy in the whole region. As we say in Venezuela: *nadie nos quita lo bailao* (nobody can take what we've learned away from us), although there's a lot that we need to evaluate critically and learn from our own experience.

— JANUARY 17, 2019

Venezuela and Its Singularities: A Conversation with Reinaldo Iturriza

Reinaldo Iturriza has engaged with the Chavista project in a wide range of roles. A blogger acclaimed by Hugo Chávez, he went on to become Minister of Communes and Minister of Culture. He has written Chavismo Salvage (Wild Chavismo), *and at present is completing a new book called* Caribes *while working at the National Center of History and as a communal agricultural worker in Lara State. In this interview, Iturriza addresses some of the most difficult questions facing Chavismo today. These include the dialectic between internal democracy and leadership in the PSUV party, the rural comuneros that are facing off with the regional oligarchy; and its allies in the government; and the perception of Chavismo internationally.*

Hegemonic historiography interprets history as developing linearly, implicitly looking for continuities. By contrast, your reading of the Chavista phenomenon points to singularities and ruptures. Can you explain this to us?

This is indeed a key point. Conservative historiography makes an enormous effort to demonstrate Chavismo's kinship with the most "backward" elements of Venezuela's political tradition. Internationally, there has certainly been an attempt to dispel the phenomenon by relating it to the so-called "populism" of "backward" countries that is supposed to have emerged once again. It focuses attention on the figure of the leader and relegates the popular classes to the background. Tacitly, the latter are considered incapable of political activity and the same goes for our countries too, which are presented as predisposed toward disorder, irrationality, and violence. How often one hears this kind of opinion! However, the uniqueness of Chavismo consists, among other things, precisely in popular protagonism. Chavismo is the result of an extraordinary process of forming a political subject that has its origin in the 1990s, due to a set of historical circumstances. Moreover, Chávez's leadership is itself inconceivable without that popular upsurge. Chávez is a purely popular construct: the result of a process and not the other way around. His leadership has to do with his resonance with the people, his translating the desires and aspirations of the popular subject.

Then, of course, it is possible to point to relations of continuity with the political culture of Acción Democrática [a right-wing political party that ruled alongside COPEI for many decades as part of the so-called Punto Fijo Pact]. This culture was clientelist, based on the logic of representation, and relegated the popular classes to a subordinate role, allowing "participation" only through traditional political forms (parties, unions, etc.), and privileging corporativism. The most conservative tendencies in Chavismo feel very comfortable reproducing these same practices, but, again, that is not what defines the nature of Chavismo. What is new in Chavismo is precisely everything that breaks with the old culture, giving birth to a new one. The Chavista subject is essentially Venezuela's majority population, who has historically been invisible and marginalized, who feels a deep distrust toward traditional forms of organization, and wagers on the logic of direct participation and spaces of self-government. Ignoring this leads to all kinds of errors regarding the Bolivarian Revolution.

The IV PSUV Congress (July 28–30, 2018) concluded recently and the debates were intense, even difficult at times. The most trying debate focused on the topic of internal democracy in the party, which has millions of members. One tendency in the PSUV proposed to proclaim Nicolás Maduro as president of the party and argued that (given the difficult conditions generated by imperialist aggression) he should personally select the national leadership of the PSUV. Another tendency wanted the party's national leadership

to be elected by the bases while maintaining Maduro as party president. The first proposal held the day. Thinking creatively about the present and the past, what type of party do you think is needed to build socialism in the twenty-first century? Obviously, the question of democracy (and debate among equals) is key, but it is also important that communal projects should have autonomy.

First of all, I consider it correct that the IV PSUV Congress decided to ratify Maduro as party president. Chavismo's unity turns on recognizing the president's leadership, not the other way around. Second, it's urgent to renew the party's national leadership. The best way to do it would have been to appeal to the party's bases, to cast one's lot with the bases. I do not agree at all with the idea that more democracy generates disunity. It is a fallacious argument.

Too often, the Chavista political class decides not to pay attention to the popular masses' deep discontent with the political class in general, Chavista and anti-Chavista, considering them to be disconnected from reality, without real knowledge of the problems that the population has to face every day. There is a very severe crisis of political mediation, between the party direction and its bases, which must be faced with courage and audacity. Among other things, a party of twenty-first century socialism must be one that is willing to do so. We have already had too many mid- and high-ranking politicians who ask the people to make sacrifices that they themselves are not willing to make. Instead, they take advantage of the positions they occupy to obtain benefits, perks, and privileges.

Today it seems as if the rural areas are where the struggle against the despotism of capital (and a part of the bureaucracy) is most active. Examples of such struggles include El Maizal Commune [in Lara State], the resistance in Sur del Lago [in Zulia State] and the Admirable Campesino March: the protesting peasant farmers who recently walked from rural regions to the capital to make themselves heard. Why do you think that the rural areas are now the most mobilized and active regions in this political process that, until recently, was focused on urban zones, especially in the poor *barrios*?

In each of the foci of rural struggle, organized popular-class movements are confronting the regional oligarchy and powers-that-be, who undoubtedly think that they are in a position to "restore" their power in the countryside. The popular movements are also confronting the aberrant alliance between some elements of state forces (bureaucrats, police, military personnel, judges, etc.) and those same regional power groups. It is simply unacceptable that this alliance should take place in a situation where, in fact, we are called upon to dedicate all our efforts on using arable land and must give all the support needed to the real subject of revolutionary politics (*campesinos* and communards, small and medium producers). For it is among the latter that the revolutionary government continues to operate and hold sway.

What would really be strange is if the rural situation today did not generate a popular response! The meeting of the peasants and *comuneros* with the president, and particularly everything they said during the time they had the opportunity to speak [in a national television broadcast], is one of the most important political events of recent times. I believe one could say that the majority of the country felt represented in their words: in their criticisms and demands. What we heard there is the same political clarity found in the people of El Maizal and other communes, in the people in Sur del Lago, and in general in all those who are aware that, in order to overcome this historical crisis, we will have to be able to produce what we eat.

In the international context, some sectors of the left say that they are neither with Chavismo nor with its enemies, neither with imperialism nor the Bolivarian government. In truth, that is a false dilemma, since there is a third option: grassroots Chavismo. The last is of course closer to the government, or at least is willing to form a front with the government to face down imperialism (at the same time as it expresses sometimes quite strong differences with the ruling bloc).

It seems to me that this is the typical position of those who idealize power relations. Despite all the disagreements one might have with the government, it is absolutely clear that anti-Chavismo is simply not an option. Those sectors of the Left, which you just mentioned, like to flaunt their right not to choose. But when you live in a society like ours, where we are trying to carry out a revolution—with both its wonders and its failures—and in which it is not an option to be governed by the criminals who ruled in the past (the same people who are recurring to absolutely all forms of struggle to defeat us, including assassination), then that "neither-nor" position looks a lot like imposture: "My position is not to take a position." Frankly, however, one can go light on such people. They will understand when they do their own revolution. When imperialism tries to suffocate them, they will come to understand that the only option is to breathe.

— August 13, 2018

Chávez and the Twilight of Capitalism: A Conversation with Eduardo Rothe

The improbable life of Venezuelan television personality Eduardo Rothe has taken him to such revolutionary hotspots as Paris in 1968 and Lisbon in 1974, until he became gainfully employed as a commercial fisherman and occasional smuggler. For Rothe and his audience, that life is an endless source of colorful anecdotes that bring together art, spontaneity, and revolutionary practice in a way worthy of the Situationist Movement of which he once formed a part. Behind the legend of Rothe, who is best known in Venezuela for his TV persona, "Profesor Lupa," there is a dedicated revolutionary and internationalist. In this interview, Rothe explains his views on the Bolivarian Process.

Two centuries ago, the continent-wide struggle for independence from Spain had its epicenter in Venezuela. Likewise, the first twenty-first century revolution in the Americas happened here. What is so special about Venezuela? Why is the country so inclined to insurrection?

Historically, Venezuela has had its peculiarities: it was a very poor colony (and later an independent country) with a very small population. It was always a mono-producing and exporting economy: first leathers, cocoa, and coffee, later petroleum. So Venezuela has a particular economic structure: our country lives off of the rent and that has its implications.

Politically, however, what determines the structure of Venezuelan society is that the independence struggle was tremendously lethal here: more than half of the male population died in the war. As far as the entire population is concerned, one third died in the war. Eighty percent of the cities were looted, burned, and abandoned. All this was accompanied by the destruction of the dominating class, both those at the service of the colonial power and those who fought for the republic.

This left Venezuela in the hands of the generals who led the independence struggle, and they played an important role in forming the nation. Later this military caste was replaced by diverse power groups, but none of them had the hereditary character (or constituted power) that more consolidated oligarchies have achieved in other Latin American countries.

Venezuela is a country of improvised power, a country with governments but not with a state. The concept of nation is an extremely fragile one in Venezuela. That makes Venezuela very flexible when it comes to transformations, which may take a long time to happen, but when they happen they are intense. All this goes a long way to making possible the experiment of refounding the nation. Imagine that! What Hugo Chávez did was to re-found an entire nation, just as Bolívar founded a nation some two hundred years before.

The relation between Bolívar, the nation's founder, and Chávez, the founder of the new republic, is basically through the military. They were both military men in a very elastic society with a very particular history.

As opposed to European countries where first a people built a nation and then created a state, which then built an army, here in Venezuela the military itself created the republic. Thus, the huge importance of military personnel, who are, as Bolívar said, "el pueblo que puede" [the *people* who actually can do things] and they in turn influence the political panorama.

Much has been said about Chávez and you yourself have contributed to analyzing his legacy. How would you place Chávez in history?

Chávez belongs to what José Martí and other writers of that era called the "cosmic race" ["*raza cósmica*"]: a new people born out of a process that brought together the Spanish conquest and domination, on the one hand, and the struggle for emancipation, on the other. That unity, which came out of an oppressed people created the conditions for revolt, a lived synthesis of impending revolution.

I would go so far as to say that the necessity of revolt in a barren land, in a territory that had nothing, is what gave rise to the army of the Latin American independence struggle: the war against Spain that burst forth here more than two hundred years ago. In other words, Venezuela, poor and chaotic, was the focus of the independence struggle. More recently, the figure of Chávez emerged in this land in a new effort to free ourselves—the men and women of Latin America—from the domination of all imperialisms, U.S. and European. Chávez is thus a full expression of the cosmic race.

Chávez should also be understood as a unique historical figure. He is unique but not alone, since he has Bolívar and other historical figures as company. Chávez was born out of circumstances, but he was also shaped by history and with the full weight of history. . . . He is the product of history in a particular moment, the man who faced a golden opportunity.

But Chávez also prepared himself to be what he became. He prepared to carry out what he thought could and had to be done.

How did Chávez carry out what had to be done? He called on all the forces of the nation and all the forces of the people (which by the way, are diverse and antagonistic) to rebuild the republic. Hence, we are talking about a revolution aimed at renovating the nation, but it was also a popular revolution aiming at human emancipation. Chávez was able to bring together, in a brilliant way, those two forces in what is known as the Bolivarian Revolution, which also bears the title, not much to my liking, of "Twenty-First Century Socialism."

Chávez's genius was to unite, to synthesize those two factors: the nationalist factor and the popular factor. In doing so, he was able to advance, with contradictions but without violence, correcting the course along the way.

Obviously, the two forces that Chávez brought together in a revolutionary unity cannot live alongside each other forever. Dual power doesn't endure eternally! Nevertheless, we have had eighteen years of it. . . . This brings us to the fact that our problem is not that the state represses—which it doesn't—but that the organized proletarian forces have not yet begun to act autonomously. They aren't struggling to constitute themselves as a force aiming to reorganize the whole society.

Because this was a territory where there wasn't a fully constituted bourgeoisie, because it was so lacking in resources, because it was such a poor Spanish colony, all this made it possible for a man like Bolívar, who was a member of the *mantuano* or oligarchical class, to emerge as a representative of the whole people. Chávez was himself a synthesis [of two cultures] and, like Bolívar, he was able to mobilize all the continent's rebels to work for the unity of Latin America as a single nation. But in today's world, that project had to go far beyond the national question. Indeed, Chávez made a rich contribution to the history of those revolutions that are taking place during the twilight of capitalist society.

How would you characterize the Bolivarian Process? It's a difficult task, but I would like to hear your view.

We need to make a synthesis of the Bolivarian Revolution, which is itself a synthesis. To do so, we can consider other revolutions that also combined processes of national liberation with popular revolution. The Russian Revolution brought together a bourgeois revolution and a revolution of the proletariat and the peasant classes. Venezuela is a country where that synthesis happens as well. It happens here because the state and its institutions do not have much weight in society. That provides wiggle room for a revolutionary project that brings together both elements. Remember, for instance, that the dominating class in Venezuela, the bourgeoisie, was in a permanent process of change throughout history. It comes from the peasant class and is a result of its "revolutions" and wars.

By the end of the twentieth century, the revolutionary force in Venezuela has become the proletariat, the urban masses, and this class cannot be simply sent back to their fields after a war [as before]. Today, the urban bloc is large and omnipresent in our society.

In a marvelous way, Venezuela's working class, as is the case with the world proletariat, synthesizes in its experience all the problems of modern capitalism and neoliberalism. Here, we are living an epoch of revolutionary synthesis. For that reason, Venezuela is the object of so many attacks. That's because [the Bolivarian Process] strives for the unity of the Latin American nation, but it is also an embryo, an experimental project, aiming to completely transform society. The truth is that anything is possible here, if we don't lose sight of the goal, which is the abolition of capitalism and humanity's liberation.

We try to promote active solidarity and coherent internationalism. You have had a long trajectory as an internationalist: in 1964 you traveled to Detroit to meet with Raya Dunayevskaya and you later moved to Paris, where you were active in the May 1968 insurrection. A few years later, in 1974, you participated in the Revolution of the Carnations in Portugal. What can you tell us about the importance of internationalism today?

Revolutions are internationalist by definition. From the Paris Commune onward, there has never been a true revolution enclosed in a single nation. But there is another element that makes this revolution all the more international. Venezuela, as is the case with all Latin American countries, is a country made up of immigrants. Here, diverse waves of migration from European countries mixed with the indigenous peoples, and they, in turn, mixed with black Africans brought here through the slave trade. So, as you can see, internationalism in this revolution is not an option; instead, it is the base of our social structure and thus of our social revolution.

Those who carry out the Bolivarian Revolution come from multiple origins: they are mestizos, the cosmic race that Martí talked about. In Venezuela's revolution, we don't just commit to our salvation and to the emancipation of our people. We aim to re-found the Latin American nation, the future "Patria Grande."[2] Also, like any revolution, this one attempts to solve the great problems of the planet and humanity. Through Chávez, we cast our lot with the environmental struggle and commit ourselves to the social struggles in Europe, the United States, and beyond. The Bolivarian Revolution has been, from its very beginning, internationalist by vocation.

It would seem fair, then, that the revolutionaries of the world would support this epic struggle, this revolution, as part of the general process of liberation that the world is undergoing.

To wrap up, I would like to ask you to say something about Venezuela on the international stage. What are your thoughts about this situation of global chaos and crisis?

In today's world, we are living a terrible epoch of domination by capital and the bourgeoisie. The United States is facing one of the most profound crises in its history, and we are just witnessing the beginning of it. I think that Venezuela's struggle (as part of the general problematic of Latin America and in its relation to the United States) is key to all of that. We are struggling against a unipolar world not because we want a multipolar world in which a multiplicity of capitalist powers, such as Russia, China, India, and Brazil, emerge as players No, we must strive for a multipolar world in which the working class calls the shots. That, of course, must include U.S. and European working classes.

We are living in times of profound crisis in which the [bourgeois] fraction must step to the side for the working masses, since they are the ones who can open a path to the future. The Bolivarian Revolution, because it stands for a new structure of power in Latin America and breaks with the "backyard" logic that the U.S. imposes, is key in this. The problem is not so much the United States; the problem is the capitalist organization of the world.

We are living a transformation, and Venezuela is part of it. Perhaps we won't witness the end of it, but I'm certain that we are approaching the dawn of an epoch larger than the one marked by the French Revolution. We are in the twilight of the capitalist system. Capitalist barbarism is out in the open for all to see. It can be observed in full daylight, and we will continue to struggle to bring it to an end.

I think that Venezuela's contribution to the revolution is very important. But the commitment of all the world's peoples to defending the Bolivarian Process as a manifestation of the new epoch to come—that is much more important!

— December 14, 2018

Defending Chávez's Project Today: A Conversation with Elias Jaua

Venezuelan politician and former university professor Elias Jaua was a close collaborator of Hugo Chávez. As a student, he participated in the clandestine section of the (then) revolutionary party Bandera Roja. Chávez appointed him minister of agriculture and vice president, while under Nicolás Maduro he has been minister of foreign affairs, communes, and education. Jaua is currently a key figure in a Chavista political movement called Encuentro de Lucha Popular. He writes regularly, with a firm anti-imperialist position while defending popular power as the centerpiece of the Chavista project. Here, he talks about the initial goals of the movement that are under threat today.

You participated in the formation of the movement that, in 1997, would come to be called the Fifth Republic Movement [MVR]. That experience gives you a privileged perspective on the genesis and formation of Chavismo as a political movement in the 1990s.

I began to work directly with Comandante Hugo Chávez in May 1996. By that time, Chávez was already exploring the idea of participating in elections. The proposal on the table was to give an electoral course to this movement that emerged from the military barracks [in the 1980s] but that, beginning in 1994, joined up with all the popular and left currents in the streets of Venezuela. Finally, in 1997, the decision was taken to participate in the 1998 elections with Chávez's candidacy.

On April 19, 1997, during a congress of MBR-200 [a civilian and military movement founded by Chávez in 1982], the movement approved the forming of an electoral instrument that would eventually be called the Fifth Republic Movement [MVR]. The driving idea was that the Bolivarian project was aiming to re-found the republic. Up to that point, there had been four republics in the history of Venezuela. The MVR proposed to make a hard rupture with that history by creating the Fifth Republic.

Around that time, Chávez put us—the people who had been close to him—to work; we were developing what we called the Patriotic Circles [*Círculos patrióticos*], which were organizational structures of a minimum of five people in each barrio, in each community, in each town. These [were the first steps toward] the electoral structure that would allow us to go on to the 1998 campaign and the December 6, 1998, elections.

Around that time, the work that had begun in 1996 began to pick up speed with Chávez's tour around the country. Really, he went everywhere! I belonged to a team that went on preparing the events in which Chávez was to meet with the people, which generally were in public squares, since other institutional spaces were not given to us. We prepared meetings with local groups and generated, with the local leaders, the conditions for public gatherings. As we did this, we also worked with the folks who, at the local level, were building the Patriotic Circles.

That was in 1997. Then, in 1998, I was given the task of building the political structure and direction of the movement in the state of Miranda [the country's second most populous state that includes east Caracas]. By then there were some twenty-five thousand Patriotic Circles, and it was necessary to begin organizing the work we had done. That is when we formed the "Tactical Regional Commands" within the MVR initiative, and I was given the task, with a group of comrades, of working in Miranda and organizing the forces there. However, I continued to accompany Comandante Chávez throughout the campaign.

How would you characterize the class composition of the movement in those early days?

It was multiclassist, and it had an ideological diversity that went from the radical Left to sectors of the Right. I refer to members of the old bourgeoisie that were against the two major parties, AD and COPEI, but who were nevertheless extremely conservative.[3] Even through 1996, there were some extreme right groups or individuals who participated, but they pulled out rather rapidly. Obviously, the movement was also composed of popular forces, the popular movement, left organizations, and patriotic sectors of the military. So, to sum up, the movement as a whole had a muliclassist origin.

How did the movement deal with such great diversity?

The movement's multiclassist character and ideological diversity made it quite sturdy in a way that was needed at the time. Chávez insisted on the recognition of plurality. He was always a "factor" that generated equilibrium in the movement, focusing on the consensus: that we had to take power and re-found the republic.

Obviously, the debates were very intense. There was, however, a desire on the part of all of us who participated in the movement (and in the whole of society) to bring closure to the bipartisan Puntofijista model of government. What unified us was the goal of putting Hugo Chávez in the presidency on December 6, 1998.

However, the multiclassist character of the movement in its early days is what led to the many fractures during the first years of Chávez's presidency. What unified us early on was the goal of ousting AD and COPEI, but later, as Chávez pushed the revolution in a more popular direction, that was when right-wing sectors began to separate from the movement.

For Chávez, re-founding the state and the creation of the new republic had much to do with a radically new concept of democracy that is already present in *The Blue Book* [short book written in 1992 by Chávez, in which he presents his views on history and democracy]. I think we could say that that conception of democracy, as expressed in that early document, already points to the socialist project that would later develop in the Chavista movement. How do you see the relationship between democracy and socialism in Chávez?

Let's address the question non-chronologically. Chávez, around 2010 and 2011, began to affirm in many public addresses that "democracy is socialism, and socialism is democracy," and he said that "capitalism is anti-democratic by nature." In other words, he broke with the false dichotomy that separates democracy and socialism.

Later, Chávez went on to say that we shouldn't be talking about "democratic socialism," because socialism is, in essence, democratic. Instead, he claimed that we should talk (and think) about socialist democracy. So there, in a few words, President Chávez answers your question.

No doubt, the issue of democracy, of *demos kratia* or people's power, is a vein that runs throughout his thinking. It's there in *The Blue Book*, and it's there in the Alternative Bolivarian Agenda [*Agenda Alternativa Bolivariana* of 1996]. Chávez made philosophy and culture out of this reflection on democracy and popular power. The right of the people to speak, participate, propose, express themselves, and, of course, decide—all that was key to his thinking and his practice.

Chávez was committed to popular sovereignty, and he also understood that the leader was obliged to do what people said. Because of that, from the Right and even from certain intellectual sectors of the Left, there emerged a discourse that aimed to demonize Chávez. They said, "Chávez didn't seal agreements, he didn't make any compromises with other sectors of society, and he didn't address minority rights." But for Chávez democracy was the mandate of the majority and the recognition of the minority. There was recognition, but there were no pacts to be made when the majority spoke loud and clear.

Additionally, Chávez was always very honest with the people regarding his electoral proposals. Thus, in the 1998 campaign, he clearly called for a constituent process. After the victory, however, powerful economic and political sectors went to him and said that there had to be an agreement before going through the constitutive process. To that he said, "No, I have a mandate."

Thus, in every electoral process, he made an explicit public proposal. Later, when the people voted for him, the proposal became a mandate. Another such instance was in 2006, when he declared socialism to be his electoral project. From then on, he appealed to the mandate that the people had given him to justify going forward.

These are some windows into how Chávez brought the question of popular sovereignty into the spaces of representation, into the framework of classical liberal democracy. However, as you know, direct democracy was also important to his project.

Chávez promoted and fostered direct democracy and opened the doors for the construction of popular power so that the people would have real power, effective power. . . . That is where the communal councils came in, as well as the *campesino* councils, student councils, worker councils, and communes. It all began with the Patriotic Circles, which were already a sort of expression of direct democracy.

In the crisis-ridden decade of the 1990s, the movement that grew around Chávez pursued the ethical reorganization of politics and society. Obviously, we are facing a crisis of the Bolivarian Process, and you have mentioned that to overcome the current situation a new "historical trigger" [*"detonante histórico"*] is needed: something akin to what happened on February 4, 1992 [Chávez's military insurrection] or Chávez's election in 1998.

The movement that Chávez led in the 1990s—he said so himself on many occasions—was based on the aspirations of Venezuelan society as a whole. [People wanted] an independent and sovereign country as opposed to being subordinated to the United States' geopolitical interests and the auctioning of our wealth to that country. [People also wanted] a country with less inequality, with less poverty, and a more honest country. That is how Chávez summed up what were the goals and desires of the society. One could even say that he incarnated that collective desire.

Within the society, there was a sense that something had to happen so that a new epoch could open up for Venezuela. And that indeed happened. The year 1998 [when Chávez was elected to the presidency] marks a pacific and democratic rupture; it was a historical trigger and a break with the old, corrupt political model. But it also brought a series of emergencies and aggressions led by conservative sectors of the society. The years 2002 [with the coup d'état and oil sabotage], 2004 [when the opposition tried to revoke Chávez as president], and 2007 [which brought violent right-wing student mobilizations] were periods of intense destabilization.

Without a doubt, 1999 marks the beginning of the period of greatest independence and sovereignty that Venezuela has had in its history. It is also the period of greatest democratization—not only in political terms, but also in economic, cultural, and social terms. From the presidency and from the government, a new ethical logic emerged in the public eye. It was something that Venezuela hadn't seen before. For the first time in a long time, Venezuela had a president who was an example for the society, someone to emulate. His life corresponded with his principles. I say this because ethics doesn't only refer to the administrative arena. We are also talking about political ethics and a political identity: a coherence in discourse and practice.

Unfortunately, that logic didn't become a culture penetrating the entire state apparatus and the society as a whole.

Chávez wasn't just honest in the way he administered things. He was first and foremost a *politically* honest person. As I said earlier in the interview, he never deceived people about where he was going. He always said, "Whoever votes for me is voting for this project."

In our time, obviously all those hopes and desires that were realized [under Chávez] are, in some way, very precarious. National independence is now under threat, as we face the possibility of a military intervention, while the sanctions limit our capacity to manage our own resources and finances. On top of this, our capacity to represent ourselves abroad is also being curtailed. All that undermines our national sovereignty.

This new phase of the confrontation, which goes hand in hand with other political shifts, began with a sector of the opposition not recognizing Maduro's 2013 victory in the presidential elections. That began to have an impact on our economy, and inequality began to grow. We are in a country where poverty is a serious problem again, where hunger has reemerged, where difficulties to access healthcare and education are real, quotidian problems. No doubt there are several factors here, such as the fall of oil prices and the emergence of new political mechanisms, but the main factor is the prolonged political confrontation.

Today we are, once again, an unequal society after having reverted to the bad karma of being the country with the largest income in Latin America, but also the country with the most inequality. With Chávez, Venezuela became the country with the most equitable income distribution. Today, I don't know where we stand in the charts, but it's enough to look at the streets to see that we are in a terribly unequal society. There are sectors that accumulate, generally through illegal means, a great deal of wealth, while the people are watching their rights vanish and their living conditions rapidly deteriorate.

Furthermore, the institutional instability provoked by this long confrontation has made it so that corruption has metastasized throughout the whole social body.

So now we are facing the same dilemmas that Venezuelan society faced in the 1990s, with one difference: today we have a project and we demonstrated that it is possible to contain society's scourges, and most of all, we have a *pueblo* that is organized, has a high degree of consciousness, and is committed to reprising the path that Chávez initiated. We are facing a very difficult situation, but I believe that it's possible to begin an ethical re-founding of the country. That has to take place in the economical, political, and social spheres.

The Chavista movement is firmly unified when facing imperialism. However, internally, as is to be expected, there are different political tendencies and diverse proposals regarding the solution to the current crisis. Some people claim that the solution is foreign investment and privatizing public enterprises. Others argue that we should look to a communal solution and point to such initiatives as El Maizal Commune or the Pueblo a Pueblo plan. What do you think?

The multiplicity of interpretations to which you refer has its roots in the multiclassist character of the Chavista movement. It is a sum of currents from diverse ideological and political origins, each with different life practices. That means that there will always be tensions.

Today we are facing an enormous crisis. The pragmatic way out will naturally loom large, and it will be presented as "necessary," even if that means making the principles that are at the core of the Chavista movement more flexible.

Here, we should say that the Bolivarian model has never ever proposed eliminating private property and private investment. That wasn't the case in the Alternative Bolivarian Agenda or in the *Plan de la Patria* [2012]. The Bolivarian Revolution is a mixed model in which the state has a key role [at the commanding heights] of the economy, with a private sector that is to be subordinated to the interests of the people, and with the emergence of a sector that was initially called "social economy," but which later became known as "communal economy." That is the first thing that should be made clear.

Additionally, when we talk about the weight of these sectors in the economy, it should be observed that Chávez's main objective was to foster the emergence of an economy in the hands of the people and not in the hands of capital. He was keen to not repeat the error of European socialisms, which was statism, but on the other hand he turned away from any glorification of private property. Briefly put, Chávez's conception broke with the hegemony of private capital.

Today, there are longstanding currents—those that express that the objective of the Bolivarian Revolution was [merely] to displace the old regime (which it did), and claim that guaranteeing public education and access to healthcare was, in itself, the goal—which are becoming more visible. Their discourse turns around the idea: "socialism in the social."

Chávez always combatted the "socialism in the social" premise. When he declared the socialist character of the revolution, he made it crystal clear. He said: "I'm not talking about western European socialism; it's not just about resolving some social problems through the state's participation." That is why striving for a society where the hegemony of the economy is in the private sector is contrary to the spirit of this revolution.

The reasons adduced by the privatizing tendency are absolutely flawed. They talk about the inefficiency of state property and social property. However, the bulk of the process of nationalization happened between the years 2007 and 2008, and those are the years with the biggest GDP growth, not only in the oil sector, but also in industrial and agrarian sectors. CEPAL [The United Nations Economic Commission for Latin America and the Caribbean] numbers prove it.

The interesting thing is that the state enterprises doubled or even tripled their production in those years. This is in part because the state injected resources, which private capital wasn't willing to do. However, it was also because the whole process of nationalization inspired a collective spirit of commitment. All this meant that food production grew exponentially, while poverty was practically eradicated.

What's more, without nationalizing the steel and cement industries, which had been in the hands of transnationals, the Great Venezuelan Housing Mission [governmental housing initiative] wouldn't have been possible. Without a nationalized CANTV [telephone company], the democratizing of communications wouldn't have happened, because people wouldn't have been able to pay for the services. This is important because we shouldn't see things exclusively from the standpoint of economic profitability. The social results of the nationalizing process also need to be taken into account.

Chavismo's collective—and I have seen it in the assemblies and meetings that I attend regularly—is opposed to letting the private sector rule. We don't deny that it can participate in the economy, but we don't place our bets on the private. Those of us who defend the revolutionary project and remain committed to it—we cast our lot with the people. Can anybody in their right mind think that the private sector can save us right now, the very sector that failed to develop our economy for decades and decades?

— MAY 17, 2019

Everyday Life in Besieged Venezuela: A Conversation with Jessica Dos Santos

Jessica Dos Santos, who grew up with the Bolivarian Revolution, is a university professor and journalist. However, she is best known as a chronicler of everyday life in Venezuela. Whether focused on the weekly struggle to get running water, celebrating Christmas in the crisis, or the wild side of using improvised public transport in Caracas, her stories are always honest, heartfelt, and revealing. They show another side of Chavismo, far from the high-toned official discourse, but just as important because it is there—in the details of everyday life—that much of the future of the revolutionary process will be decided.

Much has been written in a very general sense about Venezuela's current situation. For example, we hear a great deal about the economic war, sanctions, imperialist meddling, and even communal organization and building popular power. But very little is said about daily life: for example, about the difficulties we face every day in a city like Caracas. Would you say that being a chronicler of everyday life is a political act? What happens to politics when it doesn't connect with concrete reality and when daily life is not taken into account?

I am one of those people who believe that absolutely everything in life is a political act, from the way we feed ourselves to our way of speaking. And that is perhaps the key to understanding why politics goes beyond and must go beyond party politics. Therefore, I agree with you.

I think that being a chronicler of everyday life is a political act that seeks to record the day-to-day and to lay out, in some way or other, the main episodes of the story we are living. It is an attempt to leave traces that will later allow us to reconstruct a scene. It helps us know what was happening moment by moment leading up to this or that event.

For that reason, when politics does not connect with concrete reality or does not take daily life into account, it ends up becoming an endless number of speeches that do not connect with anything. It can be empty and so contradictory as to be shameless. This inevitably generates discontent in the population or leads to a failure to see themselves reflected [in the political discourse].

For example, many parts of President Nicolás Maduro's speech during his annual address have nothing to do with what the Venezuelan people experience on a daily basis. In the same way, Juan Guaidó doesn't win people over saying that among his first political projects is the return of the RCTV channel. These are things that don't make any sense in a country with problems as serious as ours.

Alejo Carpentier said that the work of Latin American writers was different from that of writers elsewhere. Writers from our continent have to describe things (such as the bizarre and huge ceiba tree or the noisy macaw) with a lot of attention to detail, because they have not previously figured in narratives. Is your work as a chronicler something like that? Can you give us an example of a "ceiba," a unique and previously undescribed reality, in Venezuelan daily life?

Yes, my work is more or less like that. But I also have the enormous advantage of having been born in the Caribbean. Gabriel García Márquez says in *The Fragrance of Guava* that the Caribbean teaches us to see reality in a different way and accept "supernatural elements" as something that is part of our daily life. The Caribbean is a world apart. The human synthesis and the contrasts here are not present anywhere else in the world.

A "ceiba" of Venezuelan daily life? One example would be precisely our way of dealing with the complex situations that we face. For example, once a Chilean friend, who was obviously annoyed, told me that she did not understand why we take everything as a joke here. Perhaps what she and others do not understand is that this is our way of processing and overcoming what happens. But that way of dealing with things doesn't make us crazy or unaware.

For example, on the day commemorating January 23, I happened to see both marches. Then I went home and spent the whole afternoon following the events.[4] It was really tense, but in the middle of all of it, there was a lot being said on the networks and messages from friends that made me laugh without stopping. If we weren't this way, perhaps we would have lost our minds. Furthermore, our idiosyncratic way of being in the world in some way or other brings us all together.

Another "ceiba" or "macaw" would be to tell the story of how Venezuelans try to lead "normal" lives in the middle of all the abnormality that we experience. It is not normal to see the same product change prices three times a day, or the amazing speed of information in our country. Nevertheless, we're trying to change all that and come out ahead.

Street protests are on the rise again. Previously they were in rural areas, and the demands included access to food and services. But just recently this kind of protest has hit Caracas. Unlike the *guarimbas* of 2014 and 2017, these protests have an organic relation to the poor and their needs: a material situation that is very extreme. What should our attitude toward these protests be? Should we question them? Should we work to bring the protestors back to the Chavista fold?

We should differentiate among kinds of protests, separating one kind from another. In Venezuela, there have been protests for many months, and they have been triggered by the breakdown of public services and utilities: electricity, water, cooking gas, public transport. Protests [against this kind of situation] are absolutely valid and, from my point of view, should not be called into question. Rather, they must be heard, and the demands should be urgently addressed and taken seriously. Furthermore, dealing with these problems is the only way to recover the people's trust. These, then, are popular protests.

By contrast, protests that end up in acts of vandalism, protests where houses are burned, cars are turned over, neighbors are attacked, etc., those do not contribute to anything, nor do they reflect the intentions of the majority. In fact, they end up tarnishing the just claims of the people. People want services and utilities that work, a stable economy, and they want children who have left the country to return. You don't get there by destroying what we have left.

As a Chavista, you support the government, but you do so critically. This support is unbending faced with the imperialist threat, but it is coupled with a willingness to criticize a government that (from my perspective) shows signs of separating from the people. Can you help us to understand how it is to fight on two battlefronts, one against imperialism and against the opposition, and another more fluid battlefront that demands that the government provide solutions to the people's needs?

When I was a teenager I read all the Che Guevara journals, and I read them several times. In one, he wrote that those who occupy a middle position during a battle get shot at from both sides. Thus, one should always clearly choose a side.

For a long time, I tried to internalize that as an irrefutable truth. And I continue to do so. But later I came to understand that the side we choose, our side, should be that of the people. We must choose to be with the majorities, with those who suffer as we do. If the extreme positions are out of touch with the people and one ends up in the middle, then you have to accept your [middle] position and make noise about it so that things will change.

All of that refers to the internal struggle. However, when it comes to fighting against foreign intervention, then there isn't much to think about: Our home country is and must be first. And this is because of our love for it, but also because we have historical awareness. There isn't one single nation that has come out better after a U.S. or NATO intervention. In addition to that, intervention presupposes that we don't have the capacity to solve our own problems, and I firmly believe that we can.

— January 31, 2019

Notes to Section 3

1. The "Transition" refers to the process initiated after Franco's death that opens the way to the Spanish state's new constitution (1978) with a parliamentary democracy and constitutional monarchy. The Transition was, in the end, a superficial reorganization of the political sphere, leaving the interests of the dominating class (both political and economic) intact.
2. "Patria Grande" is, within the Bolivarian tradition, a term used to refer to the entire Latin American nation, the unity of all the former Spanish colonies.
3. AD and COPEI were the two parties that shared power under the Punto Fijo Pact (hence "puntofijismo"). This was the period between the fall of the Marcos Pérez Jiménez dictatorship in 1959 and the election of Chávez in 1998, in which an extremely limited representative democracy was established in the country. The period is remembered for rampant corruption, widespread poverty, and police repression.
4. January 23 is a national holiday in Venezuela. It celebrates the end of the dictatorship of Marcos Pérez Jiménez, deposed on that date in 1958 by a military and civilian uprising. In recent decades, Chavismo and the opposition have each organized separate commemorative marches on the holiday.

4

CAMPESINO AND WORKING-CLASS STRUGGLES

Venezuela's *Campesino* Struggle: A Conversation with Kevin Rangel

Born in Caracas, Kevin Rangel joined the Bolívar and Zamora Revolutionary Current (CRBZ), the largest Venezuelan campesino organization, in 2005. Today he is the organization's national coordinator, working from the city of Calabozo, Guarico State, in Venezuela's rural heartland. The CRBZ has been in the forefront of the intense struggles taking place in Venezuela's countryside where a rural population eager to till the land confronts an old and new landlord class aiming to expand its extensive holdings.

Two years into the Bolivarian Process, a new legal framework for the land was put in place. The 2001 laws opened the way for a more equitable reorganization of the rural areas, redistributing idle land to small and mid-size *campesinos*. The Venezuelan oligarchy reacted furiously, assassinating *campesinos* who were beginning to produce on once-idle land. Could you give us some background on how the Bolivarian Process impacted the rural areas?

The Land and Agricultural Development Law [2001] laid out the basis of the agricultural revolution as proposed by Chávez at a time when the strategic path of the Bolivarian Revolution was being defined. A central element of that project is sovereignty. To have sovereignty, of course, one has to make the country produce, i.e., stop being a "port" economy.

The first step in making the country productive—producing the food we need and raw materials for the country's industry—involves the land. Land tenure has important historical dimensions in Venezuela. Since the country's independence, the *latifundio* [large estate] was established as the model that would dominate rural

Venezuela during its whole history. That was the cause of the Federal War [1859–63] led by Ezequiel Zamora. The interests of the oligarchy, which governed Venezuela for many years, were there: in the land. They accumulated a lot of riches, a lot of land . . .

The *campesinos* have historically been the most combative sector of our population. They were the ones who fought alongside Bolívar. In fact, Bolívar was only able to triumph in the Independence War after he united with the Venezuelan peasants, the poor, and the black people. The same with Zamora: the main group that accompanied him and carried out the Federal War was the peasants. That is because it was for that group that injustice and inequality was expressed in the most radical way . . .

The oligarchy's response [to the 2001 legislation] was to initiate, and continue during all of these 18 years, a whole process of conspiring and bringing in paramilitaries as part of a plan to strike at the Bolivarian Revolution. Where they did it most was in the rural areas, because it was the *campesinos* who best understood Chávez's call for a total war against the *latifundio*.

Of course, it wasn't as if the *campesinos* weren't doing anything before Chávez arrived. There were conflicts over the land and they had developed projects. As an organization, we too date from before Chávez's arrival to power, but it was the context of the Bolivarian Process that brought the *campesinos* into a new scenario of struggle.

A struggle emerged in the rural areas, and the oligarchy responded by contracting paramilitaries. The "demobilization" of Colombian paramilitaries coincided with the incorporation of paramilitary cells in Venezuela. They began to operate in Sur del Lago [Zulia and Merida States]. Thus there began a war, a war against *campesinos*, which today has left a body count of more than 300 *campesinos* murdered. Those [killed] were people who were at the front of the land recovery struggle. They wanted to make the *campesinos* afraid, and they hoped our movement would stop struggling. Thus, on our end, justice for the fallen is one of our most important rallying cries. There must be an end to impunity!

The Bolivarian Revolution once had its epicenter in the urban *barrios*, but now the countryside seems to be more combative. It is there that the contradictions of the process seem to be most intense. First, there are the longstanding contradictions that pit the small to medium producers and the rural communes against the interests of old landowners and agribusiness. On top of that, now tensions have intensified between the rural communes and the small to medium peasants, on the one side, and the state, on the other. Also, it's no secret that the judicial system favors old and new landlords and that Agropatria, the state company that distributes agricultural inputs, is permeated by an anti-popular logic. What do you think is happening?

Chávez proposed not only a new Land and Agricultural Development Law but also a new institutional framework for rural development and food sovereignty. That was to be a central goal of those struggles. After the lapse of almost 18 years, the struggles have been changing, mutating. Elements of the dispute have been broadening. In 2001, we struggled against the "Adeco institutional [logic]."[1] We struggled to remove the Adecos and Copeyanos from the Land and Agriculture Ministry, and to get the Venezuelan Agrarian Federation out of the IAN [pre-revolutionary land institute] and later out of the INTI [Venezuelan Land Institute, a Chávez-era institute] and the FONDAS [National Agricultural Fund].[2]

One of the main contradictions of the Bolivarian Process is with the bureaucracy, bureaucratism, and the corruption that has been penetrating all the state's institutions, even putting at risk the state's functioning is some cases. For us, this is part of what explains the economic crisis that Venezuela is now experiencing. It is not only the enemy's actions and not only imperialism's actions, but also a question of corruption and inefficiency in the government.

With regard to the *campesino* and agrarian institutions created by the revolution, agrarian mafias have embedded themselves, which is taking away force as well as revolutionary and transformative potential from those institutions. The logic of the bourgeois state took hold of those institutions.... We have an outstanding task of transforming and overcoming capitalist state.

That is precisely something that is entering in the struggle today: the struggle against hired killings, against impunity, and also against the agrarian mafias. That's because those mafias have been infiltrating institutions, not only in the Ministry of Agriculture and Land but also the Supreme Court and the Attorney General's Office. There are members of the security apparatuses, the Attorney General's Office, the courts, and judiciary that protect the landlord class today. We didn't succeed in getting the Adecos and their culture out of our state's institutions. Today, that is one of the main problems we face.

It is necessary to overhaul and restructure the institutions. We need to reorganize from the bottom up institutions such as INTI, FONDAS, and Agropatria. Agropatria was once the transnational Agroisleña. Elements of that transnational stayed there, sabotaging the institution from the inside. This is the result of a policy that derives from a lack of leadership from those who headed up those institutions—all of them, not just the current ones. There are people who, for many years, were at the top of the agrarian institutions and are responsible for not having transformed them. They share responsibility for the situation today.

Sometimes it seems as if we can't find a popular tendency—one that favors the working people—inside the institutions!

There, public functionaries are totally déclassé. Their raison d'être, that is, the concept of a public servant, has disappeared. There are people in the agrarian institutions that are in the service of cattlemen's associations and landlords rather than of the *campesinos*.

But there is something we need to ask: Who is the main interested party? Who has an interest that in this country there should be no production? The import sector. We need to identify that sector and make it visible. They have been interfering and have lobbies inside the revolution, so that nothing works. Then if things don't work there will be chaos, there will be no production, and they will go on importing. So that's why we say there is a need to look at the way funds are assigned, so that our first priority becomes agricultural production.

More than three hundred *campesinos* have been killed since 2001 and five since May of this year. The most recent victim is a 16-year-old boy in Sur del Lago, which is a hotspot in the dispute between the agrarian cooperatives and the new landowning bourgeoisie. The state has been slow to act in many of these cases, while in others the institutions themselves have become accomplices. How should *campesinos* organize in these circumstances?

Class struggle is intensifying in the rural areas. We are facing a new wave of violence and threats against landless *campesinos* who have recuperated idle land. The truth is that the situation is even more complex than it was before. As opposed to the earlier wave of violence [in 2001 to 2003], we are not only facing paramilitarism at the service of the old landowners, but also an emerging sector that uses state forces and the state's institutions to protect and further their private interests.

For instance, in Barinas State, there have been *campesino* evictions from the land where they produce, as well as other human rights violations. These were carried out not by the hired guns of the old landowning class, but by the state apparatus. We can even identify a [Barinas] state policy at the service of the new sectors that are acquiring land. Additionally, there has emerged a practice of criminalizing the *campesino* bloc, as a way of justifying what is happening. Thus, some sectors are implicitly granted permission to jail *campesinos* without due process, and to carry out other human rights violations.

There is another element: the historical enemy of the revolution is seeking to fuel contradictions between those who are in the government and the popular base. Those in the direction of the revolution must understand this. There is an active attempt on the part of the old oligarchy to generate an internal conflict.

The revolution's most active and loyal sector is the *campesinos*. *Campesinos* vote for this project even when they are the victims of aggression from public institutions. *Campesinos* are committed to the revolution and loyal. The livestock oligarchy—especially FEDENAGAS, which is associated with FEDECAMARAS—have been working with paramilitary leaders.[3] We know that representatives of the landlords have been in meetings in the Norte de Santander department of Colombia with sectors of *uribismo*.[4]

This bloc is responsible for fueling the violence in Sur del Lago, a situation that is near the boiling point, or rather, it has already reached it! In that territory there are constant threats, mobilizations, and public meetings that the cattle-owning oligarchy has been organizing. Intimidation has become quotidian. There have been threats against members of our organization to the effect that we must abandon our struggle for the land in that territory.

This is serious stuff, since we are talking about more than 10,000 families who are participating in the struggle in Barinas, and almost 11,000 families who are struggling for their right to the land in Sur del Lago. Thus, in Sur del Lago, the hottest spot, we are preparing our response. We are not going to stay put and let our people die. There cannot be more *campesino* massacres. The people and the Bolivarian Revolution have given us the tools to defend ourselves.

The recent assassination of Kender García, a 16-year-old son of *campesino* leaders, is yet another example of the cattle oligarchy's modus operandi. To paraphrase Augusto César Sandino: The masses are patient and, for a while, will wait for justice to be made, but if that doesn't happen, then the people will take justice into their own hands. We don't want this to happen because the battle that could take shape would be worse than the one in 2001, 2002, and 2003.

Campesinos are more conscious and more organized today than they were before and they have now many more tools—tools that the revolution gave them. In this regard, we have been making a plan so that the people are aware of what we may have to do. The government must act in a much more forceful manner against the landowning class, both old and new. We believe that the revolution, in this moment of struggle, must take radical actions in regard to the property of those who threaten *campesinos* and criminalize them, saying that *campesinos* are robbing the land.

It is urgent that the Bolivarian Revolution close ranks and act in a unified manner to confront the growing attacks from the old and new landowning class. Regarding the latter—the new landowning class who wear red shirts—those have to be expelled from the Chavista bloc. We cannot let them continue in the party and at the top of state institutions!

In today's crisis, the law that Chávez put forward in 2001, which calls for an agrarian revolution, seems more relevant than ever! The CRBZ has been promoting self-organization among *campesinos* for years and it has many projects, from the Simón Bolívar Communal City in Apure, a project in a process of consolidation, to the National Productive Alliance, a project that is still being born. Let's conclude the interview by talking about these experiences.

Our organization has a campaign to defend the achievements and advances of the revolution and to carry out the revolution's pending tasks for *campesinos*. We don't limit ourselves to work among landless *campesinos*. We believe that the revolution must incorporate *campesinos* with small plots of land, the *conuqueros* and the collectives that have rescued land—as it has—but it should also incorporate medium producers who aren't enemies of the people, people who are not conspiring and whose only interest is to produce, because the key interest of the nation now is to produce, thus satisfying the population's needs.[5]

Alliances have to be made with these sectors, which joined the right because the revolution did not know how to connect with them and didn't know how to keep them with us. With this in mind, and with the objective of generating conditions for production for small- and mid-size farmers, we are building the National Productive Alliance, which is a space of confluence and work. Those mid-size farmers that are committed to producing and are not conspiring should be incorporated.

The revolution has negotiated with large capitalists who don't produce but just import: groups in line with a longstanding logic of corruption and who are not going to produce anything. The government sits at the table with them and not the real producers: the small and medium farmers. Unfortunately the latter are not invited to sit at the table. Why? I think it's obvious!

So we have been developing the National Productive Alliance to boost agrarian production. We are committed to building an ample alliance of small to medium producers. Our main objective now is to generate conditions for production, to organize from below and form territorial networks. All of Venezuela's productive potential must be brought together and unified.

That is something that the leadership of the process should do, but isn't doing. The Agriculture Ministry lost its focus. Yet *campesinos* are working from below to unify and generate conditions for agricultural production, voicing the sector's demands. Their demands are many, ranging from the landless *campesinos*' historical claim to the land to access to seeds, agricultural implements, and fuel and machinery parts for small- to medium-sized farmers.

The truth is that the revolution has to build a national majority. It cannot be that the revolution has political power and it doesn't represent a national majority. The project of the Bolivarian Revolution is a project of societal consensus, and Chávez succeeded at building that consensus. Most especially, the foundation of the Bolivarian Revolution is participative and protagonistic democracy. That should be our political focus now and it's where the CRBZ is working. That is also why we are now in a process of giving new impetus to the "Simón Bolívar" Communal City project, which fell by the wayside when the communal project became the domain of the Ministry of Communes. We believe that the comuneros are the revolutionary subject, and we place our hopes in the commune as the path to build socialism in Venezuela.

Now we see the commune as something that is not ethereal. It shouldn't be a mere slogan or mural. We believe in the commune-as-government, as people's territorial power. It is the revolutionary government that will transform the society from below, constituting what Chávez called the "new shoots" of socialism.

The "Simón Bolívar" Communal City is just that: a space where production, organization, and political revolution take front stage.

Regarding the latter, it must be clarified that the economic war shouldn't be an excuse to halt the political revolution. That is one of the issues that the leadership must come to terms with: the continuation of the political revolution. The economic war is an unavoidable feature of the present, but the emergence of new values, of new forms of organization, and of popular empowerment—all these things are more important than ever if the Bolivarian Revolution is not to lose its transformative force.

As for the CRBZ movement, we are working on the Communal City, on the National Productive Alliance, and we are also developing a current within the PSUV, a current that will work from within. It is absolutely necessary that a revolutionary current take shape within the historical party of the revolution, as a force that will help to rebuild the Bolivarian Revolution's strategic objectives and reorient us toward them.

— October 2, 2018

Reconnecting Agriculture to Our Cultural Base: A Conversation with Ana Felicien

Ana Felicien works at the Venezuelan Institute of Scientific Research and is a founding member of the Semillas del Pueblo (People's Seeds) movement. She researches in the areas of agroecology and food sovereignty. In this interview, Felicien discusses grassroots attempts to achieve food sovereignty during Venezuela's crisis years, and the importance of changing both consumption patterns and food-agriculture systems in the transition to socialism. She emphasizes the need to combat agribusiness's complex web of domination.

In the course of Venezuela's economic crisis, we have seen changes in people's consumption patterns. People are eating more plantain, cassava, and whole-grain corn, among other things, and fewer processed carbohydrates. Do you think this is just a temporary change (a return to the "traditional Venezuela," which the romantically-minded might delight in because of its picturesque qualities), or is it a real step toward greater food sovereignty? How can we work to assure that these changes in consumption and production patterns become lasting ones and thus steps toward sovereignty and socialism?

The changes in consumption patterns during these difficult times are due, firstly, to the crisis of the whole agroindustrial system, which connects production, processing, and highly concentrated, homogeneous, and commodified consumption.

In Venezuela's case, that system is also highly dependent on imports of raw materials and technology, which makes the agroindustrial system highly vulnerable and unable to meet the food needs of the population (as we have seen in recent years).

On the other hand, the new consumption pattern is possible thanks to the availability of food harvested in *campesino* production systems. With far fewer resources, these systems have proven capable of sustaining production, even in the face of all the problems of infrastructure (for both production and distribution) that peasant agriculture confronts.

These changes occurred as a spontaneous and almost immediate response in the majority of the population. Although they point to a possible revival of foodstuffs that form part of our identity, there is an even greater challenge: to overcome the colonization of our consumption that makes us in Venezuela some of the [world's] biggest consumers of wheat and a people with one of the most homogeneous diets in the tropics, despite being a megadiverse country in biological and cultural terms. This diet results from a historical process of differentiation that has separated off indigenous, afro, and *campesino* agricultural systems, while favoring imported food from the metropolis: Spain during the colony and the United States after oil came on the scene.

It is not for nothing that Venezuela signed a reciprocal trade agreement with the United States in 1939 that lasted until 1972, making possible and encouraging duty-free imports of processed foods. A wide variety of products (Kellogg's Corn Flakes and All-Bran, Kraft cheese, KLIM milk, Lipton Tea, Quaker Oats, canned and frozen meats, Coca-Cola, Campbell's soup, among other items) began to arrive, which tended to create an American-style pattern of consumption in the country. These products were distributed in oil field commissaries and in supermarkets created by Rockefeller in the main cities. It profoundly changed the way food was distributed and consumed in the country because, although the target was the middle class linked to the oil industry, the supermarket (soon) became normal throughout the country as the main space of food distribution.

To progress in transforming our consumption habits, it's necessary to understand these colonization processes and develop responses that, beyond being merely immediate or local efforts, could allow us to consolidate a more sustainable food model. However, despite efforts ranging from the agroecological movements to state institutions such as the Venezuelan School for Food and Nutrition, we have seen how the logic of dependence on food imports is reproduced even in the CLAP food distribution system, which is a project with an enormous potential for promoting consumption patterns that would reflect greater sovereignty. The key then is to promote these transformative initiatives and connect them to the principal food policy operating in this crisis situation, with a view to making this into a process of change that comes from below.

You were part of the group that started the movement Semillas del Pueblo (People's Seeds). Can you tell us about the movement's aims and what it has achieved? What obstacles and problems have you encountered? Also, what is the importance of the seed law that was passed in 2015?

Semillas del Pueblo grew out of a process of collective construction and popular debate concerning the new Venezuelan seed law. This process began in 2013, with those of us in the Venezuela Free from Transgenics campaign working with other organizations to promote a popular debate in favor of the new law and systematize it. The aim was to get the law to protect seed varieties pertaining to peasant, indigenous, and Afro-descendant groups in a differentiated system that includes—besides the certified seed produced by public research institutes and companies—the seeds, knowledge, and organizational forms of the farmers, who, as we said before, are putting food on our table. The result of this collective work was a law that, on the one hand, opposed patenting and transgenics seeds and, on the other, promoted ecological agriculture.

It was an unprecedented law for the [Latin American] region, since recent years have seen more and more concentration in the business of industrial seed production, supported by changes in national seed laws that favor this monopolistic tendency. Because the expansion of transgenic crops has been the greatest in South America, this new law has received a great deal of international recognition. By contrast, inside the country, seed importers have attacked it. Moreover, the defunct [opposition-controlled] National Assembly recently approved a new seed law, which of course favored industrial seed producers.

After the 2015 law's approval, we organized a network of agro-ecological farmers and movements that had participated in the popular debate process. This network is comprised of urban farming groups, organizations of small rural producers (from the western and eastern regions of the country), food distribution organizations that connect rural and urban areas, and researchers focused on agroecology and food sovereignty. Last year, we were somewhat weakened by a series of difficulties, and we are now reconfiguring our efforts to focus on connecting with the work being done in communes and in producers' networks with the idea of advancing seed production.

There are a number of grassroots organizational projects doing very important work in this area. They are democratizing people's access to seeds (which, just like food, have been heavily monopolized and frequently smuggled). Of these efforts, the Pueblo a Pueblo [People to People] project stands out. That project, involving community organizations in the rural and urban areas, brings together seed production, food production, and food distribution at fair prices. The project gives political content to the seed issue by connecting it to key efforts guaranteeing the right to food during the current crisis.

We continue to work hard on getting the law implemented, concentrating mostly on teaching, promoting, and activating seed production spaces. However, we have also made efforts in the areas of communication and raising awareness. No doubt there should be a greater effort in defending the new legislation and it must be done fundamentally by spreading awareness of the law. The current situation urges us to do so.

Imported seeds (especially of garden vegetables) have practically disappeared, entering into the illegal economy. Meanwhile, seeds for more traditional crops, which have always been under popular control, have become more important in *campesino* production. This is key for any project aiming to change food and agriculture. Such a project needs to prioritize the genetic resources that small farmers have maintained and will maintain, not by the seed industry. In that sense, the law is more than a law: it is a plan for action to gain seed sovereignty.

However, despite the many grassroots efforts to produce seeds, there has been almost no coordination with state institutions, even with those institutions created by our own law. Bringing the two together is a pending problem.

Constructing socialism is not only a matter of inheriting capitalism's productive forces. It is also necessary to transform them. That is because, under capitalism, productive forces are subordinated to a quantity-based system and one that promotes false or fabricated needs and planned obsolescence. Can you connect this requirement of altering productive forces in the transition to socialism with the Venezuelan context and its food system?

As we discussed initially, the current food crisis offers powerful and clear evidence that monopolistic agroindustry is unable to provide food for the majority. There is no choice but to change, and what we consume daily shows it! Today, workers are securing food through distribution circuits that are connected to *campesino* production, whether through intermediaries or through various forms of consumer organization. It's virtually impossible to buy the goods sold in supermarkets at speculative prices, meaning that this model has failed.

But to take steps toward a real transformation, it's necessary to make our food sovereignty projects more coherent. Here we have to face some challenges, such as:

1) Identifying the political subject of food sovereignty in Venezuela. This means recognizing the project of food sovereignty as a demand both of the working population (which was produced through processes of proletarization and migration toward the cities), and of the farming communities (made up of indigenous peoples, peasants, and *afrodescendentes*) who have continued to produce. Especially

important is the practice of cultivating small family plots (called *conucos* in Venezuela) as a form of resistance to the processes of appropriation, subordination, and displacement that the growth of agro-industrial production leads to.

2) Reconnecting agro-food systems to their biocultural base; overcoming dependence on imported technologies and inputs, including seeds; and struggling for the diet to become more diverse and suited to local conditions. Crops that do not require large amounts of inputs or depend on imported seeds are key in this effort as are the various agro-ecological methods used by *campesinos* to maintain them. Of course, this has consequences for urban consumers, who are called upon to reconnect our consumption habits with those processes that can lead to greater autonomy.

3) Influencing public policy so that it favors food sovereignty and not agribusiness, which tends to be involved in hoarding and smuggling. We must occupy the spaces where public policy is made and recover those spaces of decision-making that we once had. Agricultural policy, during the recent years of crisis, has been totally disconnected from *campesino* production. We have seen a large number of subsidies and agreements that favor the private sector and do not benefit the common people at all. The struggle over policy-making is very important for obtaining food justice.

In Venezuela, as in much of the world, women and children are the group most affected by poverty. What is the role of women in Venezuela's economic crisis today? I would say that, on the one hand, they are most affected by the crisis. On the other hand, it is women—young women, mothers, and grandmothers—who are often most active and creative in responding to the crisis, inventing solutions every day.

Both in the countryside and in the city, women have played the role of caregivers to the whole society. In the CLAP, in the networks of family producers, and in consumer organizations, women have assumed leadership roles. This has been one of the keys to Chavismo: women's participation is central to popular organization. It also shows us the way patriarchy shapes the economic war: the concentration of wealth, together with smuggling and hoarding of food and other products of first necessity, are expressions of patriarchal violence against the people who have benefited from Chavista social policies and are the most vulnerable ones in the current crisis. For that reason, only those solutions that break with patriarchal domination and with the use of food as a weapon of war and social control (not those that reproduce and strengthen such domination) constitute the real path to overcoming the crisis.

Colette Capriles has referred to the Foucauldian concept "biopower" in relation to Venezuela's government programs. For her, these programs are a form of social control, using food and medicine. However, that way of seeing things overlooks the real network of biopower in our society, which involves giant corporations such as Polar and Cargill, with their patents, publicity, and distribution networks. Can you comment on this?

Of the current social programs, it is the CLAP that brings together all the contradictions in our agro-food system and also the possibility of emancipation. The CLAP network distributes imported transgenic foods (with a predominance of refined goods). Also, in many cases, it creates a new level of organization that is separate from the community one. Finally, it involves subsidies to agro-industrial business for buying raw materials, and makes little or no effort to incorporate national production.

Given this complexity, it's important to see the CLAP program in context: it is a response to a crisis in which our national consumption pattern, as we pointed out earlier, is highly homogeneous, involving refined flours and fat, dependent on agro-industrially-processed foods that are distributed mainly in large supermarket chains. This is not particular to Venezuela but a global trend in which the world's diets are becoming less diverse and agribusiness is increasingly concentrated in a handful of companies that have monopolistic control of agriculture and food.

Despite this, many reports show how peasant family farming

produces more than half the food consumed in the world. As we pointed out earlier, in our country, *campesino* agriculture's contribution is also very important. Thus, current efforts to guarantee access to food must be based on that concrete reality, and they must begin to displace the spaces controlled by agribusiness that form part of our daily life: our dishes, tastes, and gardens. Those are sites of domination, and it is there that we should concentrate efforts. We firmly believe that one way of doing this is to bring together food sovereignty projects with concrete interventions in those areas of everyday life where the contradictions mentioned above are reproduced.

— September 4, 2018

Struggling Against the "Revolutionary Bourgeoisie" in Rural Venezuela: A Conversation with Gerardo Sieveres and Arbonio Ortega

From July 12th to August 1st, 2018, a large contingent of Venezuelan campesinos *marched more than 400 km across the country in what came to be known as the "Admirable Campesino March." They walked from Guanare in Portuguesa State to Caracas to raise awareness about the many problems facing small farmers, including evictions, harassment, and general neglect at the hands of state institutions. Here we learn about the march and its objectives in the voice of two of the most prominent leaders in the Venezuelan* campesino *movement, Gerardo Sieveres and Arbonio Ortega.*

How did the Admirable Campesino March come to be? What got a group of campesinos **to walk more than 400 kilometers?**

Arbonio Ortega: Our march was triggered by the deep complexities of the *campesino* situation. Criminalization of our struggle, difficulties getting agricultural inputs, murder of *campesinos*, impunity, and the lack of attention from state institutions whose main purpose is attending to *campesino* issues.

Months before we began our long march, we organized many meetings and assemblies to address the critical situation of *campesinos* throughout the country. In these meetings, we developed a plan or proposal for how to attend to the *campesino* situation. From there, we began to look for a channel to make our demands heard in Caracas. So we made a visit to Caracas. There, we called for an end to the criminalization of landless *campesinos* by the state, and we called for protecting the lives of those being threatened by the landowning class' thugs. During the visit, we also requested that *campesinos* receive agricultural inputs, particularly fertilizers, much needed for the successful completion of the first corn crop.

Upon our return from Caracas, Jesús León and Guillermo Toledo, two *campesinos* active in the movement, were killed in Palo Quemao, a recovered farmstead in Barinas, in yet another case of landowner violence [May 12, 2018].[6] As the criminalization and threats against many *campesino* leaders continued, we began to hold meetings in other regions of the country. We went to Guarico, Cojedes, Barinas, Portuguesa, and Sur del Lago, and out of those meetings emerged the plan to do symbolic takeovers or occupations of the regional offices of two state institutions: INTI and Agropatria. The last occupation was in INTI Barinas. After that occupation, we were called by the head of the INTI to a meeting in Florentino [a state-run agricultural investigation center]. The outcome was a plan and a series of agreements, but the institutions did not act upon those agreements.

It became obvious then that we had to develop another strategy to be heard. Thus, we decided to go to Caracas again, but in larger numbers, to demand that our voices be heard. In preparing the visit, we analyzed the Zamora Takes Caracas March [a *campesino* takeover of Caracas in 2006 to demand an end to impunity], as well as many *campesino* takeovers of Caracas that were carried out when Chávez was still alive. The social impact of the Zamora Takes Caracas March marked a sea-change in the *campesino* struggle, but after that there was a sort of dispersion of the *campesino* movement and the co-optation of some *campesino* organizations.

So, analyzing the history of the *campesino* struggle in the years of the Bolivarian Revolution, and reflecting on the current situation, we decided that we would march to Caracas, as a collective sacrifice and as an homage to earlier *campesino* struggles.

My sense is that the two months prior to the march *campesinos* began to face more violence from the landowning class . . .

Arbonio Ortega: Right, around that time, in a recent recovery of land in a farmstead called El Esfuerzo in Portuguesa State, thugs of the landowning class burnt the school and some warehouses. They also burned the sheds where the *campesinos* were living, and that became yet another cause for us. With this situation in mind, and in light of the upcoming two-month anniversary since the assassination of León and Toledo, we decided that we were going to go to Caracas on foot.

We began walking on July 12th and along the way we found tremendous solidarity from the very poor people living by the side of the road. But also enormous barriers and hurdles were set up by government institutions: they made parallel "*campesino*" marches, broke promises, and launched smear campaigns.

From that point forward, the story is well known. We walked more than 400 kilometers from Guanare in Portuguesa State, and along the way *campesinos* from different regions of the country joined us, while humble people living by the side of the road gave us water and shelter.

Eventually we were joined by Reyes Parra, a *campesino* leader from Barinas State, from the La Escondida *campesino* homestead, a place where we had done an assembly with more than 300 *campesinos* days before the beginning of the march. His truck carried the water needed to keep us walking. After a while, he went back home to fix his truck, which had some problems. Immediately upon his return to the homestead, Reyes Parra was killed. But we were not going to give up!

We continued, and as we went on with our march, we met with *campesinos*, workers, and social movement activists. Everybody whom we found along the way gave us the strength to continue! People gave us shelter, water, food. The alternative media committed to covering the march, to make up for the blackout from the state media, which censored all coverage.

We continued to advance, and in Valencia the column began to grow very quickly. Many more people from around the country joined us and our voice was now being heard loud and clear—not only through alternative media, but also through social media, where people began to come to our side.

We arrived in Caracas on August 1st, and groups from the social movements received us with warmth and solidarity. That was very moving! We walked toward Miraflores and found all sorts of hurdles along the way, but eventually we were able to talk to President Nicolás Maduro.

So what triggered our march? The terrible situation of *campesinos* whose voices need to be heard. And it should be known that the problems remain, and that is why we have not left Caracas. We will stay here until there is clear evidence that solutions to the *campesinos*' problems are on the way.

What you call the Bolivarian Campesino Agenda brings together the grievances and requests of the *campesino* sector. How does this agenda develop?

Gerardo Sieveres: For us, the Campesino March was a school. We began our long journey because of the problems in the farmsteads: the problem of the criminalization and judicial persecution of *campesinos*. We walked to call for an end to *campesino* assassinations and to impunity, and finally to bring to the public eye the need to regularize land tenure. We also marched to demand access to agricultural supplies.

In the 23 days that it took us to reach Caracas, we engaged in a permanent conversation and debate. In every stopping place we debated; during the long walks we talked and analyzed; at night, after the long day, we reflected. Thus, we began to make our demands more precise. Our demands began to include issues like the decentralization of Agropatria and Pedro Camejo [state company for agricultural production]. In the debate some would say, "No, those are actually decentralized," and we would say, "Yes, but we want them to be independent of the government, because the Agriculture Ministry is incapable of responding to our needs."

After hearing our demands, the president committed himself to addressing (and finding solutions for) problems in five areas: land, production, justice, public services [institutional problems], and organization. In that meeting, he ordered, in a very emphatic manner, that the lands given to *campesinos* during Chávez's presidency be given back to them. After that, work tables were set up, but frankly for a long time, not much happened.

Let's move to the main points in the Bolivarian Campesino Agenda: the synthesis of proposals that come out of assemblies, debates, and conversations in the context of the Admirable Campesino March.

Gerardo Sieveres: The first item in the agenda is "Land and New Territories." Here we are talking about safeguarding the *campesino* population and its right to produce in the territory. Basically, we want to address the *campesino* population's integrity and right to organize. We are talking about establishing a network of all *campesino* farmsteads with a view toward creating integrated Campesino Development Zones. If we are able to unite *campesino* farmsteads, we will be safer and more efficient. All this, obviously, goes hand in hand with the issue of assigning tenancy of unused lands.

We have a singer and songwriter in Venezuela, Alí Primera, who is really a universal artist. In one of his songs he says that the *pueblo* should be like a dried cow skin: when someone steps on a dried cowhide, the opposite end will rise up. That is what we understand as the project of "*campesino* territoriality": an integrated space for our struggles, but also with the long-term aim of establishing an economic *campesino* system. This economic system that would extend from the field to the stewpot. We are thus talking about having real power, about ensuring sovereign production and the satisfaction of basic food needs.

So this new territoriality is based on a productive model. And what is our model? Our productive model is the idea of "agricultural socialism," basically Chávez's proposal . . . which has, surprisingly, been abandoned. Really, nobody talks about his model!

The productive model that Chávez proposed is based on processes of collective "recuperation" of the land and socially-oriented production, with all its implications. We, the *campesinos*, with the right granted by Chávez to produce on the land, must produce to satisfy collective, social needs.

This brings us to the second point in our agenda, which is "Strategic

Production." To understand this we have to go back in history. After the massacre of indigenous populations with the arrival of the Spanish colonists, a new culture emerged: the mestizo culture. Mestizo culture results from the mixing of the indigenous peoples with the colonizers. That is how our *campesino* culture emerges.

We have a long historical and genetic baggage of colonization, but we also have the historical and genetic baggage of indigenous rebelliousness, of liberty and of resistance. In that way, we arrive at the issue of recovering our roots. *Campesino* production happens in the periphery, in less inhabited territories, in the more isolated places; *campesino* production is resistance production, but it is also sovereign production. In these isolated areas, we have the wherewithal to produce and satisfy social needs.

So when we talk about "strategic production," we are talking about producing in a planned process to satisfy the needs of people, who are facing a profound crisis and the threat of imperialism, which wants to take what is ours.

So "strategic production" means organizing and planning the crops of cassava, yam, plantain, and corn: producing to satisfy the Venezuelan people's basic needs.

The third item is "Integral and Structured Justice of the Countryside." Our proposal is that, given the justice system's inability to respond to the *campesinos*' collective needs, a process of juridical self-protection should be implanted. We have to review the existing laws in this regard; for instance, the law recognizes the figure of the justice of the peace in the *barrio*. Thus, we are proposing to build "peace courtrooms" at the local level, in the rural territories. In this system, the judge, hearing charges against a landowner who had a *campesino* killed, would be a fellow *campesino*, his peer.

This is very important, because the truth is that certain sectors of the government are using the judicial system to criminalize *campesinos*, to dispossess *campesinos* of their land. How do they do this? They make false allegations and eventually open legal cases.

For instance, on social media, government spokespeople are making false claims against us, saying that Arbonio burned a school . . . thus

Arbonio should be put in jail because he is a threat to society! Why, because he is a thorn in the side of a power group that has nothing to do with the aims of the revolution. There is another person from the Campesino March who is being called a terrorist on social media, or myself, a humble *campesino*—now in social media some are claiming that I'm selling land! All these baseless claims are made on social media to threaten us. Basically, they are threatening to press charges that would be founded on rumors that they have planted. They are, in essence, cooking up judicial "false positives." They do similar things with landless *campesinos* who occupy unproductive land.

So, when we talk about Structured Campesino Justice, we are talking about a system that bypasses the current, corrupt judicial system that doesn't want to be reformed. . . . We are talking about establishing a model for and by *campesinos*, a system that will ensure justice and peace in the countryside. It's the only way, really. We [*campesinos*] are the only ones who know our reality.

All this must go hand in hand with the development of a *campesino* militia. The objective of this militia would be to protect our territory when facing the brutal landowners' threats, the narcoviolence of those who want to build drug corridors, or the aggressions by the new agrarian bourgeoisie. So those are the three main lines of our struggle. . . . Obviously, all this must happen hand in hand with a profound reform, or even a revolution, within the existing institutions.

Gerardo Sieveres: That is certainly the case. One thing that is important to underline is that when we met with President Maduro, he talked about the need to reform the government's agricultural institutions. In this regard, what we say is that while the institutions must change, more than changing directors we must strive to change their modus operandi, their internal logic.

And this brings us to Enrique Dussel's recent visit and the founding of the Decolonization Institute. The truth is that our institutions are colonized by an "anti-people" logic. The first thing that must be decolonized in Venezuela is power, the power that resides in state institutions. The colonial behavior that operates in institutions must be eradicated. So let's decolonize institutions!

We have seen the development of a "despotic patrimonial" logic colonizing institutions in the recent past, and it must end. This is the colonized practice that currently inhabits institutions. We say that institutions operate now in a despotic patrimonial manner because these spaces employ a deeply despotic logic. From the bottom to the top, there is disregard for the law, and they do with the patrimony as they wish. What should be done with this despotic patrimonialism in state institutions? Well, the state institutions must be decolonized, eliminating these practices.

I assume that when you talk about "despotic patrimonialism" you refer to the practices associated with the emerging landowning bourgeoisie, the so-called "revolutionary bourgeoisie"?[7]

Gerardo Sieveres: Let's explain this in three historical phases.

The historical struggle of *campesinos* has been against whom? First, we struggled against the feudal lord. Then there is a second moment in which we had (and still have) a very intense struggle against the oppressing landowning class. But additionally, we are now struggling against the despotic patrimonialists of the "revolutionary bourgeoisie." They are the ones behind the terrible functioning of public institutions. That is the first block that must be overcome in decolonizing institutions with the new institute that President Maduro formed. He is our president, and we trust that he will take the right path in this regard.

What is next?

Gerardo Sieveres: We must defend President Maduro with all of our strength. He entrusted his word to us, he committed himself to solving the *campesino* bloc's problems. Thus, those committed to Chavismo, with our decision to follow Chávez's path *as clear as the full moon*, we are committed to our president and his word.[8] The commitment he made to us is a brake against the revolutionary bourgeoisie's logic of despotic patrimonialism, which is a cancer inside institutions that tends to take Chávez's project out of the picture. That bourgeoisie is breaking the moral backbone of our process. But the moral objectives cannot be broken, and we count on President Maduro for that! The rural and urban youth, all who have accompanied us, all revolutionaries, the activists in social movements, we must all walk together toward reinstating Chávez's vision.

— November 8, 2018

Building "Patria":
A Conversation with Sergio Requena

Born in 1974 in Puerto Ordaz, in the industrial heartland of Venezuela, Sergio Requena is a worker at CVG CARBONORCA.⁹ He had a key role in forming the "Productive Workers' Army," a voluntary initiative working to jumpstart stalled or abandoned industrial plants (both state-owned and worker-controlled). Since 2016, the organization's "Productive Workers' Battles" have become a reference among those committed to rebuilding the industrial muscle of the nation. The project has brought hundreds of workers together and put some twelve industrial plants back on their feet. Of the twelve Workers' Battles carried out by this volunteer brigade, eight happened while Requena headed CORPIVENSA and was able to channel some state resources to the initiative.¹⁰ Today that support has dried up, but the struggle continues.

I would like to begin by asking you to give us a brief overview of the situation of Venezuela's state-owned factories today.

As is the case with most of Venezuela's productive apparatus, the state enterprises are in crisis. Furthermore, those enterprises are fragmented and disjointed: each plant, each factory, has its own specific objective, its own logic—meaning, there are many isolated initiatives. Each is on its own, with nothing bringing them together in a network, because there isn't a national production plan, nor is there a plan that would organize even the whole state-owned sector.

To make matters worse, there are some deliberate obstacles put up to production from within, from the enterprises' leadership. So the main problem is that there isn't a centralized production plan, but add to that the fact that during the crisis (and the disorder that comes with it), some particular economic interests have surfaced, and you get the picture.

[State firms form] an archipelago of islands, each with its own little ruler, who single-handedly decides if the enterprise will produce, under what conditions, what happens with the product, etc. Additionally, he decides who they will contract to acquire raw materials and services. In general, a director will contract outside of the state-owned enterprises, and will do so with the aim of seeking personal economic benefits.

When President Nicolás Maduro launched the Economic Recovery Plan, he referred to the fact that there are many companies producing very little or nothing at all. Our view is that there are two roots to the problem: first, there is no productive plan for state enterprises; second, private objectives and interests organize production (or lack thereof) in state-owned plants.

There is another bottleneck: in many of these plants, the bosses argue that production has come to a halt because the enterprise doesn't have funds to purchase the machine parts that need to be acquired so that the operations can get back on track. But it turns out that the machine parts that have to be replaced come from abroad and must be purchased in U.S. dollars.

Historically in Venezuela, and especially in state enterprises, machines and machine parts came from abroad and were purchased in dollars. All this happened without finding out if within the country, and particularly among the state enterprises, partnerships could be found leading to joint solutions. Today, the bosses continue to request dollars (which are not available) and they justify the stalled production by pointing to funding limitations instead of looking for solutions that can be found inside [the country].

You are part of a collective volunteer project for the recovering of the country's productive apparatus, both state-owned and worker-controlled enterprises, which has come to be known as the "Productive Workers' Army." In 2016, a group of workers from the

industrial heartland of Venezuela in Bolívar State began to recover a state enterprise called "La Gaviota," a fish-processing plant. Can you tell us about this initiative?

I would like to begin by going back to 2013. It was the beginning of the crisis, and the workers of three privately-owned factories occupied the plants after the owners infringed workers' rights and sabotaged production. The companies were Indorca, Calderys, and Equipetrol—all in Guyana's industrial ring. The process of recovering the plants was collective and very efficient. Soon after their occupation, the plants were back on a regular production schedule. These three plants continue to operate under workers' control.

Three years later, in February 2016, folks from La Gaviota, a state-owned plant in Cumaná [Sucre State], invited workers from Indorca, Calderys, Equipetrol, plus others to jumpstart the fish flour plant's industrial oven. It was a five-day journey where the knowledge of each worker plus a lot of collective creativity (and sacrifice) allowed us to kickstart production. We did this with no resources beyond our knowledge and our tools. . . . Really, in five days we were able to raise production from zero to 100 percent!

During those five days, we worked long hours and slept at the plant. The work was voluntary and the whole process of recovery became a crash course—we all learned a lot, and all the workers who participated were remoralized. The fact is that each "Productive Workers' Battle" is a school in which we teach each other, share knowledge, and look for solutions collectively.

And this brings us back to what I was saying earlier: by now there is plenty of evidence that workers are capable of recovering stalled factories and that large investments are not necessarily needed, even when production has dropped to zero.

So, La Gaviota would be the first in a long and ongoing campaign to recover state-owned factories and factories under workers' control?

Yes. After La Gaviota we went to Maquinarias Barinas in Barinas State, and there we waged the second battle. In the factory, an important part of the machinery was non-operative. Actually, there was a machine room with all new equipment that had never been made operative. It was never put to use and repairs were needed. We left it at about 80 percent of its productive capacity.

Again, the collective process of getting the plant back on its feet (in fact, on its feet for the first time!) remoralized the factory's staff.

In this battle, we also implemented a parallel learning space, an initiative that is now key to every battle and that we call "Collective, Integral, and Permanent Self-Formation." We organized a workshop on freehand drawing of mechanical parts.

Then, in March of 2017, we carried out a battle in Planta Madre Wuanaguanare, a factory that produces food-processing machinery in Portuguesa State.

Little by little the Productive Workers' Battles began to draw attention. They began to be known, and we got an invitation to head up CORPIVENSA, a state initiative to promote industrial and productive sovereignty in the country. During the seven-month period that we were in CORPIVENSA, we were able to carry out eight "productive battles." Since we had institutional support, we had extra muscle. Of the eight productive battles that we carried out during that period, four were in gas cylinder plants, and one was in a Nutrichicha plant that produces rice-based drinks for the School Alimentation Plan. We also waged another battle in La Gaviota, and finally a battle at the Amuay Oil Refinery in Falcon State.

We have had twelve productive battles in total, and we have begun to call ourselves a "Productive Workers' Army." Some 2,200 people have participated in these battles, so we feel that we are an army that can be deployed to any plant, in any state, to raise productivity.

Our army is very varied . . . made up of both active workers and retired workers, both workers from the public and the private sector—in short, people with very diverse experiences. But the most important thing is that it is a group made up of revolutionaries who want to overcome the current crisis.

When you go to a factory, your main goal is to jumpstart

production, but the educational process is also very important. Can you tell us more about this?

First, I should clarify something. We don't only repair machinery, we also repair consciousness. There is a mystique to the whole process.[11] When the Productive Army goes into a factory, a process of remoralization begins. The plants' workers participate in the recovery of their factory and transform their own reality. This practice of doing (this praxis, if you will) opens the way to what Che Guevara called creating the new man and the new woman. Jumpstarting production with our own hands, with limited resources, getting the factory back on its feet, yes, all that is important. But if we do that and we fail to remoralize the workers, then the plant will fall back into its earlier slumber.

Raising morale is through praxis that is key for us, but we also foster parallel collective educational activities, as I said before when we mentioned the ongoing "Collective, Integral, and Permanent Self-Formation" that we undertake. During the Productive Battles, we share experiences—skills acquired through work—and we also address organizational problems.

As a result of this, the plant's workers get organized in workers' councils, in feminist brigades, and in Productive Workers' Councils [CPT].[12] Ensuring that some form of organization grows out of the experience is fundamental, as workers' organization is the only thing that will guarantee continued production in a plant.

Basically, our main goal is to break with the inertia that installs itself due to bureaucracy: inertia that ends up killing production. After we leave, there must be internal conditions (not only material conditions) to continue the work, and that is why we emphasize organization.

The "Chinese Model" has discursively entered the Venezuelan public sphere.[13] By contrast, your model is a socialist model that points to workers' control and seeks to bring solutions to our problems from below and from within—it could even be called a Guevarist and patriotic model, couldn't it?

We refer to our effort, our collective epic struggle, as an "Admirable Campaign," a term that recalls Bolívar's campaign for the liberation of Venezuela's western regions [in 1813]. We understand that there is now a crisis, with some elements of conspiracy and economic war. Yet on top of that, there are serious management problems in public enterprises, corruption, and other interests that don't contribute to a solution. Faced with this complex situation, many are looking for solutions elsewhere.

For our part, we cast our lot with the people of Venezuela. The gaze of Venezuela has historically been directed to the exterior: people felt that we couldn't solve our own problems. Hugo Chávez offered a brief respite from that logic; with him, we were able to see what we had, we recognized ourselves. I think it is time that we begin again to acknowledge that we can do things, that we do have skills. Our productive apparatus has practically come to a complete halt, but there are thousands of men and women who are committed to coming out of this crisis, and they have incorporated themselves to the Productive Workers' Army. These workers do not want to be spectators. They want to be subjects again, reactivating our participatory and protagonistic democracy.

So indeed our proposal is patriotic. We believe that we can do and make things—that we aren't doomed. We have a strong conviction that the people, the workers, the working class . . . together we can bring ourselves out of the crisis that we face in the industrial sector and elsewhere. We are the ones who will build the sovereign and emancipated *Patria* [homeland] that Chávez aspired to create, with the protagonistic participation of the people. We are convinced that we can do this, that patriotic Venezuelans can do this, although we will always welcome with wide open arms comrades from other countries, people who are committed to socialism. But this is a war that we have to wage and that we must win. Only the people of Venezuela can solve the problems of Venezuela, and from our point of view this must be done with Chávez and with commitment to participatory and protagonistic democracy.

One of the most intense debates within Chavismo right now is the

debate about the "ethical referent" and the need (since Chávez's death) to point to exemplary experiences that might bring the project out of the stagnation that we are facing now. There is a mystique around El Maizal Commune and the Admirable Campesino March, but in the working class, in the industrial sector, the Productive Workers' Army has become a referent as well. Can you talk about this?

When we refer to ethical referents, we must talk about revolutionary coherence, and revolutionary coherence is a kind of North Star that guides our praxis. Our objective is to help to recuperate the productive apparatus of the nation. For this to happen, as I said before, there must be a process of remoralization and organization, which is key to the success of our initiatives.

In the Productive Workers' Army we teach by example, with a praxis that brings together political and social commitment with work. So we hope that we will constitute a school for the workers with whom we work, arm in arm, during the Productive Battles.

Sacrifice is, like it or not, an essential part of our epic struggle. We often travel for thousands of kilometers to get to a factory; we leave our family behind; we sleep very little and when we do, we sleep in the plant.... All this tends to change the plant's dynamics. We can actually say that we, the hundreds of men and women of the Army, teach by example. The sacrifice that a Battle entails is key to a shift toward a revolutionary ethos.

All this, of course, happens with President Chávez as a guiding light. His example fills us with strength day in and day out. He taught by example and he sacrificed himself for us. In return, we commit our lives to our country.

— November 16, 2018

Campesinos Defending Chávez's Project: A Conversation with Andrés Alayo

For more than two months in the summer of 2018, members of the Campesino Struggle Platform (Plataforma de Lucha Campesina), a Chavista organization bringing together small producers fighting for land rights, have been camping out in front of the Venezuelan Land Institute (INTI) in Caracas. There, dozens of campesinos *are engaged in ongoing conversations about the situation of the country and the injustices that they are facing in rural areas. They also work on documents as well as organize marches and meetings. Andrés Alayo is one of the key leaders of the Campesino Struggle Platform. In this interview we talk to him about the history of the Chavista agrarian revolution.*

I would like us to begin with the Venezuelan Land Law of 2001, which marks a turning point in the Bolivarian Revolution. The law sought to preserve and improve the lives of Venezuela's small agricultural producers. However, it also met with a furious response from the landowning class, which reacted with an astonishing degree of violence.

The Land Law was a powerful attempt to guarantee people's lives in the rural areas. The Independence Wars [1810 to 1823], the Federal War led by Ezequiel Zamora [1859 to 1863], and the Bolivarian Process are the key milestones in our struggle to build a sovereign nation and achieve social justice. The Land Law got the Bolivarian Revolution going, but at the same time, along with the Hydrocarbons Law and the Fishing Law, it provoked the 2002 coup. That's the case because the Land Law impacted the interests of the rural oligarchy. It opened the way for a new understanding of property.

Not surprisingly, implementing the Land Law unleashed terrible violence from the landowning class, which was allied with the most reactionary sectors of our society and also with Colombian landowners... it marks the beginning of a series of bloody practices that, little by little, begin to enter Venezuela's rural areas, leading to hundreds of *campesino* deaths.

The law brought with it a profound change in land tenure in Venezuela. For the first time, thousands of previously landless *campesinos* had access to the land. The Land Law represents an enormous step forward in the process of democratizing the land, which until then had been in the hands of a handful of families.

The spiral of violence began in November 2001, when FEDENAGA [national association of large livestock owners] President José Luís Betancourt publicly tore up the law in a symbolic gesture. It was a war cry. The first *campesino* to fall was Licino Lago, from the Caño Caiman homestead in Sur del Lago [in Zulia State]. To date, oligarchic violence has led to the deaths of some 350 to 400 *campesinos*.

But for those of us who are *campesinos*, we don't give up. Our calling is to produce, and Venezuela's landscape began to be reconfigured during the revolution. At that time, [because of the previous oil booms] the country imagined itself as the "Saudi Venezuela." It was the country of "plenty" which nevertheless expelled millions of *campesinos* from the rural areas and forced them into the growing slums of the large cities. However, in the early years of the 21st century, the situation began to change and people started to go back to the rural areas. They began to occupy unused land, making thousands of small homesteads. In villages, *campesinos* gradually constructed their humble homes, their *caneys* [open bungalows with thatched roofs], and they shared production spaces. In that way, there emerged a culture that puts life at the center of things.

So, on the one hand we have a wager for life and for the democratization of the land and, on the other hand, we have the landlords' culture of death and terror.

To understand the agrarian revolution as it has developed within the Bolivarian Process, it is important to consider the different periods that have shaped that struggle, from the enacting of the Land Law in 2001 right up to the present.

The process of democratizing the land can be put into different periods. The first years were characterized by an enormous popular momentum. Hundreds of *campesino* cooperatives were formed, and the Venezuelan people witnessed thousands of cases of vacant land being occupied, and we celebrated it.

It was at this time—beginning in 2002 but especially in 2003 and 2004—that the true enemies of the people begin to show their faces. They are the landowning class, but also the nation's courts, the judges who make common cause with landlords, and the local police. . . . These latter groups and institutions were quick to collaborate in the eviction of *campesinos*. That was a time when the popular movement was advancing, but it was also a period characterized by a great deal of repression that favored the oligarchy.

By 2006, they had killed dozens of *campesinos*. The law was there, granted us rights, but the repression was on the rise and impunity was rampant. In those circumstances, we organized the march, "Zamora Toma Caracas" (Zamora Takes Over Caracas) in partnership with the Ezequiel Zamora Campesino Front. The goal was to denounce the landowners' rampant violence, on the one hand, and the state's inaction, on the other. On that summer day, tens of thousands of *campesinos* (many of them on horseback) occupied Caracas.

The truth is that the state's institutions—the Prosecutor's Office, the Office of the Ombudsman, the courthouses, the judges, and the justice system as a whole—never showed much willingness to bring to justice those responsible for murdering *campesinos*. That is something that, even today, pains us and makes us indignant! The period when the popular movement was on the offensive ended with the march in Caracas.

Around 2006 or 2007 a new period begins, with a change in the government's policies toward the rural areas. Around that time, state businesses begin to emerge, and these enterprises begin to directly assume control of occupied lands. The peak of this period is around 2008 and 2009, and it lasts through 2012.

Here we are talking about a time when the grassroots initiative is no longer center stage. Instead, the state takes the lead, recovering many vacant farming estates. This includes (to mention just a few): Hato El Frío and Hato El Cedral in Apure; La Compañia Ganadera Inglesa in Apure, Guárico, and Falcón; La Vergareña in Bolívar State; Hacienda Bolívar-La Bolivariana and Hoya Grande in Sur del Lago, Zulia; the whole Valle de Turbio in Lara; and La Productora in Portuguesa.

All these estates passed over to the direct control of the Agriculture Ministry. Thus, as an outcome of the process of recuperating vacant and underproductive lands, the Venezuelan state became the largest agricultural landholder. We are no longer talking about vacant land being occupied by *campesinos*. We are talking about public, state-operated enterprises.

In this process, a large contingent of *campesinos* became wage workers for state enterprises.

This is the period when the oil bonanza reached its peak. Oil prices rose to historical records, and that meant that a lot of resources became available. An important part of it was invested in agriculture. During this time, for instance, the Pedro Camejo plant for farm machinery was founded, and thousands of tractors, harvesters, and other heavy machinery were imported into the country.

The AgroVenezuela Mission was also created during this phase, while enormous resources were earmarked for rural investment. The budgets of CVAL [state agriculture corporation] and other state enterprises figured in millions of U.S. dollars, with the aim of developing an infrastructure to support production. This is also the time when Chávez ordered the compensated expropriation of Agroisleña [seed and agricultural input corporation], which then became Agropatria.

So we could say that 2006 through 2010 were the years that brought to an end the scenario defined by the 19th century plantation.

Would it be correct to say that this last period you refer to closes with Hugo Chávez's illness?

Yes, this period came to an end when Chávez's illness began. Around 2012 we started to witness the dwindling of the state agricultural enterprises and, shortly after, a process of gradually dismantling them began.

The truth is that between 2011 and 2016, the state had vastly reduced resources, and the government chose to privilege other sectors [that were not agriculture]. Investment and credit for *campesinos* plummeted, and the building and maintenance of rural infrastructure came to a halt. It was a period of evident decay and was accompanied by the active dismantling of the large state agricultural enterprises such as CVAL. These state businesses had been built with enormous human effort and huge investments, so it was a serious setback for agricultural production.

This period's dynamic became even harsher in the last couple of years. Around 2016, the imperialist attack on Venezuela became more aggressive. During this time, the nation's food security became a public issue, and the contradictions between reform and revolution became more obvious, side by side with the more evident revolution-counterrevolution contradiction.

As far as the reform versus revolution contradiction is concerned, we find sectors of the government that are overtly aiming to restructure land ownership based on "strategic" partnerships with private capital, be it national or international. These sectors claim that *campesinos* don't know how to produce, that they are lazy by nature, that the stilted agrarian development is the fault of the small producers themselves.

According to this group, the *campesinos* received millions of dollars in credits, machinery, land, etc., but they weren't able to operate efficiently with those resources. To state the obvious, that is false, since the bulk of those resources didn't go to the *campesinos* directly, but rather to the enterprises that we mentioned earlier or even to the private sector.

These [reformist] sectors believe that the Land Law should be abrogated and the struggle against large plantations needs to stop. They are against *campesinos* occupying idle land. All this is no secret! They publicly affirm that it is necessary to ally with private interests to be able to produce.

What characterizes the government's agricultural policy today is that it works to consolidate an agro-industrial model led by supposedly patriotic business people. In our time, private businesses with a lot of resources (of unknown origin) are beginning to pop up, and they are on the fast track. To mention just a few of these businesses: El Tunal, JHS, Ebenezer Group, and Los Tres Grandes. All are private agro-industrial enterprises, and they have become powerhouses extraordinarily rapidly!

On the flip side of the coin, small producers and communards are witnessing the disappearance of the state's social and productive presence in the *campo*. We should explain here that the state has a monopoly on seeds, machinery and other inputs, even agricultural credits. It is the state that administers them, but the state's presence in the rural areas is practically null, leaving *campesinos* exposed to dangerous mafias that buy supplies.

The priority in agriculture is now large capital, both new and old. As it turns out, the government is casting its lot with those producers whose aim is exporting, not with the *campesinos* who provide produce for urban, internal markets in Venezuela.

One of the heroes in this "special period" in Venezuela—the period characterized by imperialist attacks—is the *campesino*, the small producer in the rural areas. Even now ocumo, yuca, ñame, plantain, topocho, and fruits are always available in the markets, and they are produced in terrible conditions. That is to say, there are crop thefts, skyrocketing prices of agrarian inputs (which are managed by the state but sold through black market channels), scarcity of fertilizers, mafias that operate in the rural areas, and police repression. In fact, small producers have supplied the cities with food while there were no other sources of staple foods. In doing so *campesinos*, with their hard work, have hampered the possibility of a social explosion, which is one of the U.S. State Department's aims.

Many of the state's "productive partners" are active in the long-standing counterrevolution (whereas others are newcomers). Who are the new owners of Hato Garza in Barinas State, an enormous pig farm that was formerly state property? They are the same people who in November of last year killed Tomás Ribas, a *campesino* activist who was safeguarding the infrastructure from pillage and privatization... . These are the state's "productive partners"!

The state has given preferential treatment to Alejo Hernández, owner of El Tunal, who is known as "El Tornillo." Recently a video showing him calling for an uprising against Maduro went viral. . . . He is the "spoiled child" of the current wave of these "productive alliances"! The government had awarded him 5000 hectares in Portuguesa.

This is a huge contradiction! The small producer and the communard have demonstrated that they can produce and deliver, and they have also proved their commitment to the revolution. That being the case, why is it that the state is privileging large private capital? Why is the state channeling resources, almost exclusively, to the agrarian capitalist sector? And through what channels have these private "investors" accumulated their fortunes?

We are facing a covert politics of restoration [of the old order]. The discourse goes as follows: the state is not able to maintain public enterprises due to the economic crisis. That means we have to turn over the state's enterprises to private "investors," since they have capital, knowledge, relationships, and professionals who can guarantee that the businesses come back to life. But we must ask: what is the cost of all these resources that we are handing over to the private sector?

One of Chávez's most important legacies was that he opened the path to building a sovereign economy in a strategic alliance with the *campesinos* and the communards. Chávez's stated objective was to build the communal state. However, with these alliances that are taking shape we are getting further and further from that objective every day!

So this period is a very dark one, not only due to the imperialist blockade—which itself creates serious problems—but also because the policies that are supposed to foster internal production contradict the objective of attaining collective sovereignty. The government has chosen the agro-industrial model, which has many limitations if we consider that the aim is to satisfy the needs of the majority in a time of imperialist siege.

In this period, our main slogan should be: "Produce to resist!" That's because there is no possible resistance and no fighting army if it doesn't have food. And the food for an army must be produced in a sovereign way here in Venezuela. Only the small producer, the *campesino*, and the communard can guarantee that. To resist the imperialist attack and the internal restorationist tendencies, we must guarantee agricultural practices that are also capable of resistance. To be honest, there is no other way.

Just a few days ago, hundreds of people from the Plataforma de Lucha Campesina and other organizations gathered in Caracas. They marched with the slogan "Against assassinations, plantations, and paramilitarism." The march also sought to defend the *campesinos'* **right to the land and to have access to agricultural supplies, which is all the more important in the face of the imperialist blockade. Can you tell us something about this march and what was at stake in it?**

On August 6, we marched against paramilitarism and the targeted assassinations of *campesinos*, to bring an end to impunity, and in defense of *campesino* and communal life.

This march happened one year after the meeting between President Maduro and the Admirable Campesino March. Twelve months ago, dozens of *campesinos* came by foot from Portuguesa State to Caracas to protest the grave conditions in rural Venezuela. Even though the media sought to criminalize the march (and despite the lies disseminated even by state media), we arrived in Caracas on August 1, 2018.

Thousands of committed Chavistas came out to greet us. But we were also received by a huge contingent of riot policemen as if we were the worst *guarimberos* [violent, right-wing protestors]—as if our intention was to assault Miraflores!

We met with President Maduro on August 2, 2018, and there we reached some important agreements, which in turn became presidential orders.

The first point concerns the land. All the land that has been taken from *campesinos* should be returned. That was a clear order that the president issued. However, out of 111 cases that we brought before the president, only 28 were resolved, while another 15 are in a process of review for the granting of the titles. The rest are still in a process of investigation.

The second agreement was about justice for the victims of targeted assassinations. Between 350 to 400 *campesinos* have been killed since the Land Law was signed in 2001, and their killers enjoy absolute impunity.

Since we began the Admirable March on May 12, 2018, there have been assassinations of 19 *campesinos*. Most recently, six members of the CRBZ were killed in Ticoporo. We expect to learn the truth and to have justice for all our dead! Impunity must cease to be the state's policy. A revolution cannot live side by side with impunity: *justice* is a synonym of *revolution*.

The third agreement, which was backed up by a presidential order, was to put an end to the judicial persecution of *campesinos*. Hundreds of *campesinos* are facing legal cases because they produce in lands desired by people who are more powerful or have better connections. Maduro assured us that the day after the meeting Supreme Court Justice Maikel Moreno would initiate a process that would eliminate all the cases involving judicial persecution of *campesinos*. We are still waiting for that process to begin, and a growing number of *campesinos* have been criminalized since.

The fourth point of agreement was the "Crop to Crop Sowing Plan." The plan was for cultivating forty-five thousand hectares during the "Summer Growing Season" [the Venezuelan summer coincides with the dry season that begins in October], but nothing came out of that promise. For the Winter Season [beginning with the May rains], we presented a plan for cultivating thirty-seven thousand hectares. The government approved twelve thousand hectares for planting beans, corn, and rice, but it was later reduced to seven thousand. Of that, we received seeds and inputs for 1700 hectares.

The fifth point concerns the making of a *campesino* congress. The idea is to hold a congress to build unity within the *campesino* movement and to develop plans to face the challenges that the current war scenario presents. The Agriculture Ministry, the National Constituent Assembly, and the vice presidency were to coordinate this project with us, but there was never an agreement about how to proceed.

Now there is a new (more grassroots) effort to organize the congress. We hope that this effort will succeed. The aim is to build a large *campesino* movement that will guarantee, on a local level, the defense of the revolution, making the rural areas into a socialist vanguard.

The August 6 march in Caracas was organized to defend those agreements, on the first anniversary of the presidential orders.

The Admirable Campesino March last year ran into a number of hurdles before it reached its destination, and the same could be said for the recent march in Caracas.

The police attempted to prevent our march from advancing. There were confrontations with the police, where the willingness of the *campesino* movement to struggle became clear. The marchers were indignant because the impunity [enjoyed by those who have killed *campesinos*] makes us angry, as does the judicial harassment of *campesinos*, and the state's neglect of the rural areas.

They wanted to prohibit a peaceful march! To that we said, "Nobody will prevent our advance!" So we advanced through Caracas, and we broke through three police barricades. Our initial aim was to get to Miraflores, but to avoid conflict we ended the march in front of the National Constitutive Assembly [ANC], where we delivered a document to Diosdado Cabello, its president. In that document, we made a balance sheet of all the agreements struck earlier with the president. It was a kind of status report. We also delivered the report to the office of the president.

There, in front of the ANC, we had a political rally. We sang, danced, and shouted our slogans. We also read our report in public.

In doing so, we were defending Chávez's legacy and the orders that President Maduro gave on August 2, 2018.

There are institutional actors that don't like to see the *pueblo* expressing itself. They are the same people who want to make the country believe that all is well. . . . We say to them and to President Maduro: "Take a tour around Sur del Lago, around the Andean *páramo*, talk to the producers in Trujillo, go to the Portuguesa plains, get yourself to Barinas and listen to the *campesinos*. Go to the street, Mr. President!" Maduro himself told his ministers to visit the *campesinos*, to talk directly to producers in the rural areas, and to do so without cameras and without mediation. Anybody who visits the rural areas in Venezuela will find very difficult conditions, on the one hand, and a tremendous willingness to defend Chavismo, on the other.

— August 31, 2019

The Role of the Working Class in Venezuela's Crisis: A Conversation with Pedro Eusse

Pedro Eusse began his militancy in the Communist Party of Venezuela (PCV) in 1979 at the age of 17, when he was working in a chicken factory. Currently, he is a member of the political bureau of the party, where he coordinates labor and trade union issues. Eusse is also the General Coordinator of the "Cruz Villegas" Class-conscious Current of Workers and of the National Front of Struggle of the Working Class (FNLCT). In this interview we asked him about the plight of the working class in Venezuela, and how they might contribute to overcoming the current crisis. We also inquired about the PCV's analysis of the economic measures announced in August 2018 by President Nicolás Maduro.

In Venezuela today, with the economic crisis and its many dimensions, including inflation and emigration, what is the importance of workers' struggles? Beyond the standard discourse about producing more, what solutions can the working class offer? What is the role of the workers in a situation in which the socialist project seems to be falling out of view?

For the PCV, the working class's most important task now is to defend the country against the heightening aggression of the international Right led by U.S. imperialism, with its economic, political, communicational, and diplomatic blockade, as well as the threat of a military attack against our people. If the plans of imperialism and its lackeys against our country were to be carried out, the consequences would be catastrophic for our people and for Latin Americans in general.

The interests of U.S. monopolies would be imposed, with great loss of life. National sovereignty, territorial integrity, peace, the revolutionary achievements of the Venezuelan people—although precarious at present—would all be at risk. Even the very existence of Venezuela as a nation-state is at stake. Workers' struggles that are focused on particular economic and social demands would basically make no sense if the United States and its puppet governments were to wage war against Venezuela and impose a neoliberal, pro-imperialist government.

From our perspective, the most important contribution the working class can make is to accumulate forces—and do so with independence and class autonomy—with the aim of leading a broad patriotic and anti-imperialist front. We cannot talk about "the socialist horizon falling out of view," because up until now there has not yet been a "socialist horizon" in Venezuela! It's one thing if the reformist petty bourgeoisie talks about socialism and another thing altogether if the conditions are really there to build it.

For us, the first step toward socialism is achieving a favorable correlation of forces, so that the working class and working people can come to power in Venezuela—and that does not yet exist. We must create such a correlation of forces, but first we have to defeat the pretensions of imperialism and its extreme-right lackeys. Of course, we should recognize that it's not because Venezuela has a socialist revolution that the United States and its satellite governments attack us. No, a socialist revolution isn't in process here. What we have is dependent rentier capitalism. The real reason they attack us is because the United States needs to regain full control of the strategic resources of this country and consolidate its dominance in Latin America, in the context of a dispute over world hegemony that is taking place between U.S. and European imperialism and the bloc of emerging powers, led by China and Russia.

What do you think will be the short-term and long-term impact of the new economic measures (including the monetary reconversion, the anchoring of the Sovereign Bolívar to the Petro, and the new minimum wage) on the purchasing power of Venezuelans?

As far as the Venezuelan government's recent economic measures [announced in August 2018] are concerned, we are not deluding ourselves: they are fiscal, monetary, and currency exchange measures that do not impact the structural causes of the crisis. In other words, they are reformist measures. Of course, some of these reforms, such as the minimum wage hike, are positive but very insufficient. The PCV and the National Front of Struggle of the Working Class [FNLCT] have said the following: "Adopting the new minimum wage and transforming workers' income into salary—permanent demands of the PCV and the class-conscious trade unions—are positive but insufficient steps in the face of the high cost of living due to inflation."[14] Moreover, the prices, which were set by agreement between the government and bourgeois groups (even monopolistic ones) without the participation of the workforce or the people, turn out to be very high for Venezuelans.

For this reason, we continue to propose a policy of raising the labor power's value and establishing, on the basis of the new minimum wage, a sliding scale of salaries that would reference the consumer price index of goods and services that constitute Venezuela's basic goods basket, in compliance with the Constitution's article 91.[15] This, in turn, would oblige Venezuela's Central Bank to fulfill its constitutional mandate to regularly publish the consumer price indexes. At the same time, we need to establish an institutional and social system for controlling costs, prices, and profits in which workers, organized communities, and the people in general would participate in a binding way.

A new form of social protest has emerged in recent months. Instead of the violent protests against the government (like the 2014 and 2017 *guarimbas*) now there are often popular mobilizations that aim at pushing the government toward positions that would favor workers and *campesinos* over employers and landlords. Most notable are the electrical workers' strike, the nurses' strike, the pensioners' protest, and the Admirable Campesino March. Interestingly, however, it seems to be the struggles of peasant and

rural communities that are most successful in going beyond mere grievances to present a political vision and form spaces of resistance. How do you explain this? Why does the epicenter of the revolution now seem to be in the rural areas?

The first thing is that the violent actions of the Right in 2014 and 2017, which were identified as "guarimbas," should not be confused or compared with the legitimate struggles and mobilizations of the workers, peasants and the popular movement. Additionally, it is very important that the working people mobilize in defense of their rights and that they also transcend immediate economic objectives. Of course, there are sectors of the peasantry and some rural communes that are carrying out interesting struggles against landlords (old and new members of that class) and against the bureaucrats who are in league with them.

The *campesino* struggle, which is on the rise, is defending the progressive achievements made by what is known as the Bolivarian Revolution, particularly those made during the administration of President Chávez. It has also raised some even bigger goals in terms of overcoming agribusiness and obtaining sovereignty in the face of the transnationals that control agricultural inputs. That is what was proposed by the "Nicomedes Abreu" Class Conscious Peasant Current [under PCV leadership], which, together with the Peasants Struggle Platform, organized the Admirable March.

But this kind of struggle that develops and takes shape on a path of national and social liberation needs to unite with the struggles of the working class, where there are forces that fight not only for immediate economic and social objectives. We are really enthusiastic about the *campesino* struggle's advances. This is because in a country where agricultural production has fallen, increasing our dependence on imports (and exacerbated now by a lack of foreign currency and also by the imperialist blockade), what genuine rural producers can achieve is of strategic importance.

The PCV signed a document with President Maduro as a preliminary to supporting his candidacy in the May 20 elections. Briefly,

what is the nature of that document and, more importantly, what is the current status of the agreement?

The Unitary Framework Agreement signed between the national leaderships of the United Socialist Party [PSUV] and the PCV, at the suggestion of our party [PCV], expresses programmatic aspects of an alliance between the communists and those who are socialists. The background of this agreement is the need to confront the crisis of capitalism and (locally) the collapse of our dependent and rentier system. Unfortunately, the dominant tendencies in the government and in the leadership of the PSUV have opted for a reformism that is conciliatory with capital; they are moving away from revolutionary and progressive positions.

Today, we need to recognize that the government has not adhered to the Unitary Framework Agreement's content. For example, it has not reinstated workers illegally dismissed from the public and private sector, which was a commitment President Maduro took on publicly. Likewise, the government has allowed many state companies to deteriorate, and everything points to this being part of a strategy to privatize many of those companies. All this goes against what was set up in the document: recovering state enterprises with a new management model that would incorporate workers.

It is no secret that the government has attempted to co-opt workers' struggles by creating organizations such as the Bolivarian Socialist Workers Confederation (CBST), which doesn't have autonomy or vocation for struggle. Simultaneously, we have seen some cases of the state's apparatus repressing workers and peasants. However, despite these contradictions, the revolutionary working class and peasants continue to consider themselves Chavistas and, in electoral conjunctures, wholeheartedly support the government. In a process of change like Venezuela's, how should one strike a balance between the necessary autonomy of the workers' movement, on the one hand, and a commitment to a process of national emancipation, on the other?

From our point of view [the PCV and the FNLCT], the workers' struggle has not been co-opted by the government. Rather the government seeks to overcome or domesticate it through the CBST. This trade union confederation and, more specifically, its leadership, is an instrument of official and bureaucratic trade union reformism. The CBST exists so that there is a hegemonic trade unionism that is subordinated to the government and led by the reformist petty bourgeoisie.

In the Puntofijista period the governments of Acción Democrática [Democratic Action] and COPEI [Christian Democrat]—at the service of U.S. imperialism—had the CTV.[16] Likewise, whatever the differences, the current government now has the CBST to legitimate and rubber-stamp all its decisions. All this is very problematic, because it does not help to develop class consciousness among the workers and does not help create a working class capable of confronting the owners, the bourgeois state, and the capitalist system, in the drive for the revolutionary transformation of society.

Thus, the "Cruz Villegas" Class Conscious Current of Workers and the FNLCT propose to strengthen the labor movement and class-conscious trade union movement, and do so with independence and autonomy in the face of capital, state, and the bourgeois and petty bourgeois parties. However, we are aware that, when facing the serious imperialist threat that now looms over all of Venezuela, unity of action is needed, as is the participation of all the diverse workers' sectors in a broad patriotic anti-imperialist alliance.

— September 10, 2018

Notes to Section 4

1. *Adeco* refers to the members of the Democratic Action party (AD), one of the two political parties that allied to govern Venezuela between 1958 and 1998. The *Adecos* were notorious for the clientist and corrupt practices they employed in institutions and communities.
2. *Copeyano* refers to members of the Christian Democratic Party (COPEI), one of the two political parties (the other was Democratic Action) that allied to govern Venezuela between 1958 and 1998, through an agreement known as the Puntofijo Pact.
3. FEDELAFAS is the national association of large livestock owners, whereas FEDECAMARAS is the Venezuelan business association or chamber of commerce. The latter was directly responsible for the 2002 coup that ousted President Chávez for 47 hours before he was returned to office by a mass popular uprising.
4. Uribismo is the fascistoid current in Colombian politics that continues the project of former President Álvaro Uribe Vélez, in power between 2002 and 2010.
5. *Conuquero* refers to a person engaged in subsistence farming or very small-scale agricultural production.
6. A *recovered farmstead* is a plot of formerly unused land that has been occupied by landless *campesinos*. The 2001 Land and Agricultural Development Law laid out the basis of the agrarian revolution and created the legal framework for granting Venezuela's landless *campesinos* the right to secure or "recover" land in this way.
7. "Revolutionary bourgeoisie" is a term used by Venezuelan Agricultural Minister Wilmar Castro Soteldo. His use of this term has generated controversy within Chavismo, as it was interpreted as a defense of an emerging bourgeoisie in the Bolivarian Process.
8. As Chávez's cancer worsened, he declared Maduro to be his successor, meaning all Chavistas should support Maduro as a future presidential candidate if he were to die, as indeed happened. In a dramatic final speech in December 2012, Chávez said: "My firm opinion, as clear as the full moon—irrevocable, absolute, total—is ... that you elect Nicolás Maduro as president."
9. CARBONORCA is a state-owned plant producing anodes, a component needed to process aluminum.
10. CORPIVENSA is a state institution charged with encouraging industrial sovereignty and productivity.
11. In progressive Latin American contexts, the term *mística,* or mystique, refers to nonmaterial values such as morale, hope, and confidence.
12. A Productive Workers' Council (CTP for its Spanish initials) is an

organizational figure promoted by a February 2018 Constituent Assembly law. CTPs are meant to encourage production in a plant or factory, be it public or private.
13. The term "Chinese Model" is used in Venezuela to refer to the Chinese mixed economy. Some Venezuelan leaders think that Venezuela should pursue the same path involving a pact with national and international capitalists. In consonance with this project, Chinese officials are assuming some advisory roles in Venezuela, encouraging "development" initiatives such as Special Development Zone: territories where certain laws do not apply to encourage foreign investment.
14. The Cruz Villegas Class Conscious Current of Workers is the organization of trade unionists and labor leaders within the Communist Party of Venezuela. The National Front of Struggle of the Working Class is an independent trade union confederation that takes a position close to that of the Communist Party of Venezuela. In the interview, Pedro Eusse refers to how the government's decree of August 2018 is apparently positive because it rolls back the government's longstanding tendency to convert an important part of workers' salaries into bonuses, thereby reducing nominal salaries and, consequently, the size of pensions. That surreptitious way of reducing workers' nominal salaries has long been opposed by the Venezuelan Communist Party and allied organizations.
15. Venezuela's Bolivarian Constitution of 1999 indicates that a minimum salary should be equal or higher than the "basic market basket," which is the cost of all the basic goods needed by a family of four.
16. The Confederation of Venezuelan Workers, or CTV, founded in 1947, is a federation of trade unions. It was initially a combative organization. However, it eventually became coopted by Venezuela's right-wing political parties. The CTV participated in the 2002 coup d'état against Hugo Chavez.

5

IMPERIALISM, FASCISM, AND THE DEFENSE OF BOLIVARIAN VENEZUELA

Venezuela's Missile Crisis: A Conversation with Juan Contreras

Juan Contreras was born and raised in Caracas's 23 de Enero barrio, famous for its revolutionary political activism and internationalism. A graduate of Venezuela's Central University, Contreras was active in the revolutionary organization Bandera Roja, under the direction of Comandante Geronimo (Carlos Betancourt) in the late 1970s. Today he heads up a community organization, Coordinadora Simón Bolívar, in the heart of working-class Caracas. Here Contreras looks at the historical precedents of the February 2019 coup attempt—recently defeated at the time of the interview—reminding us of all that is a stake.

The idea that politics inevitably involves a struggle over historical meanings received spectacular confirmation in recent weeks. That's because the political crisis that we are in the midst of right now—following Juan Guaidó's declaring himself president—saw the opposition trying to evoke the memory of the pro-democracy rebellion that began on January 23, 1958. How do you understand this effort of Guaidó and his imperialist masters to appropriate that historical event, which was essentially a leftist victory, in the name of a coup d'état?

I would begin by saying that there would never have been a February 4, 1992 [when Hugo Chávez tried to take power by insurrection] without [the democratic rebellion of] January 23, 1958. If indeed it's true that the opposition and the right-wing Venezuelan oligarchy have been trying for some time to appropriate symbolic dates such as January 23 or February 12 [Youth Day], it's still true that those events are symbolic for our people.

The great protagonist over all these years has been the popular masses, whose trajectory of struggle reaches a long way back. There is a powerful historical current that goes back to [indigenous leader] Guaicaipuro who struggled against the colonizers, to José Leonardo Chirino who fought to establish a republic and to abolish slavery, to our nineteenth-century liberators Francisco de Miranda, Simón Bolívar, and Antonio José de Sucre, and to Ezequiel Zamora with his call for freeing the land and people in 1846. We could also include the democratic rebellion of January 23, 1958, the Caracazo of February 1989, and the civilian-military insurrections of February 4 and November 27, 1992.

We descend from all this! That historical legacy is the work of our people, and it has accompanied us in these times as one of our important strengths. Well, that legacy belongs to the people and not to a few "leaders" who are bowing down to the designs of U.S. imperialism. To rally their followers, they have to use the U.S. flag! They even call for an invasion, when all of us know that even in the twenty-first century there are no bombs that kill only Chavistas or hunt down only Chavistas!

That revolutionary historical legacy is the antithesis of everything that the opposition is doing today. What they are doing doesn't have any basis in our revolutionary history, because that history is marked by a high degree of popular participation. The popular masses paid for this struggle with their lives: they paid a high price in blood. That is to say, the struggle during all of these years and even centuries—500 years of struggle, in fact—has been the work of the poor people: the Bolivarian and Chavista people.

In examining the international panorama, would you say that Donald Trump is taking a step away from the Middle East to recuperate U.S. power in its so-called backyard? Arguably, what is going on in the continent today appears similar to Ronald Reagan's attempt to roll back the advances of the Latin American Left in the 1980s, which involved U.S. intervention in Grenada, Guatemala, Nicaragua, and El Salvador. How would you interpret, from a geopolitical standpoint, our current situation?

Imperialism, Fascism, and the Defense of Bolivarian Venezuela

I would like to begin by saying that what is happening now is quite similar to what happened in 1962 during the Cuban Missile Crisis. Fidel Castro had a conversation with Che Guevara, and Che told him that the crisis would unfortunately be resolved from above: Cuba would not have a say in the missile issue. Indeed, the meeting happened in the upper spheres of world power, between the USSR and the United States. Cuba was not an actor in its own history. It is possible that we may be in a very similar moment in history today. History is cyclical, and there are episodes that repeat themselves.

Why does today's situation recall the Missile Crisis? Well, after the meeting between Putin and Trump, a shift in the geopolitical chessboard began to take shape: the United States starts pulling troops out of Syria (although troops still remain there), and more recently a withdrawal of troops from Iraq was signed by U.S. authorities. Thus, it would seem that, from a geopolitical standpoint, and when faced with an important crisis, the current relations of power are such that only the big players can sit at the table: our government doesn't sit at the table. I believe we could be facing a situation in which these two powers reach an agreement: what is happening in Syria points to that and the developments in Venezuela could be the other side of the coin.

Venezuela is the "backyard" of the United States, while Russia needs control of Syria and the region around it to ensure the construction of a gas pipeline. . . . In *barrio* slang what we are facing might be a *cambalache* [exchange]: I let you have Venezuela, and in return you let me have Syria. This resembles what we saw in 1962.

We could also look back to the 1980s, as you suggest. That was the era of the U.S.-led intervention in Central America. And that disastrous episode seems all the more recent when we learn that the U.S. advisor for the Venezuelan crisis is Elliott Abrams. He is a well-known figure, with a warmongering history. Abrams was convicted for his participation in the Iran-Contra affair, but he also supported counterinsurgency in El Salvador and Guatemala, and he encouraged the Panama invasion. All this reveals the United States' undeniably hawkish attitude toward Venezuela. There is no doubt about it: they are determined to have full control of their "backyard."

That takes us back two-hundred years. The Monroe Doctrine [1823], which was designed by John Quincy Adams but got James Monroe's name attached to it, can be summarized with the phrase "America for the Americans." It was a warning from the United States to Europe: any European participation in Latin America would be considered by the United States to be an act of interference. That doctrine is alive and well today, two centuries later.

The current confrontation has two elements. The obvious one has to do with the United States' open interest in our resources, but I would dare to say that more important than that is the United States' deep antagonism to Bolivarian doctrine, which is the one that has oriented this political process for the past two decades. Bolívar wanted to construct a bloc of republics as one nation. . . . [Tellingly] when reflecting on this in the 1820s, Bolívar said: "The United States appears destined by Providence to plague America with miseries in the name of liberty."

We are going through this first hand once again. Two hundred years later, the confrontation continues the logic of the Monroe Doctrine: the United States' pretensions to control what they always considered their backyard. And just as at that time Venezuela was in the vanguard of the independence struggle, so today we have to play again the role of a continental vanguard.

In Venezuela, what is at stake is not only the destiny of the Bolivarian Process, but also the destiny of Latin America and the Caribbean as a whole. Together they make up what Bolívar called "Meridional America." It is an open battlefield in which the destiny of Latin America and the Caribbean is at stake.

As Bolivarians and Latin American patriots, how should we respond to the imperialist offensive that attempts to generate conflicts among nations in the region? You mention that U.S. imperialism is directed at Bolivarianism. It aims to break continental alliances using governments such as those of Brazil and Colombia, which now are towing the U.S. line. How can we counteract the United States' efforts to undermine Latin American unity?

Here we have to go back to Bolívar once again. He sought to

integrate the Latin American republics, aiming to make them into one single nation. By contrast, the Monroe Doctrine tries to divide our peoples. Today, we see that they are determined to do so once again. We only need to look at the rise of figures such as Colombia's president, Iván Duque, who represents the Colombian oligarchy and the interests of the Global North, or Jair Bolsonaro, who represents the ultra-right of Brazil, or Mauricio Macri in Argentina.

The rise of these figures marks a setback for the Left in the continent, compared with the two previous decades in which the processes of building Latin American unity were advancing. Clearly, we are now going in reverse inasmuch as these new governments are imperialist puppets. They are the local representatives of U.S. interests, and their aggressions take place not only on the frontier, but also in the sphere of public politics and media campaigns, working constantly to divide Latin America.

In contrast with diplomacy on a state and government level (which is often penetrated by foreign interests), there can also be "people's diplomacy." In other words, the popular sphere should try to coordinate and organize itself [across national boundaries]. The International Assembly of the Peoples that is going to happen at the end of February in Caracas could be an important step in this direction, if it's not co-opted.[1] People's diplomacy is the way to resolve this conflict and avoid confrontation amongst sister nations.

How to push for integration? It can only be achieved from below, in the popular sphere. There are so many projects in Latin America that should be brought together! *Campesinos*, factory workers, the indigenous peoples, students, and *barrio* dwellers. There is a local saying here in Venezuela: "lo que es igual no es trampa" [If there's a level playing field, things are fair]. Our enemies believe in diplomacy from above and they try to attack the Bolivarian Process with those tactics, by pitting governments against each other, and with the threat of a military intervention. Our self-defense has to work in the opposite way: it has to be like the people and reach beyond borders. Bolivarianism is equivalent to the ideology of popular continental unity.

We should not fall into isolationist positions but rather work with those who struggle and those groups that break with chauvinist attitudes—which, although not new in Venezuela, need to be overcome. In Colombia there are the *guerrilleros* of the ELN [National Liberation Army] and in Brazil, there are the *campesinos* of the MST [Landless Workers Movement], who have a long trajectory of struggle. I think that those kinds of groups are the ones that we can count on and with whom we must work. Pursuing popular integration and fraternity would allow us to consolidate the process of continental integration in the face of the disintegration that the United States wants to foster.

Defending the country doesn't have to be limited to responding to media attacks or mustering legal arguments. Those kinds of defenses often risk becoming part of a spectacle. There could also be a popular response, which would advance the revolutionary process and have nothing to do with pacting among power groups.

I think there are three elements that have kept the Bolivarian Process going during these twenty years. First, there is the historical memory of the emancipation struggle that took place 200 years ago and the Bolivarian teachings that accompanied it. This is one of the most important legacies that our people have. It has accompanied us during those twenty years of the political process, where it serves as a kind a guiding light.

Second, there is the well-known "unity of the civilians and the military." There are people-in-uniform, on the one hand, and people-who-are-civilians, on the other. Yet in the end it is the same popular mass. Some members of the popular classes went to the military because of conviction or because of a career, but it is the same popular base. The "uniformed people" go through the same stuff that the civilians live through too, which is something we should be aware of.

Third, there is the disposition for change that the Venezuelan people have shown. That disposition for change has been evident since the Caracazo rebellion of February 1989, where people went to the street and buried the International Monetary Fund's prescriptions.

That popular revolt against the neoliberal policies that the IMF was trying to foist on our country cost us about 5000 lives.

Those same people who led the revolt and in 1998 elected Chávez as president of Venezuela later approved the new constitution with a new presidential period. On October 7, 2012, they reelected President Chávez for the third time, and on April 14, 2013, being loyal to Comandante Chávez, they elected Nicolás Maduro as president of the Bolivarian Republic of Venezuela.

I think that in this [trajectory] you can discern the effort that the Venezuelan people have been making. The Venezuelan people's disposition for change has continued, and it is not limited to Chávez's leadership. It has its own life apart from the direction of the revolution: the Bolivarian Process's "political-military leadership."

In Venezuela, the popular masses said, "Enough!" They are the ones that got the political process going and they are the ones who believe in the revolution. There is a wide swath of the population that took seriously Chávez's calling for a communal state as a way to advance toward Bolivarian socialism. They are the popular masses, with a history of struggle. It is these people who make history. As brilliant as certain individuals may be, as important as Bolívar and Chávez are for us today, they are just pieces of straw caught up in the whirlwind of revolution.

In Venezuela, the people said "Enough!" and organized themselves. Despite all the things that we can criticize, I am convinced that there is a solution, and that solution is with the people. That is to say, the path forward for the Bolivarian Process is with the popular masses, with the organization of our people: workers, farmers, indigenous peoples, students, and the popular sectors from the *barrios*. Our way out is with them with us. There is no solution possible through high-level negotiation with power groups. There is no solution that involves accepting the blackmail from the North. The solution is with the people. And it's with the people that one has to negotiate, sit down, and talk. There is no other way!

— February 16, 2019

Either Washington or Venezuela, Savage Capitalism or Socialism: A Conversation with Luis Britto García

Luis Britto García is arguably Venezuela's most highly regarded public intellectual. A firm supporter of the Bolivarian Process, he has authored numerous plays, novels, historical investigations and film scripts, and is also an incisive commentator on politics in the region. Here, Britto García talks about the short- and long-term defense of Venezuela's sovereignty.

Many people on the left criticize President Nicolás Maduro's government, but that criticism has nothing to do with a desire to join the ranks of the right-wing opposition or its foreign allies. In the face of the imperialist attacks going on now against Venezuela, we need to defend the country and stand up against interference. Do you agree?

I have repeatedly claimed that, when both internal and external forces of reaction make a double attack on our country and use all legal and even illegal resources they have at hand, we must all come together to Venezuela's defense and in the defense of its authorities and the political coalition that maintains them legally in power.

There may be differences and internal debates, but we can't hesitate when faced with these alternatives: it's either Washington or Venezuela, invasion or sovereignty, savage capitalism or socialism.

You have written about Simón Bolívar and have pointed out how his example remains relevant today. What would Bolívar do in our time? As Bolivarians, what should we do in the present?

That's right. I did a meticulous examination of both Bolívar's ideas and his actions in relation to society and the economy in my book *The Thought of the Liberator: Economy and Society* [2010], and in numerous articles and other works. If Bolívar were here among us today, he would do the same as he did when he was alive: first of all, he would make every effort to defend (with arms if necessary) Venezuela's sovereignty: the right of our people to choose our own government.

He would attempt to organize and unite Latin American and Caribbean peoples against imperialist domination. Also, in the economic sphere, Bolívar did not hesitate to carry out the largest confiscations of goods in Venezuelan history. He seized all the royalists' property, in the form of either land or other goods, and distributed it among patriotic soldiers, in accordance with the services they had rendered (though it could also be used collectively).

Bolívar said that the nation has property rights to its underground minerals, which is a principle that still holds today and must be defended at all costs. In 1814, long before his trip to Haiti, Bolívar began to eradicate slavery. He also fought against racial discrimination, with his "Angostura Speech" [1819] proclaiming that in contemporary Venezuela "nobody should be mistreated for the color of his skin." If we say that a slave is someone who just ekes out an existence, making just enough to survive, then Bolívar's struggle today would be to overcome both extreme and relative poverty.

To carry out these measures, Bolívar did not hesitate to take radical and extreme steps (nor should Bolivarians hesitate to do so today). Let us remember his declaring a "War to the Death" [in 1813]. Bolívar today would continue with the project of Latin American and Caribbean integration, as he did with his Amphictyonic Congress in Panama, where the United States only got to participate thanks to Francisco de Paula Santander's influence. Anyone who calls himself a Bolivarian today must follow—and if possible extend—the practice and thought of Bolívar. If we don't do so, we'll become a colony again.

How do you evaluate the global response to the imperialist onslaught we are experiencing these days? Can we see ruptures

in the United States' hegemony and evidence of a new, multipolar world?

For me, there is an evident break in the United States' hegemony. The United States has moved its industries abroad to take advantage of cheap sweatshop labor. In so doing, it has deindustrialized the country and plunged its own workers into misery. China is today the world's leading economic power; Russia has reemerged as a great power after the decline that came with the Soviet Union's dissolution. Europe is trying to become independent, despite being occupied since the mid-century by a network of NATO bases. The Middle East eludes U.S. control; after decades of interference, the United States has only managed to make chaos.

I have pointed out that, historically, revolutions have always emerged in the fissures created by the clash of the hegemonic powers at the time. The United States emerged taking advantage of the struggle between England, France, and Spain. The Soviet Union took advantage of the clash of European powers during the First World War. The same goes for the People's Republic of China, which benefited from the fighting of the Second World War. Later, Cuba used the confrontation between the United States and the Soviet Union. Today, the hegemonic struggle between the United States, Russia, and China offers us an opportunity to consolidate Venezuelan sovereignty.

After dealing with this imperialist attack and coup d'état attempt, which is our most immediate problem, what should the Maduro government do in the medium and long run?

I think that there is no way to get out of our immediate crisis without advancing in the revolution, and that is also the key to going forward once we have recovered. That's to say, we can only face down imperialism after we have dominated the local oligopoly formed by a dozen companies that monopolize the import and distribution of basic goods [in our country]. And we have to subjugate the handful of actors that run the oil smuggling business and are involved in paramilitary infiltration.

We will be able to face external threats once we have cleaned up the internal theatre with a control of the whole administration—at all stages of its operation—and have installed an integral computerized control in real time of prices and costs of economic operations. We must sanction the many acts of corruption and clean up the companies and institutions where this kind of activity is rife. With these measures, popular support for the socialist project will become unbreakable. On the other hand, if such measures are not taken, it's to be feared that the economic war will erode this support, which maintains itself now only through great sacrifices.

— FEBRUARY 5, 2019

Venezuela's Constituent Assembly and the Rise of Fascism: A Conversation with Julio Escalona

Born in 1938, Julio Escalona began his revolutionary activity at an early age in the MIR (Left Revolutionary Movement). Later he helped found the urban guerrilla OR (Organization of Revolutionaries) and its political arm the Socialist League. A professor of economics in Venezuela's Central University, he has also been part of Venezuela's United Nations delegation. Today, while continuing to write and reflect, Escalona serves as a member of Venezuela's Constituent Assembly. In this interview, he shares with us his thoughts about class struggle in the Venezuelan countryside and the menace of the Ultra Right in Brazil.

Recently you wrote an article about the resurgence of fascism in our continent, as embodied in Brazilian presidential candidate Jair Bolsonaro. You hypothesize that, if the economy continues its chaotic course and the pauperization of Venezuela's masses goes forward, a fascist option could emerge here. Can you tell us about this?

As long as the welfare state existed and relations of power evolved under it, fascist projects were impeded. There have always been fascist practices: violence, torture, violations of human rights, attacks on democracy.... They've always been present in Venezuela but without being the usual political method. What's been usual in Venezuela has been a combination of forms of struggle: there was an authoritarian government, which was maintained by concessions to people and workers, and was buttressed by repression in what was called "the war against insurgents."

Today, in global capitalism, finance capital has become hegemonic. Financial capital cannot coexist easily with democracy because it liquidates the spaces of interclass negotiation, which was the social and political basis for representative democracy. Liquidating those spaces of negotiation means that there are two options: either a move toward fascism or a growing popular movement, which is what the Chavista period represented in Venezuela. The option that in fact emerged here was that of the popular movement and the practice of participative and protagonistic democracy.

Moreover, our popular struggle relied on something Chávez developed, which was both the worldview and the practice of solidarity. The practice of solidarity could be developed because people could see the advantages of solidarity, but it led the empire to realize that the way to defeat Chavismo would be to defeat the concrete practice of solidarity here: stimulating individualism and promoting egoist solutions.

To do that, imperialism worked to make Venezuelan society chaotic, destroying forms of organization and relations of solidarity. That is what has been happening in Venezuela: a process of destroying relations of solidarity along with a reawakening of individualism through what is here called *bachaqueo*, which is in essence the individual solution. Individual solutions of that kind are only possible by damaging the collective, which is precisely what capital tries to do.[2]

So we have entered into a process in which individual solutions have not exactly won out, but they have been strengthened and the fabric of solidarity has begun to weaken. One thing goes hand-in-hand with the other: you weaken the social fabric and relations of solidarity, at the same time as you strengthen individualism. That's what's underway right now in Venezuela.

Fascist experiences tend to result from a frustration of the popular movement. The popular movement had begun to emerge in Germany. The Communist Party got to be very strong there. However, defeating the communists and the socialists in Germany led to fascism. This is so because the liberal position, especially the neoliberal position, is based on the weakening of the state, but above all in the weakening of the state in its role as a representative of the population's interests. At the same time, the state is strengthened as a vehicle of repression and persecution.

That's how we get to a situation of a fascist kind, since [it amounts to] strengthened power that is located above society, which decides people's rights and determines what is done and not done, while forcefully encouraging one to focus on oneself. It tells you: it doesn't matter if you kill, it doesn't matter if you torture, it doesn't matter if it's a dictatorship. But you can work things out for yourself.

In Venezuela, the Right is trying to frustrate the Chavist process because they know that frustrating it will lead to a reaction in the opposite direction. State power, which Chavismo used to respond to popular demands, could be used to repress. This would go hand-in-hand with a fascist demagogic discourse—showing how you can enrich yourself and live better. That discourse tells you: you shouldn't be so stupid as to think about other people!

Faced with this, what is the government doing?

The government should confront this situation. It has the political and legal tools, all the necessary instruments to confront the Right's main tactic today, which is permanently raising prices. The Right does this because it's what hurts people the most. As a result, you cannot buy a kilo of meat. Nobody can buy it! That's the truth! Nor can you buy a kilo of chicken.

That's to say that the basic goods that people use can't be bought, but neither can you get anything else. When they become aware that the people are eating vegetables, then they raise their prices. Wherever they see that the population is beginning to turn, the Right immediately hikes up prices to reduce people to a situation of defenselessness.

Salaries were raised significantly as a result of the measures taken by President Nicolás Maduro, and when they became aware of this, what did they do? They raised prices to such a degree that salaries now don't allow you to buy anything!

The government has to confront inflation, and it possesses the means to do so. It can establish a new relation between the Bolívar and the Petro and raise the real salary. Those are steps that can be taken. They are not easy of course, because [businessmen] will begin to hoard basic goods. However, the government also has the instruments to solve these problems . . .

On the subject of fascism, in 2017 we saw a fascist uprising. It was in the face of this fascist outbreak that President Maduro called for a National Constituent Assembly (ANC), which had two tasks. The first was to change the correlation of forces to end the fascist insurrection. That was successful. However, the ANC also was charged with writing a new constitution. Can you tell us how the ANC is working internally? Has there been a debate in commissions and is the new constitution being developed?

The idea that the government had in convoking the ANC was, as you said, to defeat street violence. The Venezuelan people understood this clearly and massively went out to vote for it.

But the question of violence was not properly understood. People have said: "peace triumphed." However, what was defeated was street violence, so the opposition changed their form of struggle and began a battle on the economic front, which is where we have not been able to defeat them.

So we defeated the street violence but not the economic war. One form of violence was ended, but other forms became stronger. It's there that they have hit most hard. That's the case because while the street violence jammed up the city and created chaos, it never had the people's support.

For that reason, defeating street violence was easy. Maduro did what one does in that sort of situation: appeal to the people. Convoking the ANC was a way of mobilizing people, and that was correct. Nevertheless, where we have not been able to mobilize people is in the struggle against the economic war.

Winning that struggle would require making people conscious of the nature of the problem. It's a question of awareness because the

Chavista movement, the Bolivarian movement, has enough people to deal with the economic emergency. Yet it's there that we have failed, in mobilizing people to confront the economic war.

Additionally, the government has not taken the steps to limit prices and keep basic goods from disappearing—in effect, all the things that make up the economic war. If it's a war, that means it cannot be resolved only through dialogue. In a war, of course, there are spaces for dialogues, but only if you have both sides wanting to negotiate. But what in fact happened was that one side wanted to talk and the other side pretended to want to do it, They went to the table and made agreements that they immediately broke, making the government appear ridiculous in front of the population.

The government said, "We agreed on such and such prices." What's more, the businessmen signed it and it came out in the official bulletin, but they broke the agreement immediately. Breaking the agreement has to be punished by the state, but it hasn't done so! For me, that is the most serious problem that we have now, because it could cause the population to lose confidence in the government.

Up until now, the government has been strong, because it has maintained people's confidence. That is what the recent elections proved. If that confidence is broken, then we might have a critical situation.

Fascist spaces now exist in Venezuela without having had either the opportunity nor the leadership to go forward. The internal Right [within the government] is working to open opportunities for fascism, while, from the outside, imperialism is working to find the leaders who can direct the movement. So I think the political struggle in Venezuela has to face the possibility of a fascist movement emerging—one that would have a base in the country. . . . That danger exists in Venezuela, and I think it is our most serious problem now.

What is happening with the ANC? Are the commissions meeting? Is there debate?

The ANC has been working and there is ample evidence of that. The commissions [work groups by area, such as economy, gender, etc.] are the ones that have most of the work for now, but those are closed-door spaces.

The problem, from my point of view, is that even though the ANC has approved open debates in the street, in the barrios, in rural areas, etc., these debates have not happened. A void exists, and it has to be filled soon! The debate internally within the ANC cannot remain inside the four walls of the assembly chambers. The leadership, the heads of commissions, the delegates, everybody must go out to debate in public squares, in the barrios.

I myself have been to open meetings, but initiatives like that have occurred as a personal project. They are not enough. According to Hermann Escarrá, who heads up the Constitutional Commission, eighty percent of the constitution's text is ready, but where is the debate, the open debate? I assume that this problem will be solved. The truth is that nobody has to ask for permission to debate.

Now, what you should understand is that class struggle expresses itself in all societies and in all spaces of society. Thus, class struggle is also found within the government. I'm not making an accusation; it's simply a fact. There is a very active class struggle in Venezuela, and it expresses itself within the government, within labor unions, and within all communities. It's necessary to overcome the closed-door tendencies in this class struggle.

In recent months, popular Chavista movements have begun to question the government. They insist on being heard, and they want the government to rectify its errors. The best-known case is the Admirable Campesino March. Can you tell us about this new phenomenon—these rebellious movements that are emerging within Chavismo—and particularly about how Venezuela's peasant movement might help to revitalize and rebuild the Bolivarian Process?

The emergence of the *campesinos* in the public arena is very important. Indeed, it is the most important political event in recent times.

Campesinos are a key social element in Venezuela. After all, they form part of a long struggle and they produce our food. In Venezuela, much of what we consume daily is *campesino* production. The old landowning class, the agribusiness sector, produces to export. The emerging agrarian Chavista bourgeoisie, which is for now midsize, does the same. Actually, even some of the *campesinos'* production ends up in Colombia as a result of paramilitary networks. *Campesinos* have been denouncing this.

We have three very active borders in Venezuela. The one with Colombia is the most active, but we also have important borders with Brazil and with the Caribbean islands. In a small boat, you can reach many Caribbean islands. It's very hard to control the ocean, and there is a lot of open-ocean smuggling of agricultural products. Of course, the contraband is sold in exchange for hard currency, for U.S. dollars, which is a draw.

This is a very serious problem. But despite the large amount of contraband, the fruits and vegetables that we eat daily are still produced by *campesinos*.

The government must sit and dialogue, as equals, with the country's *campesino* organizations. The Admirable Campesino March, as important as it is, is not the only expression of *campesino* organization today. There are many, many *campesino* organizations in the country that must be heard.

There will be a Campesino Congress to address these issues. It probably won't happen this year due to the elections. Most likely it will be next year, probably in January. The Campesino Congress must directly address class struggle in the rural areas and try to resolve this struggle in favor of the Venezuelan nation, in favor of the people, and, by the same token, in favor of the *campesinos* who produce what we eat.

To go forward, it's important that *campesino* organizations develop as spaces of unity and political consciousness. They must unite the *campesinos* in the struggle against large landowners, pushing for an alliance with the state, making the state come to their side. If that doesn't happen, the problem of the rural areas will not be solved, and we will not be able to solve our problems related to food supply and prices. The solution lies in the *campesino* bloc, which the Venezuelan state must listen to, offering real solutions.

Today, there is an open struggle between the large and medium agrarian bourgeoisie versus the *campesinos*. The only actor that can solve this very serious crisis in favor of the *campesino* bloc is the state. So the state, the government, must act! Only the state can solve this situation, as it has the police, the apparatus of repression (a part of which, by the way, is actually participating in the smuggling business and is connected to non-*campesino* interests).

Can you tell us more about the importance of class struggle in the countryside today?

There are two very important factors to consider today in analyzing class struggle in Venezuela. The first is a *campesino* bloc, which is growing in organizational terms and also making demands that are just ones. This is not a problem; we should see this as a blessing!

The second factor is the struggle between the *campesinos* versus the large and middle landowning class. Finally, there is [a third] factor: mercenary forces (as well as, in some cases, state forces) are participating directly, and they are not siding with the *campesinos*. These mercenary forces are already in action: they steal and even burn farmers' crops.

All this is not being talked about, but it needs to be known. The violence created by anti-*campesino* groups is leading, once again, to displacement of *campesinos* toward urban areas. These displaced *campesinos* are entering urban pockets of poverty.

We should understand that big capital and especially finance capital aims to take control of all spaces. There is a very real process of privatizing war, and that is why it is important to point to the growth of mercenary forces. We must understand that finance capital—a supranational power with local relations—is operating here.

When mercenaries come to the scene and displace *campesinos*, they are acting on behalf of supranational interests. The mercenary forces in Venezuela aren't a bunch of petty criminals. They form part of a strategically organized project, and their mission is to take over the Venezuelan countryside. The class war in Venezuela has an important mercenary component.

So again, in this open and intense struggle, the government must side with the *campesinos*.

We know of your deep concern for the fate of the Bolivarian Process...

It is a well-known fact that Venezuela is a region of particular geopolitical interest for imperialism. This is not only because of our natural resources, which are important enough, but also because there has been a revolution here. The example set by a profound process of change is a serious problem for them.

Venezuela has been able to defeat all imperialist offensives, and that represents a challenge for them. Imperialism is intent on defeating the Bolivarian Process. That is why this process is of great importance for the peoples of the world, and if it was defeated, it would begin to close off revolutionary paths. That is also why I believe that international solidarity with Venezuela is a revolutionary duty for internationalists.

— October 26, 2018

Venezuela in the Continental Labyrinth: A Conversation with Amílcar Figueroa

In the 1970s, Amílcar Figueroa was part of the Party of the Venezuelan Revolution (PRV), an insurgent group that split off from the Venezuelan Communist Party and is widely credited with developing the ideology of Bolivarianism that influenced President Hugo Chávez. A committed internationalist, Figueroa worked with El Salvador's National Liberation Front (FMLN) in the 1980s. Recently, he was honored with a U.S. Treasury Department sanction for his support of the Colombian guerrillas. Figueroa was president of the Latin American Parliament (PARLATINO) between 2006 and 2008. As a historian, he has written several books, including El Salvador: Su historia y sus luchas *(Ocean Sur, 2009) and* Chávez: la permanente búsqueda creadora *(Trinchera, 2013). In this interview, we asked him to explain the Bolivarian Process in the current continental context.*

Recently, Colombia has entered NATO (North Atlantic Treaty Organization) and soon Iván Duque, an ultraconservative close to former president Álvaro Uribe, will become the country's new head of state. Can you analyze the consequences of this, both on the continental level and specifically for Venezuela?

The triumph of Duque must be situated, just like the Venezuelan situation, in the complex panorama of the Latin American situation, which unfolds in the context of an overarching struggle between reform and counter-reform, revolution, and counterrevolution. Moreover, all this push and pull must be understood in the context of the United States' recolonizing offensive.

Regarding Colombia, it's clear that the most reactionary Right has long been in control of the state. The Colombian state was reactionary, anti-popular, and pro-imperialist with Uribe, with Juan Manuel Santos, and it will be so with Duque. The differences between the three leaders are subtle.

Obviously, for reasons that must be examined with precision, the Santos government facilitated—or rather allowed—the conversations and the peace dialogue in Havana. As is well known, the outcome of the dialogues was the incorporation of the FARC [Revolutionary Armed Forces of Colombia] into electoral politics. But let's not be fooled: the Santos government was a warmongering one, wielding constant violence and repression against the popular movement.

The issue now is whether the Duque government will recognize the Havana agreements, which were already being cast aside by sectors of the Colombian establishment and were being systematically broken by the Colombian state even under Santos's presidency.

It's true that the peace so desired by the Colombian people scored some important successes with the Havana agreements, but the overall situation of violence and social injustice remains in place. Now that Duque, a representative of the most retrograde sector of Colombian politics, has taken center stage, we are likely to see an even more complete rollback of the peace agreements. That, in turn, could send the Colombian nation back into an overt conflict of large dimensions.

Will Duque's presidency alter the relations of the Colombian government vis-à-vis Venezuela?

Things are not going to change much: Duque, Santos, and Uribe share the same views regarding geopolitics. The latter two represented a continental vanguard in their anti-Bolivarian (and anti-Venezuelan) project, and Duque will continue to be part of this drive. It is not, in the end, a question of individuals but of the Colombian state, which has long been in the service of U.S. interests.

The incorporation of Colombia into NATO (an issue that, by the way, had been brewing for a while) further threatens peace in the continent. For Venezuela, this is quite serious, since it reinforces the offensive against its government.

In the last few years, Venezuelans have repeatedly experienced the consequences of Colombia's being the United States' beachhead on the continent. Colombia joining NATO was the logical step after installing seven U.S. bases in its territory in 2009 and making additional agreements (less public but disclosed) between the U.S. military and Colombia that turn Colombian territory into a potential platform for U.S. Southern Command's military actions.

However, we should keep in mind that in the June 17 elections more than eight million Colombians rejected Duque and also said no to war; they did so by voting for Gustavo Petro. Those eight million votes do not even express all the dissent, since the electoral system in Colombia is highly problematic. This means that the parliament is not going to be absolutely submissive to Duque's project. They won't give him a blank check, neither for the reactionary establishment's agenda regarding Colombia's internal politics nor its agenda regarding Venezuela.

It is evident and worrisome that so many people point the finger at Colombia to explain all of Venezuela's problems. According to this way of thinking, everything bad—from violence to smuggling—is caused by Colombia. Could you tell us something about this?

Leaving aside national chauvinism, which is surely a problem in Venezuela, the spilling over of paramilitary practices from Colombia to Venezuela is real and a very serious concern. It endangers spaces of popular organization.

As far as smuggling is concerned, there has always been an illegal market on the Colombia-Venezuela frontier. It only exists because there is complicity on both sides of the border and from both states. Smuggling is a practice that has a direct relation with private appropriation and accumulation of wealth in a lumpen or mafioso context.

Latin America is in a process of political regression and the Bolivarian Process' leadership generally espouses a kind of

"realist" reformism which erodes the original revolutionary project. Can you talk to us about the relationship between the overall continental regression and the Venezuelan leadership's tepidness?

The reactionary counteroffensive taking place in the continent must be examined with care and precision. It began in 2009 with the coup d'état in Honduras, and from then on we have seen imperialist interests advancing in a series of big steps. This led to a new balance of forces in the continent. In Venezuela, things began to change with the September 2010 parliamentary elections, in which we lost the popular vote. Whether people acknowledge it or not, that event initiated an internal shift. Then, in 2014, there was a real turning point in the Bolivarian Process.

That March, negotiations began between key representatives of the Bolivarian government and the bourgeoisie. The most powerful capitalist in Venezuela, Lorenzo Mendoza, became the public spokesperson for "production," and the government made tremendous concessions to the sector that he represented. The new balance of forces coupled with the fascist Right's violent emergence in the 2014 *guarimbas* was what immediately triggered the negotiations. However, it was the financial boycott and the war on different fronts against Venezuela that caused the Bolivarian leadership to assume that backing off from revolutionary goals was the only way to maintain control of the government.

The death or even assassination of Chávez, who had an impressive capacity to find creative (and popular) ways out of difficult situations, has had an enormous impact on the revolutionary process. Henceforth, with an unfavorable correlation of forces, reformist positions became hegemonic within the government. Furthermore, this revolutionary to reformist shift is not confined to Venezuela. I believe that, as a whole, the continental Left's leadership assumes that there are no conditions to advance. Their analysis fails to take into account that a profound capitalist crisis of global dimensions spawns tremendous violence and enormous suffering, thus creating exceptional conditions for an anti-systemic struggle. On the other hand, the Bolivarian

Process's leadership (and that of the continental Left) assumes that capitalism is very strong. As a consequence, they think that changes can only be small and gradual to avoid social confrontation.

How would you characterize the Bolivarian government today?

When Chávez was leading the revolution there was a constant creative search that proposed profound reforms. He opened a path of deep revolutionary transformations. But after his death, and when the correlation of forces became unfavorable, much of the Left and its leadership assumed an attitude of class reconciliation. With this shift, the Bolivarian Process abandoned its radical character and began sliding toward a Keynesian model and a social protectionist project. For example, there are many discourses in which Nicolás Maduro calls himself "the protector of the people." In other words, the government's objective now is not that people take power and transform the social and economic structures. No, it is rather to generate social welfare policies from above.

Of course, this is not the whole story. Those in power do not constitute a perfect and unified bloc. However, there is no question that reformist positions are the most common ones in our political leadership.

How can we imagine a "left-solution" to Venezuela's current crisis?

To imagine renewing the strategic path toward a revolutionary horizon with mass participation has much to do with making advances, taking spaces, and developing concrete work from a class-based perspective.

Working people must take on many tasks. The proletariat in this stage has to accumulate forces. That is because whatever our aspirations and critical analysis of the situation, it's impossible to do anything without organization. No matter how much imperialism has advanced on the continent and reformism has spread in the country, we need to develop a conception that allows new political referents to emerge: leaders who will take up working people's revolutionary goals.

Thus, our tasks include building an overarching movement that consolidates the spaces that the popular resistance movement has created. This would be a movement influenced by Chávez's proposal of popular power, the commune, and workers' councils. All this has to be consolidated to defend what has already been achieved at the same time as the great objectives of the revolution are revived. Simultaneously, there needs to be a process of political education focused on the historical revolutionary process and on bringing back to the foreground the desires that were unleashed by Chávez, which are latent in much of the Venezuelan population.

The truth is that most of the people of Venezuela do not want to return to the past and they aspire to build a society of equals.

— July 11, 2018

The Worldwide Struggle Against Fascism and the Role of Marxism in the Struggle: A Conversation with Néstor Kohan

More than any other living thinker, Argentinian intellectual Néstor Kohan has worked to recover the tradition of Latin American revolutionary Marxism, a trajectory that he argues stretches from Julio Antonio Mella and José Carlos Mariátegui to Che Guevara, Fidel Castro, and Manuel Marulanda. Kohan has also developed an interpretation of Capital: Critique of Political Economy *that puts commodity fetishism at the center of the work at the same time as it emphasizes the political and revolutionary character of all of Marx's texts. Kohan has supported the Bolivarian Process from its beginning.*

In this interview, we asked him questions about the crisis that is engulfing the whole continent, with Venezuela as its epicenter, and for his views on how to struggle against fascism in Venezuela and elsewhere.

What is happening right now in Latin America seems to have a lot in common with Operation Condor, which aimed to roll back the revolutionary tide of the 1960s and 1970s. Today, U.S. imperialism wants to wipe out the "Pink Tide" that began at the start of the current century. Do you think the analogy is relevant?

In the decade of the 1970s Operation Condor was born. There is a lot of investigation about it and a lot of evidence. An Argentinian investigator, Stella Calloni, wrote a very good book about the operation, and a Paraguayan victim of political persecution found documents in Paraguay that prove its existence. Intelligence agents of the Augusto Pinochet dictatorship also made declarations that ratify its existence, and finally there are declassified documents of the CIA that confirm it too. In effect, there was a coordinated international project put in place to carry out repression on a continental scale. In other words, there was a right-wing internationalism, a counterrevolutionary internationalism.

On a rhetorical level, the counterrevolution employed nationalist language. In every country they even talked about defending the "national self" ["el ser nacional"]. That was their preferred jargon, but their practice was internationalist, and their combatants and agents operated in many countries. For instance, the terrorist of Cuban-American descent Félix Rodríguez not only assassinated Che Guevara, but later participated in the counterinsurgency in El Salvador. There are films of Rodríguez on a helicopter shooting at the troops of the FMNL in El Salvador.

Another terrorist of Cuban-American descent, Luis Posada Carriles, put a bomb in a commercial airplane, killing many civilians. He also operated in several countries. Many of these terrorists did their work in several countries. The bomb that killed [Chilean economist] Orlando Letelier in the United States was set off by agents of the Chilean intelligence. They were, arguably, internationalists.

The "clandestine detention centers"—that was the juridical terminology used in Argentina—also worked on an international level. In Buenos Aires, there was an extermination camp, a torture camp. (I call it that, because there's no reason to use the juridical terminology; let's speak without euphemisms.) Well, one of those camps for torturing and "disappearing" people was called "Automotores Orletti," because it was run from an auto repair shop. They gathered there the foreigners they had kidnapped from countries near Argentina (Chileans, Uruguayans, Paraguayans), and they sent them back to their respective dictatorships. In other words, Operation Condor worked on a continental scale. Who directed it? The United States. One of its main heads was Henry Kissinger. That is a well-known fact.

So where did Operation Condor come from? The National Security Doctrine, that is how they called it, which was nothing other than a counterinsurgency doctrine, imported from the French torturers in

Algeria. The United States applied it in Vietnam.... The practice used by the United States in Vietnam, for instance, of throwing prisoners alive from airplanes, which was part of the Phoenix Program, well, that same practice was used in Argentina. They threw the revolutionaries captured by the military and the navy from airplanes into the Río de la Plata. And they also combined it with the same form of massive torture that was used in Algerian torture camps, including the systematic rape of men and women, during the French occupation.

So those were the two doctrines, French and North American, which were taught in the counterinsurgency schools in Panama (run by the U.S. military's SOUTHCOM), and in the war school in Rio de Janeiro in Brazil, after the 1964 coup, and in Buenos Aires too.

What was Operation Condor trying to do in the broad sense? It was [imperialism's] reaction to three things. First, to the huge revolutionary insurgency, the huge "social rebellion" of the 1960s, which went from the Vietnamese Revolution to the Algerian Revolution and the Cuban Revolution. It also included the youth rebellions that took place in Mexico, Tokyo, Rome, Berlin, Berkeley, and Paris (which was the most famous one). In effect, Operation Condor was a response to the 1960s social rebellion. It was a response, as well, to the emergence of Third-World national liberation movements, because many countries, nations, and communities that had been French, English, Dutch, U.S., or Japanese colonies gained independence between the end of World War II and the late 1960s, or even the end of the 1970s, if we consider the case of Angola.

So the counterinsurgency doctrine that expressed itself in Operation Condor (but not only in it) was an organized response. First, it was a reaction to the "social rebellion" of the 1960s and the global emergence of Third World national liberation movements. Second, it was a response to the declining profit rate, which was felt especially sharply with the oil crisis, or "petrodollar crisis," of 1973 and 1974. That economic crisis was itself the outcome of the rebelliousness in the workforce. In effect, counterinsurgency tries to curb the consequences of the falling profit rate. Third, there was the overall aim of disciplining the workforce, imposing mechanisms of super-exploitation on Third World workers, and finishing off with the welfare state (the so-called "golden age of capitalism" that had lasted little more than thirty years in Western Europe: from the end of World War II through the crisis of the early 1970s). The aim was to be able to make a capitalism-in-crisis function again.

In sum, Operation Condor was imperialism's political reaction to these three issues. . . . It was a project that produced a strong social response and a lot of conflict. In other words, imperialism did not have an easy time implementing it.

Are we seeing the same thing today then? Is there an Operation Condor of the twenty-first century?

Today, the counterinsurgency project continues. There is some continuity and some discontinuity. I believe that we are seeing a new attempt to apply the [old] counterinsurgency doctrine in different conditions. Why does this happen? Because rebellions reemerged, as responses to neoliberalism, which was applied at the end of the 1970s. The rebellions emerged after twenty or so years of neoliberalism.

First, there was the Zapatista rebellion in 1994. Then came Hugo Chávez's emergence in Venezuela. There was also the ongoing political-military insurgency in Colombia and the survival of non-capitalist relations in Cuba. That wave of rebelliousness against neoliberalism extended to the World Social Forums in the early twenty-first century. And it got more radical when Chávez declared the Bolivarian Revolution to be socialist. . . . To the Zapatista's question, "Is there a world where all other worlds fit?," the World Social Forum responded: "Another world is possible." Then Chávez raised the stakes. He said that that other possible world must be a socialist one. And he added, it's "Twenty-First Century Socialism."

So what is "Twenty-First Century Socialism"? The question was an open one. In my opinion, it is a weakness of the progressive movements to not have defined Twenty-First Century Socialism, to have stopped short. However, I think we should be cautious in our answers, because from my point of view there are no preestablished models about to how to make the transition from capitalism to socialism, of how to initiate the transition to socialism. There are no models.

Many paths were proposed to Chávez. Some people suggested that using self-managed industries was the right path, as was done in Yugoslavia. Others proposed to follow the path of market socialism, as Deng Xiaoping had done in China. Still others, including me, suggested working with Che Guevara's project and his Budgetary Finance System. In other words, a transition to socialism based on Popular Power, on participative democracy, but also with a centralized economy. Venezuela has an apparatus that offers certain advantages when it comes to applying this system. Its situation is more favorable than Cuba's, where the economy was based only on sugar.

Venezuela has nothing less than [state oil company] PDVSA, which could, with its oil resources, coordinate a series of activities, not only those relating to the oil profits but of collective, centralized socialist production, with a centralized banking system and a nationalized [network of] large enterprises. But that had to be done not only in one isolated country, Venezuela. The proposal was that from ALBA, the Budgetary Finance System could be put in practice on a continental scale. If not in all of the countries, at least in a great many of them.

Hence I believe that President Chávez and Bolivarian Venezuela only went halfway, not because they were lukewarm or didn't understand Marxism, but that there was a shallow reading of it. They did so because there was, and there continues to be, an open debate. The debate is about the transition to socialism. It is not a new discussion. There have been at least three stages.

The first stage took place in the 1920s in Bolshevik Russia, where not everybody was in agreement as to how to move forward. On the one hand, Nikolai Bukharin proposed market socialism. On the other side was Yevgeni Preobrazhensky, who proposed an economy with centralized planning. Meanwhile, V. I. Lenin tried to find a political solution, reconciling the two.

That very rich debate [about the transition to socialism] from the 1920s reemerged in the decade of the 1960s in Cuba, where Charles Bettleheim proposed market socialism together with Carlos Rafael

Rodríguez, who had a somewhat more pro-Soviet attitude. On the other hand, Che Guevara, supported by Ernest Mandel, proposed the Budgetary Finance System. As Lenin had done before, Fidel opted for a political solution that tries to maintain the alliance between the two tendencies as Lenin had done in the Bolshevik Russia of the 1920s.... He tried to keep the pro-market current and the central planning current both within the revolution's sweep.

The third phase of this debate is the one that exists now. It's the one that has been going on in Venezuela and I think in the Bolivian process too. It's a debate that is going to happen in any Third World or peripheral country that wants to leave capitalism behind. It is an open debate. It's not a failing or a problem that the debate is there. The progressive governments in Latin America—in the Venezuelan case it's a government that stands out for its socialist intentions—have raised this debate. It is still an open one and has not been resolved.

Following up on that, let's look critically at our movements and political process in Latin America, which are all in crisis now. Would it be fair to say that these progressive movements are in trouble because of their failure to connect with the Latin American revolutionary tradition and with the practices that derive from Marxist theory?

Are you asking whether Marxism guarantees that we will have successes and triumphs? Is that what we are talking about? I believe that Marxism is a political identity, a conception of the world and of life. It is a multilinear and materialist conception of history, a philosophy of praxis, and a dialectical method, but in itself it does not assure [that we are on a] revolutionary path.

Marxism is a tremendous tool that allows us to understand how capitalism works as well as the elements that bring it into crisis. It allows us to understand the mechanisms of exploitation, domination, dependency, and imperialism. Yet merely appealing to Marxist texts does not guarantee a revolutionary outcome.

As an Argentinian, I know a tremendous number of Marxist intellectuals who can quote from classical Marxist works, but in practice they have reformist positions! And as far as Venezuela is concerned, they have very ambiguous positions! Some don't know if they should support the Bolivarian Process. Or they don't want to admit it because they are embarrassed by their own positions, but they support the imperialist offensive using quotes taken with tweezers from Marx's texts. They don't define themselves clearly against imperialism, and yet they employ apparently Marxist rhetoric. For that reason, appealing to Marxist texts is not sufficient to confirm that you're going in a revolutionary direction.

I believe that revolutionary Marxism must be accompanied by a firm revolutionary project and not just a reading of the texts. In that sense, I believe that Bolivarianism is an emancipatory continental project that could [fill that role]. That is what Chávez tried, and it is what the Colombian insurgency tried to do (along with a lot of other people in the continent). I believe that the synthesis of Marxism and Bolivarianism is the best assurance that we can have a leftist solution to the crisis, one that questions capitalism. In other words, confront imperialism and not make any concessions. And that is not going to be achieved only by quoting the classical works of Marxism.

It is necessary to study Marxism, but it's not enough. Marxism is needed because it makes things clear. It is necessary because it is a theoretical and scientific tool and critical method, but it must go hand in hand with clear political positions. Again, in Argentina there are political currents that quote Marxist texts, but when imperialism attacked Syria and Libya, and now Venezuela, they have very ambiguous positions. They declare Nicolás Maduro to be a tyrant. They declare Muammar Gaddafi to be a tyrant—whom they lynched! They say Saddam Hussein was a tyrant! In other words, in the name of Marxism they end up being the shock troops of imperialism. So studying Marxism is necessary, but it has to go hand in hand with revolutionary positions.

Recently, you wrote that the Left today has no "Kremlin" and no "Vatican." Still, some people now consider Russia and China to be models, or they look to those emerging powers for help. What kind

of support can such countries provide to a socialist project, and what is it that we shouldn't expect from them?

I believe there are no models. That is why I used the expression "we are without a Vatican." It could also be expressed by saying that we don't have a Mecca or we are without a great synagogue. In other words, we [on the left] are without a world reference point. That leaves us, to a certain extent, orphaned from a theoretical and political standpoint. But it also has an advantage, because there is no need to subordinate ourselves to anybody. We don't have to follow a strategy that has been cooked up and digested in another country. We have to elaborate our own revolutionary strategy.

In that sense, when you ask about the role of Russia and China, I would say that here we can appeal to the teachings of Marxism. Antonio Gramsci arrived at an important conclusion when FIAT workers struggled alone against their bosses. They lost their battle against capital. Gramsci expressed this conclusion both in the *Prison Notebooks* and even before he was imprisoned. He concluded: alliances are necessary, because if the revolutionary class struggles alone, it will lose.

When Gramsci dealt with the question of hegemony—the ideological, political, and cultural project that has to do with building alliances—he was systematizing Lenin's concept of "social force." Both Gramsci and Lenin were conscious of the need to build a revolutionary social force. We cannot depend on an individual. It's not a question of President Maduro being either the new world leader or an incompetent person who cannot make the revolution go forward. That is a mistaken perspective. I think that if the Bolivarian Process triumphs with Maduro at its head, it's because it has a social force that accompanies him, drives him, and of which he is part. There is a long debate in Marxism about the role of the individual in history. The individual is very important, but one man alone cannot change history. Social forces must be built, and alliances must be established at a national and international level.

In this sense, there are two important historical examples to consider. In the 1960s, the Cuban Revolution confronted the United States, and this was done through two levels of alliances. On the one hand, there were alliances made with the USSR, with which there were many differences and polemics on a theoretical, political, and ideological level.

These contradictions went so far that the USSR even tried to organize a coup against Fidel Castro! It is public knowledge by now, and it came from what was known as the "micro-fraction," headed by a man named Anibal Escalante. It was an attempt to do a coup d'état from within the Cuban Revolution from the Soviet side.

There were also conflicts during the Missile Crisis, when Nikita Khrushchev decided unilaterally to withdraw the missiles from Cuba, leaving Cuba unprotected when faced with the United States' voraciousness. Despite those conflicts, Castro and Che Guevara fostered alliances with the USSR, and with the countries that were friends of the Soviet Union. On the other hand, the Cuban Revolution also established alliances with the countries of the Non-Aligned Movement.

This is a very important historical precedent because sometimes you don't have to share a hundred percent of the objectives with your allies. Yet if an alliance allows me to confront imperialism, then the alliance can be established. But an alliance should not be confused with the project itself. That is the key.

For the second historical example, we have to go back in time. It is the Latin American Independence Wars that took place at the beginning of the nineteenth century, headed up by Simón Bolívar in the continent's north and by General José de San Martin in its south. Both leaders established alliances. For instance, they made alliances with the British Empire, which was a monstrous empire, colonialist and genocidal, but it was opposed to the Spanish Empire, their main enemy.

None of the Latin American liberators—neither Bolívar nor San Martin, nor anyone else—believed that England would help out in a selfless or disinterested manner. It was a tactical alliance in the struggle against the Spanish Empire, which was the principal enemy. However, it was completely distinct from the project of emancipation and independence. So, as far as Bolívar and San Martin's projects of liberating indigenous people from serfdom and Black people from slavery, in fact none of these projects was subordinated to the alliance with the British Empire.

In other words, Bolívar and San Martin used international alliances at the beginning of the nineteenth century and the same thing happened during the Cuban Revolution in the 1960s.

Nowadays, should we make alliances with China and Russia to put the brakes on Western imperialism, which is out of control? I believe it is legitimate to do so, because these alliances may give us some breathing space. They may counteract U.S. military power, which is superior to that of the Nazi empire. In fact, the Nazi empire was weak when compared with the U.S. military today.

Dwight Eisenhower identified a "military-industrial complex," and Paul Sweezy, Paul Baran, Leo Huberman, Harry Magdoff, and other U.S. intellectuals analyzed what they called "military Keynesianism." The military-industrial complex, which needs permanent war to keep the economy going, is far more powerful than the Nazis were. To be able to confront it and stop our enemy's advances, it's valid to make alliances, not only with Russia and China, but also with countries of the Third World.

Does that mean that Russia and China should establish the political and ideological framework for our path forward? No, that shouldn't be the case, because they are capitalist countries. The truth is that they have no interest in socialism. In China, the red flag is an empty symbol. Today's China is not going toward socialism, and Russia ceased being socialist a long while back. In other words, a geopolitical strategic alliance shouldn't be confused with our taking on their project as our project, because their objective has nothing to do with Latin American socialism.

It's obvious that the United States wants to seize Venezuela's resources, but probably more important than that, it wants to bury Bolivarianism and eliminate everything it stood for. We are witnessing a kind of fascist mopping up operation aiming to

discipline the working class so that it won't rise up in the future. What do you think Chávez and Bolivarianism stands for today? What makes those legacies so important and so dangerous?

Why does the United States attack Venezuela? I agree with what you said in the question. Everybody speaks about oil, but we should recall that President Chávez and the Bolivarian Revolution mobilized the whole continent and put the objective of socialism back on the agenda of social movements, which weren't connected to the socialist project at that time. The Zapatistas never talked about socialism, and in all the World Social Forums nobody spoke about socialism either. They only criticized neoliberalism.

Chávez brought people back to speaking about socialism. And he didn't just say the word. He tried to make strategic alliances; he created new institutions; he gave life to MERCOSUR and the CELAC.[3] Really, Chávez was a political force, what classical Marxism calls a "vanguard." He headed up a process that has to be eliminated for that reason.

It was not for nothing that the Santa Fe Documents in the 1980s declared that Washington's strategic enemy was Gramsci—that is, liberation theology—and Bolívar. But if Bolívar was a historical figure who died in 1830, how could he be an enemy today? That's because Bolívar is the ideological source of both the Colombian insurgency and Chávez's Bolivarian Process.

Together, Venezuelan and the Colombian revolutionaries drew from Bolivarianism. Therefore both processes had to be finished off. They were obstacles for U.S. imperialism, with its project of installing military bases in the continent and reconquering its "backyard" in a time of world crisis.

Now the United States has managed to disarm the Colombian insurgency—letting that happen was a strategic and geopolitical error on the part of the popular forces—and they have managed to assassinate Chávez. (His assassination is something very probable, although nobody has the proof. It's very likely that they used the newest generation of biological weapons to put an end to Chávez's leadership.) So, in that way, I think that the United States hopes to regain control of their backyard and take Venezuela's oil resources, because it is one of the main oil producers worldwide.

But at the same time, they want to neutralize Chávez's example as a leader and Venezuela's vanguard role. It's a role that wasn't being played by Brazil, and couldn't be played by either Bolivia or Sandinismo.

What is fascism? It's a capitalist response that is not only confined to Venezuela, Colombia, or Brazil, but is rather a worldwide response. Faced with fascism, I think we need to reprise the offensive spirit in the international revolutionary camp, which includes not only Marxists and communists, but also all the national liberation movements and all the anti-colonial and anti-imperialist struggles on a worldwide scale.

I think that's what needs to be done. It's not only about defending Bolivarian Venezuela, but rather confronting fascism everywhere, including in Europe, Africa, and Asia. It's about confronting imperialism on a worldwide scale. I think we have to retake the offensive, leaving behind fear.

I am referring not only to the fear of physical death and invasion, but also the fear that operates in the ideological sphere. For example, the fear of using powerful concepts like colonialism, imperialism, exploitation, dependency, and super-exploitation. I think we need to overcome not only physical fear but ideological fear [which leads to] the ideological disarming and the "social-democratization" of Marxism.

How many Marxists speak of Marx but in practice act like social democrats? That's an obstacle to advancing and to being able to respond to fascism. I think that the postmodern void can be filled either with fascism or with revolutionary Marxism, and a revolution that moves toward socialism and communism. I think that the postmodern void has to be criticized, and one has to confront fascism by recovering the best of the revolutionary tradition.

— FEBRUARY 22, 2019

Economic Downturns and State Violence: A Conversation with Andrés Antillano

Andrés Antillano is a social psychologist and professor at the Universidad Central de Venezuela in Caracas, where he holds the Criminology Chair. He investigates violence and the conditions that favor it, examining these issues from a class perspective.

For years, the Bolivarian Revolution attempted to offer a new approach to police activity, working to develop a new model based on social justice. These policies, unfortunately, have been rolled back during the crisis. In this interview, Antillano, who is also a human rights activist, walks us through the historical relation between economic fluctuations, government policies, and police repression.

The hardline approach to crime has had a cyclical history in Venezuela. When the economy shrinks, reducing the average income, then police activity becomes more repressive. That's what happened toward the end of the Fourth Republic, when an undeclared "war against the poor" began. In recent years, police policy and practice in Venezuela has been turning once again toward the hardline approach. How do you understand this?

The hardline policies that you are pointing to and the discourse justifying repression have to be understood in terms of class struggle, not just as a response to crime. Disregarding the class factor would lead to mechanical and naive interpretations.

In Venezuela, it is easy to show how the increase in police repression and in the incarceration rate—the repression of the poor in general—goes hand in hand with periods of economic downturn due to squeezed oil profits. The thesis of Pierre Bourdieu about the left hand and the right hand of the state becomes a reality. That is, when the state loses the capacity to redistribute as a mechanism of containment and control of the poor, then it opts for the right hand, which brings in hardline policies: repression, containment, police violence, and vamping up the criminal justice system.

Venezuela is no exception to this pattern. We have seen how, in times of economic downturn, repression against the popular sectors increases as a mechanism with various functions. The first function is to contain, repress, and intimidate, using systematic terror on the popular classes, which are the ones who feel the crisis most sharply. The weight of the crisis falls on those in the barrio, and so the police send them a clear message to not rebel, quelling any possibility of disorder in the face of deteriorated living conditions.

Furthermore, these policies aim to please middle-class sectors who consider insecurity to be one of their main concerns. With "public order" and "security" as the stated goals, police repression becomes a means to acquire political legitimacy in the eyes of the middle class.

Finally, in Venezuela as elsewhere, these repressive policies are connected to economic control and distribution in grey markets. During a crisis, repression goes hand in hand with the regulation, reorganization, and access to illegal markets, where practices of extortion are closely tied to the police. Thus, when diverse groups struggle to take charge of illicit distribution networks, police violence usually takes sides with some particular interest.

All this occurs, I contend, cyclically in Venezuela, and we can see it taking place in recent years.

In this regard, we can distinguish two periods in recent history. When Chávez came to power, it ended a period of growing prison population in Venezuela. The prison population had gone up in the 1980s, a decade of economic downturn and reduced oil profits (in effect, it represented the downswing of the oil profit cycle). Prison population rose in a sustained curve during the 1980s, hand in hand with an increase in police repression. I insist that both mechanisms, police repression and incarceration, coincide with this idea of controlling, intimidating, and disciplining the population that is excluded as a result of the economic downturn and structural adjustments.

With Chávez this repressive cycle stopped, and with it the tendency to increase prison population. The incarceration rate fell. Also, under Chávez, repressive policies toward the poor were explicitly rejected, both in the discourse and in reality. It was understood that these policies were functional to the neoliberal program that former governments had maintained.

Through most of Chávez's presidency, prison population remained more or less stable and police violence declined. With Chávez, there were no police operations of the kind used in the 1980s such as "Plan Unión" ("Union Plan"), which were sometimes referred to as "social prophylaxis" (a term that reveals their ideological and political nature). Arrests without warrant, so common before the Bolivarian Revolution, went away, and the number of deaths at the hands of the police dropped too, while torture episodes and repression of protests fell significantly.

Contrary to what is said by the international centers of power, Chavismo was not only the most democratic project in its moment, but it also made human rights key to its program.

This is interesting because on the left we have always had suspicions about human rights since they are framed as liberal achievements associated with the bourgeois revolution. I think this has to do with the historical context and conditions in which Marxist-Leninist thought took shape, in countries where there was little tradition of human rights and individual liberties such as Russia and later in Third World countries. For example, the position that V. I. Lenin had about this question is very different from that of Rosa Luxemburg, for whom the idea of democratic liberties and rights is central.

The Left, or a part of it, has seen human rights as an instrumental question, but it seems to me that Chavismo put it in the center of the debate with the claim that it is not possible to reach equality and social emancipation without respecting rights, because respect for rights is all about respecting the rights of the poor.

Infringing human rights is, in fact, usually the violation of the rights of the most vulnerable, of the poor. That is what is happening here. Police never infringe the rights of the bourgeoisie. The bourgeoisie is always able to defend its rights, whereas the rights of the poorest are easily cut back. So Chavismo put human rights and democratic liberties in the center of its political project and that, in turn, leads to repressive policies going into abeyance.

However, we began to witness a shift around 2010. First came the "Madrugonazo al hampa" ["Wake-up call to the criminal underworld"], with aggressive police repression very similar to that employed in the Fourth Republic. Along with it were massive detentions of poor youth from the barrios, and a rapid growth in prison population.

This led to filling up of prisons. The prison population went up from about 20,000—the lowest in the continent—to more than 50,000 in a few years. It more than doubled! By 2014, coinciding with the decline of oil profits, this tendency became firmly established, with a turn that didn't just involve massive imprisonment but also systematic killings of young people from the barrios, first at the hands of the OLP [Operation for the Liberation of the People] and now with the FAES [Special Action Forces].

From my point of view, all this has to do with the logic that I mentioned at the beginning: the dynamic of containing and disciplining those sectors that are the first to suffer the severe effects of the economic crisis, [and] a form of governmental legitimation for [middle-class] sectors that call out for security. So, the state's legitimacy ceases to depend on its policies of redistributing wealth or its social reforms, but rather on guaranteeing security—what's more, carried out in a questionable way. Additionally, we should mention that there is a sector of capital that is attracted by, and directly benefits from, these hardline policies.

To understand the situation now, it might be useful to describe the general political context in Venezuela, especially with regard to the Chavista project and how that project has survived or been transformed during the crisis.

Sure, the hardline repressive policies that we have been discussing are part of a larger shift and new rhetoric against the poor that has unfurled over the past few years. The human rights issue has to be understood in this context.

In effect, we have witnessed a drift away from the centrality of the poor, the poor as the historical subject, which was at the core of the Chavista project. Now, in various spheres we can observe how the poor are no longer considered to be the historical subject. There has been a process through which at first the poor became simply an object and then they became a problem or even an enemy.

So this marks a shift away from the original revolutionary discourse in which the *pueblo* (people) was the subject, to a discourse where the *pueblo* is a beneficiary object or a kind of receptacle. All this indicates a radical discursive shift. The *pueblo* is no longer the historical subject, the subject of the Revolution, nor the agent of transformation. Now the *pueblo* is understood to be a helpless object that needs tutelage. It has to be reprehended, led, protected, and, above all, domesticated. This is a discourse that has emerged in many arenas, and in the most diverse spheres of government.

The next step is to make the *pueblo* into an enemy. This expresses itself in diverse forms. For example, when the Right won the 2015 [parliamentary] elections, the problem was the people "who lacked political awareness" or "the ignorant people who voted for hunger," etc. It was a missed opportunity to do a very serious self-critique about the nature of the policies that the government had been implementing. The political leadership chose to turn the *pueblo* into the victimizer rather than engaging in the critical reflections that could lead to making the necessary corrections.

Another example has to do with the "economic war" discourse. The economic war transforms the historical discourse of Chavismo. Now it is no longer big capital that is responsible for the economic situation, or corruption, or mistaken economic policies. Instead, it's the people, the poor, the *bachaqueros* [people who resell goods purchased at state-subsidized prices]. Who is to blame? Who is responsible for the tragic economic situation? The *bachaqueros*. They are the problem, they are the ones who make merchandise disappear from store shelves. They are the ones who are responsible for the price hikes. The problem is not the Mendozas [the family that owns Alimentos Polar, the largest food monopoly in Venezuela and the maker of the popular PAN corn flour brand], but the barrio woman who buys three packages of PAN flour, one for her family and two to resell for survival.

So we encounter a [new] discourse in which the *pueblo* is no longer the agent of transformation, it is not the subject of history. Instead, the *pueblo* is presented as an obstacle in history. This, of course, goes hand in hand with a process of growing disconnection between the Chavista direction and its social base.

Returning to the 2015 elections, the key to correctly interpreting them is not focusing on the defeat in itself, but rather how the defeat and the discourse that emerged as a response to it reveals a rupture between the class components that had defined Chavismo until then. There was an electoral defeat, and what's important is the degree to which it came from barrio sectors and rural areas—the strongholds of Chavismo.

The disconnect between the government and the people goes hand in hand with the idea that the *pueblo* is no longer the historical subject, but is rather an obstacle to the revolution.

So there was a change in the discourse and a significant rise in repressive policies dictated from above. This goes along with the diluting of another element that is central to Chavismo: democracy and participation. Democratic participation has shrunken, going from electoral processes [where Chavismo primaries have vanished] to the exercise of local participation. We see participative democracy being weakened by top-down mechanisms: "transmission belts" that the government uses to deliver orders and organize clientelistic policies. These break down the mechanisms that allow for a real exercise of power by the people.

We have seen how first communes and then even communal councils vanish from the official discourse. Now the only organizational expression legitimated by the official discourse is the CLAP [Local Supply and Production Committees, responsible for distributing subsidized food], which is not a mechanism of participation. Without passing any judgment on the CLAP, it is no more than a mechanism for distributing food, a clientelist, assistential mechanism. It is not Popular Power in action.

Thus, I think that we could put these repressive policies in a broader context of policies and discourses that seem to indicate a shifting of the government and of certain sectors of Chavismo away from the class coordinates that had been key to the Bolivarian Revolution.

Returning to the issue of repressive policies, you have argued that not only are they ethically unacceptable, they are also incapable of controlling crime. In recent years, the actions of special forces units have led to thousands of extrajudicial deaths, but this hasn't reduced crime.

These policies are not only inefficient, but they are also actually counterproductive. First, they don't achieve their declared goals. In other words, these policies do not reduce crime. Let's look at two strategies that have been used in the last ten years: massive incarceration and massive destruction based on the execution of poor people.

The policies of mass incarceration, which began with the "Madrugonazo al hampa" in 2010, meant that the prison population more than doubled. As a consequence, prisons became insidious mechanisms for reproducing criminal activity that, until then, had been disorganized delinquency. Prisons, in effect, worked to organize the existing but decentralized criminal activity.

By the way, the social basis of *barrio* crime should be addressed here. The Revolution was based, to a great degree, on creating redistributive mechanisms. It so happens that these mechanisms didn't reach all sectors of society. *Barrio* youth didn't participate in communal councils or in social missions, so they didn't benefit from the process.

This produced a gap between, on the one hand, the generations that had experienced the last years of neoliberalism and were able to improve their living conditions during the years of the Bolivarian Revolution and, on the other hand, the youths who weren't directly incorporated.

The gap between these sectors is often not only intraclass, but also sometimes intrafamily. It's the gap between the father, a worker whose living conditions decayed during the last years of neoliberalism, but whose situation improved with the Revolution, and the son who has no way of finding a half-decent job. These intraclass gaps, which are often invisible to traditional statistics, have to be taken into account to understand why crime persisted during all the years of the Revolution.

That's the social base for the phenomenon. Then, we have to consider the effects of the mass incarceration policies that began at the end of the last decade and how they ended up priming these groups that had been left behind by inclusion policies that didn't reach them. Much of this disenfranchised youth were involved in a disorganized or unstructured small-time crime, and the policies of mass incarceration bring all these precarious subjects together, fostering a reorganization of crime.

Thus, prisons become crime factories, as has happened before. In other words, when the Venezuelan penitentiary system went from twenty thousand to more than fifty thousand prisoners in less than three years, that generated favorable social conditions for the emergence of criminal structures inside the prisons that are later exported to the world outside.

Around 2012 and 2013, criminal groups began to have a much larger, structured capacity to carry out crime. They did it in a more organized, efficient manner. At that time, kidnappings for ransom began to increase. Criminality went up, and it was no surprise.

The state's response—at a time when the economic conditions were clearly deteriorating and the generational gap was rapidly widening—was to begin policies of systematic extrajudicial killings, first expressed in the OLP campaigns and now with the FAES.

From mid-2015 through the end of 2018 more than fifteen thousand people died at the hands of the police. That is really a scandalous number, particularly when one puts faces to these numbers. We are talking about young men from the popular sectors, the sons of the women who organize the CLAP or the Communal Councils in the *barrios*. These were the folks who were not yet included in the Revolution's initiatives—instead, they were killed by "iron-fist" policies.

A side effect of these policies is that they began to give rise to new practices of territorial control by organized crime, which begins as an attempt to defend themselves from police incursions. To do so, they increase their firing capacity for the sake of defense, which they do very efficiently, paradoxically, by purchasing weapons from the police. This, in turn, leads to an increased capacity for extortion, etc.

Briefly put, the string of repressive policies has generated an efficient reorganization and an escalation in the criminal capacity of these groups.

In the face of this dire situation, what do you think should be done?

I don't like proposing formulas. I think it would be very irresponsible to prescribe magical solutions.

The current policies, no doubt, go against the original ideals of Chavismo. This Revolution's program focused on inclusion and the recognition of the poor as the subject. These policies are maintained in part because some sectors of the population approve of them. When the OLP was launched, it was supported by large sectors of the population. In terms of electoral cachet, the beginning of the OLP was quite useful. At that time, everyone except the communities where the OLP did its work supported the initiative. Those views, of course, shifted later.

By the way, the OLP began in mid-2015. In terms of political cachet, we can see clearly then that in those communities where the OLP intervened—in poor *barrio* sectors where, as I said before, Chavismo had always won—there was a tremendous electoral defeat. That is the case of the polling centers in Cota 905 [a Caracas *barrio*], where Chavismo had always won, but beginning in 2015, people decided not to vote for Chavismo.

What's the solution? I have the uncomfortable role of revealing what is going on, but society must define its strategies. The solution to this problem has to come through a democratic debate among the *pueblo*.

— JANUARY 22, 2019

Solidarity Isn't a Slogan, It's a Process: A Conversation with Vijay Prashad

Vijay Prashad is an Indian historian, journalist, and Marxist intellectual. Among numerous books and articles, Prashad's The Darker Nations *stands out for its thorough account of Third World organizational efforts during the 20th century. Today, he is the chief editor of LeftWord books and heads up the Tricontinental: Institute for Social Research. In March 2019, Prashad was in Caracas for the International Peoples' Assembly and found time to respond to some of our questions about the history of internationalism and how to do solidarity with Venezuela and other countries under imperialist siege.*

There is a long history of international solidarity, but as far as South-South solidarity goes, one important landmark is the Non-Aligned Movement—starting with the Bandung Conference in 1955 and then its first summit in Belgrade in 1961—which brought together governments from what we now would call the Global South. Could we talk about what that legacy stands for today?

There are two reasons why we should understand this. It's important to see that when Karl Marx and Frederick Engels wrote the *Communist Manifesto* in 1848, they wrote, "Workers of the world, unite!" But in 1848, the workers of the world couldn't communicate with each other. In fact, the first telegraph between India and Britain only came in 1870. So it would be a bit silly to look back and say that the First International of workers set up in London, or even the Second International, were really internationals. After all, in the colonized parts of the world, workers movements really didn't get going until the second half of the 19th century and later.

So it's really important that in telling the story of internationalism in the South we become not too enthusiastic about small connections in the "ancient time." By the "ancient time," I mean the 18th and 19th centuries. All that would be quite silly, because the real connection begins in the period right after the Russian Revolution. Strikingly, the Russian Revolution, the USSR, took a decision that was quite out of time. In 1919, a hundred years ago in March, [it] invited people from across the world to create the Communist International. The Communist International was made up not only of European trade unionists, radicals, and so on, but also people from as far away as Argentina and Puerto Rico. Initially, it involved mostly the Western Hemisphere, and the various parts of the former Russian empire that had been colonized. . . . Turkmenistan and such.

Then in 1920 [in the Second World Congress of the Comintern] many more people came from around the world (and you know, the real heir to this movement was the Tricontinental Conference that was held in Havana, Cuba, in 1966).

In 1928, the bourgeois anti-colonialists met in Brussels in the League Against Imperialism meeting. I'm saying all this to point to the fact that the history of international struggles—of solidarity with and among people who had been colonized—is only about a hundred years old. A hundred years in the large scheme of things is not a long time. For that reason, I don't think we are ready to be judged regarding the utility and value of anticolonial solidarity across boundaries.

It is of course important to say that, in the 1950s, when new states emerging out of colonialism like India, Egypt, Ghana, and Indonesia created the Non-Aligned Movement—with its first summit in Belgrade in 1961—that was a different kind of process, because it involved countries: it was an intergovernmental movement. They had now taken state power, and they were trying to change the routines and institutions of the world order. It was a much different scale of discussion. They had an incredible vision for an alternative—it was called the New International Economic Order, which was passed by the UN General Assembly in 1974.

Imperialism and especially U.S. imperialism consistently tries to undo these South-South alliances. We have seen how U.S. imperialism operates in Latin America and its attitude toward Venezuela, which is particularly aggressive now. Can you tell us something about how imperialism works in the broad sense and then move into the particulars of the Venezuelan situation?

Imperialism is not a static phenomenon. What we had in the 19th century and into the early 20th century is different from what we have now. At that time, production was mostly inside nations. You had the Ford Motor Company located in the United States in competition with Daimler located in Germany, and most Daimler cars were built in Germany, while most Ford cars were built in the United States. They were competing for resources in third or fourth or fifth countries and for markets and finance, etc. That was a form of intercapitalist rivalry, and it pushed countries to use their political, military, and economic power to get an advantage over other countries. That was the classic form of imperialism in the old days.

From the 1960s onwards, the old factory form began to dissolve. You saw factories being disarticulated and the emergence of the so-called "global commodity chains." General Motors began to produce most cars outside of the United States. German cars were as often finished in Germany as in the United States. . . . The whole structure of world production changed.

This had an impact on imperialism, because from the late 1960s onwards [there emerged] a much closer alliance between what we call the Triad: the United States, Western Europe, and Japan. The Triad didn't come together with equanimity—they didn't agree on everything—but there was a certain understanding that the United States was the first among equals; that new trade regimes had to be created and enforced; and that Third World [projects] such as the New International Economic Order had to be destroyed.

It was in this realm that imperialism has sharpened its teeth. Now aerial bombardment was not necessary. It all came in the writing of trade laws, [in determining] how finance should operate and money should move. An entire infrastructure was created almost behind the scenes by a group of seven countries, using the General Agreement on Trade and Tariffs [which spawned the World Trade Organization in 1995]. In the 1980s, they imposed new regulations on property rights.

All this narrowed the ability of Third World countries to develop, to be able to trade with each other, and exercise their right to finance. A new set of "institutional asphyxiations" was created by imperialism. It was very smart, because now you didn't have to show your gun. It was there, but it was hidden, because you now exercised power by saying, "Sorry, we are not going to finance you," particularly after the debt crisis in the early 1980s.

Countries like Venezuela are so vulnerable. . . In 1974, when Venezuela "nationalized" its oil resource, it actually didn't do it. What actually happened is that the companies told the government: "You nationalize the oil, because we don't want to deal with it anymore. We don't want to invest in your country or take the risk. You invest and take the risk. We just want the profits." That is the new structure of imperialism.

That brings us to the present. Right now, it seems like there is an intense effort to strangle Venezuela's economy and topple the government (to say nothing of killing off the socialist project). I would like your perspective on both the risk of direct military intervention in Venezuela and on other less visible forms of violence, like economic sanctions.

When the Soviet Union collapsed, the United States actually began to feel that there was going to now be another century of complete domination [that it would lead] on behalf of the Triad. Actually, the United States is quite generous to its Triad partners: it's not as if it wanted everything for itself. It wanted growth of the corporations, because that was seen as benefiting the United States and its allies. They thought that what was coming was a hundred years (who knows even a thousand years!) of capitalism dominated by the United States and its allies.

But [instead of that simple capitalist success story] there was enormous demoralization after the collapse of the USSR. . . . There was a huge demoralization, because so many of the countries that had previously experimented with socialism and had transitioned, now began to collapse one after the other into debt, disorder, and so on. So the United States began to talk about a few countries that it called "rogue states" which needed to be taken out. Then after that would begin the thousand-year rule! They identified Iran and North Korea, among others (you know, any country that seemed odd and wasn't allowing the commercial order determined by the World Trade Organization to manage things).

Of course, what began to be evident is that there were contradictions. These contradictions are uncomfortable—they are in bad taste!—such as the Iraqis saying, "Look, we fought the war on your behalf against the Iranians, and now we want payment for the destruction of our country." Then they invaded Kuwait, and that bothered the Triad, so it went into Iraq. [Another example is] Yugoslavia, where you see that, as the cement of socialism began to break down, very toxic forms of nationalism began to appear. Then Yugoslavia was bombed into destruction.

The wars continued, bewildering wars. They were in principle wars to finish off the remnant countries—not socialist countries by any stretch of the imagination, but countries that were resisting the will of the Triad led by the United States. It is wrong to idealize these countries just because they were being bombed by the United States. Some of them had very dystopic internal relations (even if they were being attacked for other reasons). It was a surprise, but we understood that the war was a way of saying: "Let's get rid of the walls around Yugoslavia, and let's open it up to the IMF and the World Trade Organization. Let's get those markets and those workers."

The United States got embroiled in the wars on Iraq and Afghanistan in the early 2000s. It took its gaze away from South America. It lost sight of the plot and didn't see what was happening. In one country after another, diverse social movements, indigenous peoples, and popular masses turned to elections. And in one country after another, they elected left-wing people!

Honestly, if the United States hadn't been so involved in Iraq and

Afghanistan, it might not have allowed this to go all the way. After all, it does have this idea—which has come up again recently—that South America is its backyard. But by the time it turned its gaze back here in 2002 and tried the coup in Venezuela, it was already too late. Although there were differences between the Workers Party [PT] in Brazil and the experiment in Venezuela (such as working at different paces), nonetheless they were on the same page.

In Venezuela, Chávez [realized] that you cannot build a new project inside a country: it has to be regional, and you need new trade policies. Venezuela understood how imperialism was working: it was the imperialism of finance and trade, and so it attempted the ALBA project involving regional governments and states.

The United States attempted to break that project many times. Look, Venezuela doesn't have the kind of oil that the United States needs and desires. It is not coming for the oil resources! It is coming for this project, and it has done a very good job. Honestly, the most impressive coup d'état that it did in this period of social media was the [2009] coup in Honduras. There was also, earlier, the coup d'état in Haiti, where it just absented Aristide twice, and in the rest of the continent it pushed [the leftist wave] back little by little.

But it wasn't just U.S. imperialism, and not being aware of that is one of our weaknesses. It was also that new social forces came in that the Left was not fully cognizant of. For example, Pentecostalism and various [other] forms of aspirational desire from below. Things were being reshaped and people were moving in directions that were outside of the ideology of the new Pink Tide and the Bolivarian Project.

I think there are two big dynamics that have weakened this project. It isn't just imperialism. There are these internal developments that were contrary to the dynamic of a strong Left, and, of course, you have the collapse of commodity prices. But what I want to highlight here is that it wasn't the collapse of commodity prices alone that create this problem.

There are a couple of other things that I would like to say on this subject. One is that socialism takes time in a poor country, and this is a poor country. It has never been a rich country. It is a poor country with a lot of oil, just like Nigeria. It's rich in resources, but very poor in terms of the distribution of wealth and aspirations and hope and so on. Socialism takes a long time, and basically ten years is not enough.

Thomas Sankara used to say, "He who feeds you, controls you." But this country imported most of its food. There was no freedom yet. It was going to take thirty, forty, fifty years to get there. Capitalism took hundreds of years to develop. Socialism is always attacked within two, three, four, or five years, and not just by the capitalists, but also by people on the left who get impatient and angry, because it doesn't meet their own dreams and utopias. It's a very ugly process, because you are desperately trying to create new forms, and in the meantime you must be sure that people are not hungry.

That is the first point. The other one is a political question: the United States was very craftily able to set legal boundaries around countries, where they said, "Well, we are going to sanction you because you did this wrong." Obama's decree in 2015 opened the door, and then from that door they add another sanction and another, and more and more. And since they control money, its movement, and how you are going to buy and sell your own goods, then you are really caught in a vise, and nobody is going to come to liberate you.

If tomorrow this government falls and a U.S.-backed government comes in, what will the Chinese and the Russians say? Pay us back in cash. The truth is that Venezuela is not in good shape, whether the Bolivarian government remains or a U.S. puppet government comes in. The Americans will not have the money to pay back the Chinese and Russians. That is just not going to happen! If the [newly installed] government were to say that we need to renegotiate our loans, that is a bad precedent, so Americans don't want that. You've got to face up to the fact that there are some serious economic challenges, and it's very tragic that the oligarchy and others don't see that. They are being reckless with their own country. I think they will pay a huge historical price for that recklessness.

Finally, I would like to ask you about international solidarity these days? How should it be done, especially in relation to Venezuela?

Solidarity with the Bolivarian Process has to begin by demanding the end to all interference. Now interference is a complicated word under the new imperialism. It means no military intervention, that is one point. But does it mean that there should be no embargo? Yes, that is another point. No economic sanctions? That is another point. Also, finances should not be blocked, and Venezuela's own money should be available to it. Of course, all that is important.

But I'm saying there is more than that: solidarity must help countries have food security, total independence in relation to food. You know, Cuba needs solidarity to help it produce grains, and it doesn't produce enough potatoes either, nor does it produce anywhere near what it consumes in terms of wheat or rice. These problems are solved through human connections. We have to really work together to provide food security. Hunger is a weapon often used by imperialists. They make you hungry, and then they tell you, "Take the aid." It's very crafty, so this is the thing that has to be overcome.

This is not news to anybody. Chávez spoke about the problem of food all through his political career. It was very important for him to think about how to feed the country. Like, is it possible to feed this country with domestic grains? Also the problem of feeding animals. He talked about this stuff all the time. Fidel Castro, toward the end of his life, had this dream of creating organic food for animal feed that is produced now in Venezuela. These kinds of options must come to be. In that sense, solidarity should not be thought of as a slogan; solidarity is a process. You have got to build solidarity by providing interesting new thinking about how to solve problems of hunger and how to organize society.

— MARCH 16, 2019

Notes to Section 5

1. The International Assembly of the Peoples was held in Caracas from February 24–27, 2019, and it brought together over 400 activists, politicians, academics, journalists and other personalities from across the globe in the defense of Venezuela's sovereignty and self-determination.
2. *Bachaqueo* refers to the widespread practice of acquiring subsidized products (i.e. cornmeal, toilet paper, etc.) and reselling them at higher prices.
3. CELAC (Community of Latin American and Caribbean States) is an organization that promotes the integration and development of Latin American and Caribbean countries. It was founded in Caracas, Venezuela, in December 2011, and it is composed of every country in the Americas with the exception of the United States and Canada.
4. Mercosur is a South American trade bloc established in Asunción, Paraguay, in 1991. Its full members are Argentina, Brazil, Paraguay, and Uruguay. Venezuela is a full member but has been suspended since December 1, 2016. Associate countries are Bolivia, Chile, Colombia, Ecuador, Guyana, Peru, and Suriname.

6

FEMINISM, GENDER, AND RACE

Women and the Crisis in Venezuela: A Conversation with Gioconda Mota

In early November 2018, just weeks before this interview took place, a group of feminist researchers released a groundbreaking report on the situation of women's human rights in Venezuela titled Desde Nosotras *(From Us). This 250-page report—with hard data and thorough analysis—reveals the key challenges facing the political, economic, health, as well as sexual and reproductive rights of Venezuelan women today. This independent report comes out of the ranks of feminist Chavismo and aims to improve the gender politics of the Bolivarian government.*

We sat down with Gioconda Mota, who, with Alba Carosio, coordinated Desde Nosotras. *Gioconda is a longtime activist for women's rights and the rights of people with disabilities. She is general coordinator of Entrompe de Falopio and a founding member of the feminist network Red La Araña Feminista. Gioconda is also the director of Hay Alguien Allí, a foundation for the exchange of information regarding autism.*

Since the beginning of Venezuela's Bolivarian Process, some progressive reforms have entered the country's legal framework. For example, the 1999 Constitution guarantees women's economic rights, while a 2007 law affirms women's right to a life free of violence. Can you contextualize some of these advances for our international readership?

If there are important advances in the Bolivarian Process regarding women's rights, it is in improving the existing legal framework. On the one hand, the Constitution of the Bolivarian Republic of

Venezuela has a groundbreaking article, Article 88, which recognizes that housework generates value and wealth, and that "social security" should be granted to homemakers. Additionally there are laws and norms that address the right to having a life free from violence, particularly the 2007 law, which represented an advance at the time and still does, ten years later.

We can also point to some victories in the area of labor, such as the 2012 labor law, which guarantees maternity leave and breastfeeding rights. Nonetheless, there are some aspects of the legal framework where there haven't been any advances despite [grassroots] mobilization. That is important to mention because all the legal advances so far have gone hand in hand with organization and demands from the feminist movement. They have happened with a lot of pressure from below, with debate, and with mobilization and action.

So what are the pending issues that are still a priority in the legal realm? The issue of bodily autonomy, the right to legally interrupt pregnancy—that is an urgent struggle. There is a great deal to do in the realm of sexual and reproductive rights, which implies access to sex education throughout the whole schooling process, access to contraceptive methods, etc.

Also, in the political realm, issues of parity and alternation should be brought to the forefront. We are a country where there has been an extraordinary process of political awakening, and women have been the most active participants in it, but there haven't been positive measures put in place so that women can participate politically in equal conditions.

That happens through norms and laws. It doesn't happen spontaneously in a sexist, patriarchal society. There have been important oversights in this regard and even some steps backward. Up until 2007, there was a law establishing a minimum of 30 percent participation for women in representative posts. Venezuela's Supreme Court eliminated it on the basis of it being discriminatory. Then came a promise that a fifty-fifty parity law would be brought out in the National Assembly . . . but it didn't happen.

Finally, another important field for struggle is in the realm of

Feminism, Gender, and Race 319

dissident sexualities. The Venezuelan state does not recognize same-sex unions, nor does it recognize trans identities. There have been some steps regarding dissident sexualities, but they actually have been very timid, and they haven't been put into practice.

So, as you can see, there are many fronts of struggle remaining.

The report on women's rights that you produced points to the critical problem of gender violence. The document says that in 2016 (the last year in which the state published statistics) there were 97,858 formal accusations of gender violence. Of those, only 14,863 went to court and a mere 1,277 resulted in guilty verdicts.[1]

In Venezuela, politics on the state level fails to grasp the structural problem of gender violence. This is a deep cultural problem: violence against women has cultural and economic roots, and the battle against it should be multidimensional. As I indicated, there have been some legal advances regarding access to justice, but the results have been very limited. In part this is due to there having been practically no advances in the area of prevention, and prevention must go hand in hand with a cultural transformation.

That, of course, seems like a gigantic undertaking because it is the struggle to bring down patriarchy itself! However, that doesn't mean that specific steps can't be taken that would open up a path toward cultural transformations. For example, reforming school pensums and teacher formation, developing media campaigns, controlling media to eliminate sexist stereotypes, etc.

The spaces that reproduce and consolidate sexist and patriarchal culture in our society must be changed. We are convinced that, with a coordinated effort, we will be able to first reduce and eventually eliminate this societal scourge. But the truth is that, since the state hasn't made an analysis of the structural problem of sexist violence and domination, solving this problem isn't really on the government's agenda. That is why the advances are so slow.

As I mentioned before, the area where we have advanced most is in the legal framework. However, we should also take a close look at what's really happening in the judicial system: the legal framework is established and a new kind of institutional [framework] emerged with it—this includes a special prosecutor's office specialized in gender violence, public defense lawyers focused on the issue, gender offices to orient the police forces—but that hasn't changed the character of the administration of justice, which is sexist to the core. We find ourselves face to face with a situation where the main lawbreakers are those who operate the justice system. If we look at the situation case by case, we can quickly see that some 90 percent of the cases were dismissed and, as the numbers that you mentioned show, the rate of conviction is well under two percent. In fact, the degree of impunity is overwhelming.

The sad truth is that women go to the justice system expecting (and, of course, needing) a legal solution. There, however, they run into many obstacles (from reporting the aggression to investigating it and bringing it to trial). Along the way, they suffer a process of revictimization and institutional violence against women that crushes them once again.

Faced with this situation, what has the state done? The state has injected resources into the education of public officials, but this educational process has, for many reasons, not yielded the desired results. Since the problem hasn't been solved, a new set of strategies must be developed so that women don't find themselves in a labyrinth of revictimization whenever they seek justice or protection or both.

Now a proposal for reforming the 2007 law against gender violence is making the rounds. It's a proposal that comes eleven years after the [initial] law was passed, and with the years we have learned of its limitations and oversights. This reform proposal, which comes from the feminist base, calls for real punitive measures to be taken against the public officials who don't abide by the law in investigations and procedures associated with gender violence. Nowadays, if an official ignores a blatant case of gender violence—a femicide, for example—nothing happens! So the reform proposes to punish those who disregard or discard complaints.

Gender violence is one of the most serious human rights problems in Venezuela today. We are talking about some 120 reported femicides in 2016. If you compare that with other Latin American countries, the numbers may be considered relatively low, but we have to take into account that there isn't a monitoring institution (nor a coordinated effort) to track cases of violence against women. So we know that this number underrepresents the problem.

Further, when we talk about femicides, we should also take into account maternal mortality rates, which we [the feminist movement] consider indirect femicides. We are talking about 756 maternal deaths in 2016.[2] So, again, attention to women's human rights continues to be one of the most urgent issues that our society should address.

Together with Paraguay, Venezuela has the most backward legislation regarding abortion in the whole continent. Although the struggle to make abortion legal here precedes the Bolivarian Process, the Chavista feminist movement has staged important mobilizations during the past year or so, demanding that women gain control of their bodies.

The decriminalization of abortion is a historical struggle and a global one. The feminist movement in Venezuela was demanding the right to voluntarily interrupt a pregnancy long before the Chavista era (all taking place within the framework of the right to bodily autonomy and the right to decide about our bodies).

After all, we should decide how many children we want to have and when. But there has been very little willingness to pay attention to this issue from above. Year after year, we make our demands for the decriminalization of abortion. We organize street actions and we present technical reports such as CEDAW. In truth, the feminist movement has made all sorts of demands and proposals.

In Venezuela, the only case in which abortion is legal is when there is a very high risk to the life of the mother: that is the one and only justification! This year, feminist Chavistas—the autonomous movement, not the institutionalized one—tried to make their demand to decriminalize abortion heard. We marched and rallied; we made a petition to have our demands discussed in the National Constituent Assembly; and we delivered reports and proposals. Members of the assembly received our petition, and we were told that a debate about the issue would be opened in the constituent platform. That was back in June and still nothing has happened!

In general, there is little receptivity from those in power, and that is due to the religious baggage of decision-makers. That doesn't just mean their pure, inner religious beliefs but rather their calculations regarding the vote count and how the decision to support decriminalization would impact their personal political careers. Nonetheless, there is a collective effort to decriminalize abortion, and we will be heard!

You referred earlier to a contradictory political situation of women in the Bolivarian Process. On the one hand, during the past twenty years there has been an explosion of women's participation in spaces of local or *barrio* level organization (committees, communal councils, communes, CLAP). On the other hand, the participation of women in higher spheres of politics and power is very limited. For instance, less than one out of every four high government positions (ministers, parliamentarians, constitutional deputies, and governors) is held by a woman. What is going on here?

First, we should make it clear that the expansion of women's participation in public life and political activity in the Bolivarian Process is totally unprecedented. Why is this important? To get a mass of women out of the sphere of domestic labor—out of the private universe and into the sphere of political engagement—that is a big step forward. When women began to participate in communal councils, in social organizations, in committees, when they became engaged in educational missions . . . all that was very important. It was a process of empowerment and [a process of generating] autonomy.

On the other hand, the government has made "feminist socialism" a rallying cry, saying that our revolution has "the face of a woman." At the same time, it emphasizes that women are key to the revolutionary tasks. However, this discourse should be analyzed from a critical perspective, because it turns out that women reproduce gender roles in the context of community participation.

What does this mean? If we fail to insist that male counterparts assume equal responsibility in community participation and care work, then women will be the only ones who organize, who administer the distribution of food in the *barrio*, and who coordinate health care or cleaning projects. The way things are, the role of women as unpaid caretakers is being projected from the domestic, private sphere onto the community level and into the public sphere. This means that our analysis of this phenomenon, which empowers women but also increases their responsibility as caretakers, must incorporate a critical perspective as well.

Additionally, as you mentioned, this flourishing of participation doesn't necessarily mean that women enter decision-making spaces—spaces of real power. A culture of masculine representation prevails. So, for example, even though women are the majority in the PSUV and the majority of those organizing committees and communes, at the end of the day less than one out of every four positions that involve representation or power is held by a woman.

That means that we are not participating in the political sphere in conditions of equality. Also, when we see women in ministerial roles, they don't run strategic areas such as economy or oil. Instead, they end up assigned to areas such as [the Ministries of] Women, Tourism, and Indigenous Peoples that are generally considered less important in our society. (That is not only a cultural conception: if you look at the institutions women run, it turns out they are the ministries with the lowest budgets.)

All this is very important because when women don't hold spaces of power, then our society is failing to recognize our capacities. It is a symbolic message. So, as you can see, in the area of political participation we have much to do. We need to advance so that women participate in decision-making spaces.

In today's world, 70 percent of the poor are women and girls, and the gendered character of poverty gets worse in the Global South. In Venezuela, the weight of the crisis has fallen on the shoulders of women: women are the majority of those standing in long lines,

the ones who feed large families, and women suffer firsthand the critical condition of the medical system.

Indeed, the feminization of poverty is a global phenomenon. This has to heavily weigh on women's economical life. Our society imposes on women alone all the responsibilities regarding life and care work. All that added weight falls on women, who also participate in the productive realm.

Women are often the only ones responsible for the reproductive tasks of nurturing, feeding, and caring. Obviously, no human body can take all that without being affected. This is all the more true in monoparental households with four, five, or six mouths to feed: from children to the elderly to the sick.[3] So we are talking about the singlehanded care of the family and, nowadays, also the care of the community.

What do we observe in Venezuela's profound crisis? The crisis spreads more rapidly in the world of women. You mentioned women standing in long lines to purchase basic goods, but they also search for medications for the sick, bearing the brunt of the healthcare system's deterioration. Since women are the sole caretakers, they are also the ones who have to find solutions if a baby is sick, if a mother needs blood thinners. All this happens in a context where the mere reproduction of life has become more and more complex, and it sinks women into deeper and deeper spirals of poverty.

This means that, even though in Venezuela there has been a wider incorporation of women into formal spaces of labor during the last decade and a half, that participation is now being reduced, as the other responsibilities for care demand more and more time. Therefore precarious labor is also on the rise among women.

We also have to be very clear about the effects of the crisis on the healthcare system. Maternal mortality has risen at an alarming rate. There are some numbers from 2016 that are simply terrible. Since then we haven't had any official data, but everything points to an acceleration [in deaths] of this kind. The increase from 2015 to 2016 is more than 60 percent. In that year [2016], 756 women died during delivery or in the puerperium phase, while the year before we had 457 deaths. As I mentioned, the Ministry of Healthcare has not released official data for 2017 and 2018, but we are quite aware—through news and social media—that the situation is worsening.

There is a further problem, which is access to contraceptives. Contraceptives are simply inaccessible for the majority because of their cost. Today a monthly round of the pill costs 7000 Bolívars, while the minimum wage is 1800 Bolívars. The state does not provide contraceptives, so we find a rapid growth of abortions carried out in precarious and unsanitary conditions. In the end, there are many facets of women's life that are being seriously damaged: from her sexual and reproductive life, to healthcare for her children and for the elderly.

In the last few years, we have witnessed the emergence of a feminist movement that considers itself Chavista, but that is autonomous and attempts to take the government to task on a number of issues. Can you tell us about this?

I have an optimistic reading in this regard. In the past two years, the feminist movement has been growing, with a rich diversity of left-leaning variants, and it is also intergenerational. In the past, feminism in Venezuela was associated with academics or with older women who participated in the earlier waves of mobilization for women's rights. Today, we see the emergence of a younger feminism—a feminism with ties to the world of art and culture, and a pluralistic feminism associated with university students. Additionally, there is a feminism that operates more in the street, through public exhortation rather than through institutions, and that does not seek just limited reforms, as was the case with the hegemonic tendency in the feminist current for a while. In this feminist awakening, we see that many socio-political organizations (which involve both sexes) are beginning to incorporate feminist elements into their programs, and they participate in feminist mobilizations not as individuals, as used to be the case, but as organizations.

Indeed there is an awakening with a special political nature. We are talking about a feminist movement that considers itself to be Chavista; it is anti-capitalist and simultaneously anti-patriarchal, but it also takes the government to task. When I say that it takes the government to task, I mean that the movement supports the government and in particular identifies itself with the popular and communal project of Chavismo, but it is making bigger demands because of its growing strength. All this has happened because after twenty years there are so many areas where we haven't advanced or where we have actually gone backwards. This movement has much to do.

The movement addresses the government in a multidisciplinary way. On the one hand, through the institutions, where demands and requests are filed. On the other hand, proposals are made public, briefs and documents are generated, and there is work in the realm of communication, where we now have at least two television programs addressing gender issues and more than seven feminist radio programs, in addition to websites, etc.

The feminism on the rise is also more and more committed to unity. The feminist movement is growing, and it understands itself as a social movement that supports this socio-historic, political process of great importance. But it isn't afraid to insist that the state and the government do what they must do.

— November 30, 2018

If Socialism Isn't Feminist, It Won't Be Emancipatory: A Conversation with Indhira Libertad Rodríguez

Indhira Libertad Rodríguez is a feminist researcher and sociologist. A member of La Araña Feminista (Feminist Spider network), she does human rights advocacy for women and sexually dissident groups. In this interview, Rodríguez shares with us how feminism intersects with anti-imperialist and anticapitalist struggles. She also discusses the specificity of the feminist struggle in Venezuela and the need for Bolivarian socialism to combat gender oppression.

There are some sectors of the Left that still argue that feminist and gender diversity claims can only be settled in a postcapitalist society and thus shouldn't occupy much of our time now. The current situation, in which we are under attack by imperialism, might seem the best case for this viewpoint, which is nevertheless mistaken. How can we show people the vital links between the anti-imperialist struggle and the antipatriarchal struggle?

There is indeed a tendency that comes from the traditional twentieth-century Left, which puts gender rights and women's struggles aside, apart from what is considered to be the main struggle. The idea is to separate these struggles—our struggles—from anticapitalist or anti-imperialist ones. That was a tradition of the Left in the last century, both in this continent and in the West more generally.

But I'm not sure if it is very strong these days.... What I'm seeing now is a surprising willingness to incorporate our debates. For instance, I have observed that left parties are now forming offices and teams focused on feminist issues, and this has been happening even in communist parties. So I have seen these new openings. And it has all been very interesting to me, precisely because there has been, as you mentioned, a very conservative tradition that descends from the traditional Left.

The truth is that now the Left cannot ignore the feminist Green Tide [the color green is associated with the abortion rights movement in Argentina and elsewhere in Latin America], the "Ni una menos" [not one woman less] movement, or the 8M feminist strike. These movements, which have been massive on a global scale, have forced the Left to question itself. So now the Left has had to think and debate about feminist demands, and it has had to introduce such demands into the emancipatory struggle.

But it is also true that this conservative left tradition has continued in some ways. For that reason, we need to remember that it's not possible for an emancipatory process to succeed if half of the population is not taken into account; or if (even worse) the Left participates in the oppression of that half of the population. Socialism must be feminist. If it isn't, socialism is not going to be liberatory, it won't have an emancipatory character, and it's not going to be socialism.

If we think about it, the struggle against imperialist intervention that is going on right now is an antipatriarchal struggle because imperialism expresses hegemonic masculinity. Imperialist subjectivity actually reflects and reinforces masculine domination.

An anti-imperialist struggle is, by definition, antipatriarchal. The concept of "patriarch," if we go to the original meaning, is the owner of the wife, the children, and the household goods. Yet he also dominates the whole space of the family. The patriarch exercises power and domination not only over women, but also over younger men, and over slaves, of course.

I think it is important to remember this, because precisely in imperialism we find this masculine, patriarchal subjectivity reinforced. Imperialism is power brought together and imposed on those who are weaker, and it is power that is exercised through coercion and violence.

Imperialism also implies the negation of other beings. The process of colonization was exactly that: making other human beings into non-beings. In other words, imperialism erases the condition of humanity from other human beings. It takes that premise to new lengths: imperialism is essentially masculine and patriarchal.

Caribbean societies are often sexist and homophobic, but they are also very flexible and dynamic. Additionally, among the working class, especially in the *barrios*, family organization tends to be matriarchal. How do these specific characteristics of Caribbean society affect the feminist struggle in Venezuela?

Well, I would put things differently. I would say that the Venezuelan family is actually matrilineal (what we find is, in fact, matricentrism [a society organized around the mother]). The concept of matriarchy is not necessarily correct, because a "matriarchal society" would be one in which women would hold a monopoly on power.

If we talk about matriarchy, we might also be talking about an exercise of power from the feminine standpoint. Frankly, we still have to think about how that would be done, what it entails, how it would differ from the patriarchal exercise of power. That means that matriarchy as a conception is "a construction in construction." Also, in this open debate, we must avoid essentialist attitudes regarding the feminine.

This is a patriarchal, *machista*, and androcentric society [dominated by the masculine point of view]. It turns out that one of the most evident features of our revolutionary process in Venezuela is that it put women of spaces of power. That fact, for us, does not mean the end of *machista* organization. Women [occupying] spaces of power guarantees nothing. The best proof of that is the twenty years of the revolutionary process. We find women in decision-making roles, in positions of power, and yet we find that they don't defend our interests from a feminist perspective. That is because they exercise power with the tools at hand and replicate the existing model, based as it is on the exercise of power from the masculine standpoint.

Regarding Caribbean culture, it is indeed tremendously sexist.

However, we could also ask where that's not the case. But it is true, as you point out, that here there are spaces of flexibility, in general and in terms of gender, and that is important.

Now I believe that in Venezuela and in much of the Caribbean, matricentrality is very difficult to overcome. That is because the central role of the mother in our society actually reinforces the patriarchal system. . . . The struggle against this system in a society like ours, and particularly in the popular or *barrio* sectors with their profound matricentric organization, leads to two important problems.

First, as I mentioned before, the mother's role in our society is the reproduction of the [patriarchal] system. That reproduction has no masculine face to represent it; it is apparently a woman's affair. This means, as many class-conscious feminists have observed, that women are the ones who teach in our society, and so it is women who end up transmitting sexist values.

That's not surprising, however, since the mother assumes the role of reproducing society as a whole: she does it because that is the role that the system gives her. Women are oppressed economically and sexually, and additionally, they are assigned the role of transmitting sexist values!

The other component is the identification of woman and mother. In general, this happens throughout Latin America (where, by the way, there is also an identification between woman and nation). That identification makes it very difficult to untangle the web of oppression that affects women and mothers in our society. It includes the fact that we are denied the free development of our personalities, since the only legitimate role for women is being mothers.

Thus, non-mothers are second-class women or aren't exactly women in our society.

Then, there is a second issue that is very particular to the Caribbean. Women here are often forced into the stereotype of "the Atlas woman." That is, the person who can hold the weight of the entire world on her shoulders: the woman who can deal with it all! We are talking about a woman who must work, deal with the house and children, be a community activist, and go to marches. The woman who can do it all!

That may be an extraordinary strength and may reflect the toughness that women from the *barrio* often show. But still, it is not the same as women being in important decision-making spaces in our society.

In Venezuela, there is still much to be done as far as progressive legislation is concerned, especially regarding sexual and reproductive rights and gender diversity issues. Are these struggles making any headway in the constituent process?

It is not going well. The constitutive process is very administered and controlled. The decision-making processes [are not transparent] and there is little possibility that the final text will include feminist claims and the claims of dissident sexualities. So it's not going well.

When the call for the Constituent Assembly went out in 2017, those of us in the Araña Feminista (which is part of the popular feminist movement) organized a big debate in what we called the "Constituent Coven" [*Aquelarre Constituyente*]. The "coven" had two large meetings geared toward making proposals for the new National Constituent Assembly.

Out of those meetings came what I believe to be a beautiful and rich text. That document has a range of proposals for the new Venezuelan constitution, from material to be included in the preamble to a new chapter on sexual and reproductive rights. We also propose to include new economic and social rights, environmental rights, political rights, etc. Really, the document touches upon all aspects of life and politics. That is because feminism today—after three centuries of struggle—has something to say about everything!

And I should add that the Araña Feminista's text is not the only one incorporated in the document. Yet all the varied contributions demand sexual and reproductive rights, the right to adoption by homoparental couples, the legalization of homosexual unions, the right to self-perceived gender identity for trans people, just to mention a few of our key issues.

Nevertheless, I'm not very optimistic about the final text of the new constitution. When it comes out, it will have to be subjected to a popular vote. Then we will see what happens!

As you pointed out earlier, the last twenty years have brought with them an explosion in women's participation in local, territorial organizations. Women often play leading roles in communes, communal councils, and the CLAP. However, women's participation in spaces of power is very limited. What do you make of this contradiction?

If we have matricentric societies, then it makes sense that a revolutionary process aiming to overcome representative democracy will logically bring women into spaces of organization, into spaces of participatory democracy. That is, in fact, what happened here. Women have been the most active organizers at the local, territorial level.

At the same time, the cadres of our revolution are not feminists. It took Hugo Chávez a very long time to connect with the feminist struggle. The first trigger, the event that made him recognize women as subjects, was the 2002 coup, when he saw that it was working women, women of the *pueblo*, who most vigorously demanded his return. They were in the streets and they were ready to fight.

That made Chávez—who as a military person came from one of the most patriarchal institutions—recognize this struggle as legitimate. Also important was the fact that he was accompanied by women such as María León [longtime Communist Party member and former *guerrillera* who became an important colleague of Chávez], who taught him about the feminist struggle. . . . Since Chávez had a great capacity to rectify, to rethink himself, he moved away from the *machista* framework that he had inherited.

That brings us to the 2006 World Social Forum where Chávez declared himself a feminist, and he encouraged Rafael Correa and Evo Morales to declare themselves feminists too. However, that, of course, doesn't mean that all the cadres of the revolution are feminist. Far from it! Proof is the way women's issues are so often dealt with: by making them into mothers' issues, since that is the only role that our society's imaginary assigns to women.

And so, we still have much work to do reflecting and verbalizing who we are as subjects, who we are as protagonists. We must go through a process of self-recognition regarding our roles, who we are as community leaders, who we are as social leaders, and regarding our capacity to really exercise an influence in other spheres.

We also have to break with microsexism and the logic by which one woman is the chief of the UBCh, the CLAP coordinator, the leader on the street level, but then, when the party representative comes to the community, he talks to a guy and not the real community leader. Additionally, we have to wonder how it is that we can be protagonists in the political process, but when we get home, the tasks of reproducing life [homemaking and childcare] are not shared, or that the husband is jealous and violent. Why do these patterns remain?

We must break with all this; we must cease to take over the role of life's reproducers. We must resist and creatively build other roles for ourselves, other paths. In fact, even if this struggle is one that takes place in small quotidian spaces, it must go hand in hand with government policies regarding education and broadcast media. The whole system must be transformed.

In Venezuela, the patriarchal state bureaucracy and the capitalist private sphere tend to co-opt the feminist projects, reducing the struggle to very limited demands, or interpreting them through a simplistic "woman equals love equals mother" framework. How can we fight against this tendency to appropriate and declaw feminism in our context?

In effect, the "woman equals love equals mother" formula has been used to subsume the feminist struggle.... There has been, as Fernando Buen Abad would say, a process of phagocytosis [one cell absorbing another]. Buen Abad talks about symbols being absorbed by modernity, referring to how symbols become spoils in modernity. It could be compared to the process of making the symbols and struggles into a small enterprise, and it has happened particularly with the struggles that the twentieth century Left didn't take into account. I'm talking about the things that the Left excluded, marginalized, or oppressed.

A good example of this kind of co-optation is the emergence [in the United States] of the Pink Market in WASP society: the 1980s phenomenon of integrating gays into society as long as they were consumers. Similarly, there has been a process of co-opting women's demands.

I think we have to be very leery of a feminism based on downloading [hashtags and slogans]. We have to ask ourselves if doing that will strengthen our struggles, or if it is instead about making collective processes invisible.

Here in Venezuela, to struggle against the "woman equals love equals mother" cliché, we need to mobilize on the street and we need our own symbolic production. We have to fight, collectivizing the struggle, collectivizing alternatives, and collectivizing solutions. Those are the tools that the feminist movement has at hand right now.

—April 8, 2019

A Crisis of Social Reproduction in Venezuela: A Conversation with Alba Carosio

Alba Carosio is a longtime feminist writer and activist, and a member of La Araña Feminista. She is the director of the feminist academic journal Revista Venezolana de Estudios de la Mujer, *a researcher at the Centro de Estudios Latinoamericanos Romulo Gallegos, and part of the Latin American and Caribbean Feminisms (CLACSO) work group. In this interview, we talk to her about the global crisis of care and its unique characteristics in Venezuela.*

A new feminist discourse looks at how social reproduction includes both the making of goods and services and the "making of people," which is usually assigned to women. This discourse emphasizes that capitalism depends on the work of nurturing and caring for people but, in a contradictory way, it tends to not remunerate or recognize it. In Venezuela today, reproducing life has become especially difficult, and the weight of this crisis falls largely on the backs of poor women. Do you think there is a crisis of social reproduction in Venezuela? Is it an extension of a global crisis of social reproduction, or is it *sui generis*?

I would say that the reproduction of life is in a critical situation globally. In fact, in the richest countries, there is a direct reproductive crisis due to a set of related phenomena: the disappearance of the classical patriarchal extended family, the decline of the welfare state, and the population's aging. The extended patriarchal family put the burden of care for its vulnerable members (babies, the elderly, and the sick) on women, whom the standard gender mandate identifies as universal caretakers. Extended families, with several generations of women, fulfilled the function of social security. In turn, the parents' rearing of many sons and daughters was their old-age insurance.

Contemporary families are much smaller, often containing only one generation, and they have been reshaped to include women who are now responsible for generating income, having jobs that demand time and commitment. The state, in turn, is meant to be as small as possible, and it offers little in the way of collective care (few institutions offering enough childcare hours, still less for the elderly, and virtually none for the chronically ill or people with severe disabilities). In wealthy countries, as a solution, the care work is transferred to migrant women workers. In fact, this is the reason why migration has become feminized. In the poorest social sectors, the problems aren't solved, and this leads to restricted care or neglect.

In Venezuela, the care situation corresponds to this global pattern but has been exacerbated by a crisis of services and the emigration of young people of productive age. Obviously, caring becomes much more difficult when services such as electricity, water, cooking fuel, and transport are precarious and, on top of it, people's spending power is hugely reduced. All this is made worse by the emigration of young and healthy family members, which makes it common for the sick and aging to find themselves in difficult situations, and for girls and boys to be in the care of their grandmothers.

The number of hours that Venezuelan women are devoting to the basic reproduction of daily life has increased by more than 50 percent during the crisis, with a big impact on their own health and wellbeing. Venezuelan women have always been heroic, but now they are surely the heroines of daily life. The responsibility for sustaining their families' lives falls on them, but recently, on top of that, women have been shouldered with the responsibility of sustaining the life of their communities.

Venezuelan women are the ones who, almost exclusively, take on the unremunerated distribution of CLAP food boxes; they are the ones who get water for their community; the ones who take care of the administrative process to get cooking gas and who report failures of services to UNAMUJER [institution addressing women's issues]; the ones who go from health center to health center, from pharmacy to pharmacy trying to get medicine, etc. All this means more and more hours of work and effort.

The financial sanctions that the United States imposed on Venezuela in August 2017 exacerbated an already existing crisis. What is the impact of these sanctions on social reproduction and the work of caring for families?

U.S. sanctions have aggravated an already difficult situation. Since the electricity blackouts [which happened in March, and were largely due to sabotage], and despite the good intentions of the state Electrical Corporation, there has been electricity rationing in much of the country. These problems persist because of lack of funds to buy the supplies—now more costly because of the blockade—that are needed to strengthen the electrical system. As I mentioned earlier, power outages have a direct impact on caring and social reproduction. The same goes for problems with water, transportation, cooking gas, etc. All this leads to there being less time and fewer resources to care for people. As a consequence, Venezuelan women try to make up for the deteriorating situation with more work and effort

For example, in this moment of history, food preparation has become much more traditional. It often goes from the grinding of corn (which is done in many homes), to making homemade breads, cookies, and cheese, along with other food strategies. A whole set of "alternative" recipes have emerged—no doubt much healthier than the processed foods bought in supermarkets—but they require much more work for the women involved. It's fair to say that things happen this way because men are either absent from home or have not become aware of what co-responsibility implies.

There seems to be something *machista* or at least one-sided in the government's discourse that focuses on creating a "productive

country." **Given the very dire situation we are now in, shouldn't the goal be a more holistic one that encompasses human life itself and the environment? In other words, isn't the problem really about producing life rather than producing commodities and profits?**

I would say that the project of building a productive country is necessary but not sufficient, and here it is even a bit utopian for several reasons.

The "productive country" project is not enough, because simply producing more will not improve the lives of working people, if we do not have a comprehensive approach to taking care of life, and that includes implementing a new system to sustain life and care for it (focused first on those who are most vulnerable). Additionally, all this must happen in environmentally sustainable conditions.

On the other hand, in situations such as ours, where so much time is dedicated to resolving problems of everyday life—with all the hours spent on figuring out transportation, water collection, getting fuel for cooking and looking for food, to say nothing of the time wasted due to blackouts—it is very difficult to increase production. We must acknowledge that time and human energy are finite, and it must be cared for. Human energy must be taken care of and sustained. It is not possible to produce without giving care.

Taking into account the perspective of women would be very useful for restructuring production and social life.

There is a great deal of discussion about how the Bolivarian Process has incorporated women into political life. Certainly, women have been more involved in politics during the last twenty years. In the barrios, they take on the task of organizing the communal councils and the CLAP. However, the *Desde Nosotras* report suggests that the issue is not as simple as it might seem. It turns out that the percentage of men in government positions (ministers, vice ministers, governors, mayors, deputies, etc.) is much higher. We could say that women's participation in political life tends to be relegated to tasks closer to home, and even there women take on responsibilities that are an extension of family care.

Indeed, the political participation of women ends up supporting and being functional to patriarchal patterns of politics. National decisions continue to be most often in the hands of men, and women remain involved in the community and local politics. In other words, it is understood that women participate to solve specific problems—such as the distribution of the CLAP boxes—and men formulate the strategies and decide the overall direction that will be followed by everybody. Women participate politically as an extension of their role as family caregivers, or as support for male leaders.

Venezuelan politics continues to have a patriarchal character, treating women as great universal mothers. I think there is still a long way to go before Venezuelan women are seen differently. For example, among the state governors, only three women were chosen [as candidates] in the last elections. Women who are leaders at the local level are recognized only within those narrow contexts. It is very difficult for women to escape those confines and operate in more general, national spheres [of power]. It seems as if there is a need for women to stay at the local level because someone has to do the hard daily work that political action means at the *barrio* level. They are called to do the work at the local level, but end up being supervised by men who are usually the ones giving the orders and are in the limelight.

With regard to the reproduction of life in a patriarchal society like ours, I want to mention two legal matters that are relevant to feminist struggles in Venezuela. The first is positive: Article 88 of the Constitution recognizes housework as a job, implying the right to social security (although we must note that this article also links housework to women by referring to "housewives"). The other is negative: Venezuela has a legal framework that penalizes abortion. In that sense, it is one of the most regressive legal codes in the continent. How do you reconcile these two aspects?

These are two struggles that have been real battles in the Bolivarian Revolutionary process.

With regard to making good on Article 88 of the Constitution, there have been some attempts to do so. These include Misión

Madres del Barrio [a project that focused on economic support for barrio mothers] and the Misión Amor Mayor [a project giving funds to senior citizens who never contributed to social security], which undoubtedly benefits women who had informal jobs or were exclusively housewives, but there is no specific recognition of the activity of care work in homes.

Nor are their programs based on "co-responsibility" among families, men and women, and the state. Moreover, public policymakers haven't the faintest idea of co-responsibility in this sphere. Even the feminist movement has worked too little on this issue, not pushing enough for it. During the debates on the current Organic Labor Law, there was discussion of caring and the status of care workers, that is, extending the idea of work beyond those tasks that are remunerated. We were not able to get this into the law, which continues to equate work with employment. So there you can see the conception that predominates in Venezuelan society. We continue to think that care work is not work, that it doesn't involve expenditure of energy. Care work is seen as pure love, and the most tragic part of all this is that "Only women love." It is an important debate and an ongoing struggle for feminist movements.

Regarding the interruption of pregnancy, it has not been possible to move forward either. It is precisely in the Constitution where we find one of the most important barriers. It states that "life is protected from conception," "conception" being a religious term and not a biological one. From there, we have been unable to debate the issue, often facing the argument that we are in an electoral year and so abortion is not a subject that can be debated at this time. But the truth is that, even when we are not in an election year, the debate doesn't happen. In the current National Constituent Assembly there is total silence regarding this issue, and there has been no debate or reflection on it, despite the fact that the Women's Rights Commission has the best intentions.

It is indeed a huge contradiction that in a revolutionary process there is no willingness to face the interruption of pregnancy with sincerity and without hypocrisy. The laws on dealing with it still discriminate against women, especially the poorest. There are prejudices but there is also hypocrisy and prudishness. It is a huge challenge for the feminist movement.

— July 19, 2019

Afro-Venezuelan Culture and Resistance: A Conversation with Inés Pérez-Wilke

Inés Pérez-Wilke is an activist and researcher who works on issues of Black and Mestizo cultural production, particularly improvisational performance, from a decolonial perspective. A professor at the Universidad Experimental de las Artes (UNEARTE) in Caracas, Pérez-Wilke has written and published extensively. She is part of the Caracara Research Group (focused on decolonial esthetic mediations) and heads up the Semeruco Investigation Team (focused on improvisational performance). In this interview, we asked her questions about racial identity and Black cultural production in Venezuela.

The Federal Wars in Venezuela, which took place during the nineteenth century, broke down the barriers of the old society and led to a great deal of racial integration. Since then racial issues have not been so decisive in Venezuelan society as they are, for example, in U.S. society. However, that does not mean that there isn't racism in Venezuela. Can you explain how and to what degree racism still organizes this society?

Venezuela's social configuration is more flexible than that of most countries that were once colonies. That means that people of African descent are more integrated into society, and the laws in Venezuela aren't necessarily racist, but the spaces Blacks occupy here are still peripheral ones.

In that sense, Venezuelan society has always had a double standard. There is a discourse of inclusion—ever since the incorporation of *campesinos* and indigenous and Black people in the Independence

Feminism, Gender, and Race 343

Wars and later the Federal Wars—but the opportunities that our society offers to these groups go hand in hand with a double standard.

The double standard is that you have to adapt yourself to the Creole cultural pattern on which the national imaginary has been based since the end of the nineteenth century. . . . Creole culture constitutes a (false) path of social ascension. [The belief is that] the closer you get to that Creole ideal, the more you are going to move from the society's margins to the center, without ever, of course, occupying the center, which is reserved for the power elite!

The double standard leads to a situation in which people of African descent are clearly situated in the spaces where there were formerly slave estates, like the Tuy valleys around Caracas or in Barlovento, where there were plantations producing coffee and cocoa.

If you see a map and think about class relations, you see that racism expresses itself, not in the discourse or the laws, but still, it turns out that indigenous and Black populations are on the cities' margins, in the peripheral spaces that were once *encomiendas* [Spanish colonial system that rewarded European settlers with the labor of particular groups of subject people] and plantations. There you see a clear expression of racism.

That double standard also affects the cultural sphere: our way of speaking, our way of treating the Afro, that zone between care and contempt, between the contemptuous, the comic, and the judgmental. That is the complex space where the race experience has operated in Venezuela.

Barlovento and Tuy are in the outskirts of Caracas, but Caracas itself has a Black urban culture that is quite rich. Can we talk about Black urban culture here, and about urban racialized identities?

Here there is something very important and visible. It's the relation, in urban contexts, between black communities and the rest of the city. There are, on the one hand, ghettos and spaces of coexistence, where there are specific structures, languages, festivals, and calendars; on the other hand, there is the city.

People from Black communities sometimes even say, "I'm going to the city," even if they are already in the city. They are transiting from the mainly Black community to the formally denominated city. Their ways of being in each of the spaces is different. This points to a disputed terrain, which is still important, especially for people of African descent.

I can't see it so clearly among indigenous people. Maybe it exists with some national communities like the Peruvian community or the Colombian community. (However, it happens more with the Afro-Colombian community than the Colombian community in general, which is more mixed into the city.)

So there is a tension that modifies the manner of being of a black person, in his or her community, versus how they move through the so-called city or how they move through the east of the city. The experience of moving and the way of seeing and being seen changes in these contexts. For example, they can be objects of a racist treatment in the city center.

These are things that one sees in relations that happen more or less in the same way in Havana, for example, or in Brazil. . . . The entrance of the Black person from the periphery into the places that are considered "the city" is very clear and evident, fully identified. So here we see how the discourse of the non-existence of racism is belied in a physical sense.

There is a racist tendency in Venezuela's political right wing. How is it connected to the history and structures that you are talking about?

Of course, one of the things that President Hugo Chávez did was to make the racial issue visible. The double standard here produces a situation that is very different from what people experience in English-speaking societies, where there is clearly a racialized policy and that explicit racism allows one to organize a struggle directly against it. It doesn't mean that that system is better, but it does allow you to make the debate clearly and publicly.

The double standard here makes things more difficult because when a person, militant, or group takes up the theme of racism, it is often perceived as if it were merely a fantasy. It appears to be just an invention of that group. So one of the things that Chávez's discourse did was to make [the existence of racism] explicit and visible. It made explicit the power relations that, in fact, exist regarding access to means and goods, to education, to territorial occupation for Black people over the course of our long history.

Chávez's discourse allowed us to express, propose, and make visible the links between the question of class and the issue of race. For that reason, the popular base that identifies with a racial minority sees itself reflected in the discourse. It makes that discourse its own, because formerly there had been a kind of interdiction or prohibition. The prohibition operated by means of the mechanism of the double constraint in which there is an oppression but it seems like a fantasy. So you can't speak of it. Once it's made explicit, you can take part in that political discourse: you can make it your tool in the struggle.

You have claimed that cultural diversity, if it includes political, intellectual, and social dimensions (and is not merely seen as folklore), can be a revolutionary force. Can you explain this to us?

I think that the main problem is that modernity and the capitalist world have been built on a categorical framework, on a way of seeing reality. It is the way that we have been discovering and denouncing that is really narrow, unfair, and unequal.

When I say that cultural diversity offers revolutionary potential to us, I am basing that claim on the fact that in each of our cultures and ancestral peoples there is knowledge. There are proposals about how to see the world, nature, and life that offer alternatives to modernity and capitalism. They have a great deal of potential.

Yet to acquire a profound understanding of those epistemological proposals, you have to take them seriously. Quite often, however, the place that is given to cultural diversity is the place of folklore or of conserving traditions. There is a profound lack of knowledge about their functional contents: the knowledge and technology that form part of a culture. (I refer to technology in the ample sense not only of tools for working with nature but also technology of thinking and of curing and other forms of knowledge that we can compare to scientific knowledge and have a great deal of transformative potential.)

So if you have a profound familiarity with African, Yoruba, or indigenous traditions . . . well, there you would find knowledge of biodiversity, of relations with animals, of productive technologies on many levels, links between the spiritual and the material, and radically different teaching forms. These are things that are revolutionary. They operate to directly open up, to denounce and demonstrate the limited nature of the strategies that modernity offers.

You have claimed that there is a mobile and plural space of popular urban creation in Venezuela in which the contributions of the African diaspora dominate. Why is that the case?

In urban communities, which are made by exodus of waves of *campesinos* to the cities, Black and popular immigration has been concentrated in certain sectors. There, they constitute a force, a political and social force that is clearly identifiable.

If we think of Caracas, the Black population is concentrated in centers such as San Agustín del Sur, La Vega, Pinto Salinas, and Petare. What's more, the people there organize themselves. They have generated mechanisms of organization, of self-recognition based on the African cultural patterns. The forms of struggle they deploy against the social decomposition that results from drug trafficking, violence, alienation, and endoracism have to do with seizing hold of their African roots and cultural narratives to generate activities and organizational structures—which are based on, for example, festivals or foods—to respond to urban forces that tend to dominate not only African cultural patterns but also other heritages. (The city is a very modern apparatus that efficiently erases any political force that is not useful to it.)

The practices of the African diaspora have a greater visibility and have more evident resistance than other cultural patterns [here], because they bring themselves together around a cultural pattern as a mechanism for confronting [the urban environment] and creating mechanisms of social dialogue.

The interpretation one uses depends on the framework from which one sees things. That interpretation will determine if we understand improvisation, orality, or marginalization as stigmas—as they are seen in modern society—or if they will be seen as cultural elements and community strategies that go with certain concrete aims that work for society. Everything will depend on that conceptual framework from which you read things. For that reason, you have to do a reading from other frameworks of thought to be able to advance here.

Take the case of the comparison between the oral mechanisms of transmission of knowledge and the written ones. Leaving aside the hierarchies set by academia and by publishers about non-written knowledge, it is indeed very hard for academic thought to address social processes. It gets bogged down in these contexts. It is backward and has problems getting away from pre-written texts to adapt itself to new social realities.

By contrast, oral processes, working with the most ordinary elements, can continually absorb and update knowledge, incorporating new facts that are being developed in real time, even second by second. You can see it in festivals: when people sing or improvise *decimas* [a ten-line song format used in the Cruz de Mayo festival], they incorporate what is happening at that very moment, or they refer to what has happened in the course of the year. They work on that material right there for the community. In these practices, you can see the potential of oral culture to process reality.

Marginality is more difficult to analyze in a positive sense. Yet one of the things that one finds when one works with marginalized populations of a society is how, for sure, the privileged center has more access to resources that the state administers, but to the same degree they have mechanisms of social control. They control especially the middle classes, who have codes of behavior, clothing, consumption, and discourses that are very closed and preestablished.

The elite are freer from this. They have spaces of liberty. However, among marginal groups there are also spaces of freedom. They are outside of the focus, and they have the possibility to be creative. "Gordo Edgar" [Edgar Antonio Pérez, a committed libertarian militant from the La Vega barrio in Caracas, whom we also interviewed] said a few days ago that everything new was invented by poor people, by the marginal classes. Later, what they invented is captured, coopted, and used by other people, who turn it into a commodity.

Can you tell us more about improvisation and how it operates in popular culture?

When I speak of improvisation, I am thinking in part about rituals among the African diaspora, where there are generally agreed-upon codes. An example is the "Velorio de la Cruz de Mayo" [religious-cultural Mestizo festival in honor to the cross, which is adorned with flowers], where they sing a kind of music that is typical of Barlovento that is called the *fulía* [musical style that is played with a string instrument, maracas and drum plus vocals]. The *fulía* has a basic chorus that is repeated and everyone knows it in the festival. There are moments for soloists that are four strophes and have a rhyming relation with the basic strophes.

In the *fulía* festival, all who want to participate in this form of improvised expression can participate freely. Everybody sings in front of a cross. They make an arch in front of the cross, and everyone who incorporates him or herself in the arch can improvise a strophe for that *fulía*, using some very simple codes so that everybody can take part. Normally there is a token—it could be a flower or an instrument—which is passed [from one person to another]. The one who sings is whoever has the instrument. . . .

So there is a whole apparatus that is prepared in advance, but it is all geared for the participation of everybody in an improvised way. Everyone who takes part using codes that are very simple brings a new perspective, generating a reinterpretation of what is happening in the present. It could be a re-interpretation of the community, of the person herself, or of life. In these events, it often happens that many themes are discussed: gender, race, history. Perhaps there could be a discussion about barrio gangsters. Using song forms, people improvise on themes that concern the community.

As I see it, improvisation is an apparatus for collective creation that allows one to deal with themes that are important, or forms that are important, or questions of the community, based on simple structures that allow everyone to participate.

Cedric Robinson, in his book *Black Marxism*, points out that despite the participation of black people in most of the rebellions and revolutions in Venezuelan history, they never projected a future African or Black state, as happened elsewhere in the continent. Instead, Black people, poor whites, mulattos, and indigenous people joined together in a broad class struggle. Is it true that this tendency toward integration into class struggle persists in Venezuelan society today?

I think the discussion about *mestizaje* [cultural mixing] in Venezuela—and that has developed elsewhere in Latin America as well—is important. It's related to the discussion of the Creole cultural pattern. Indeed, there has been a wager for homogenization and an erasure of Black struggle through the nationalist discourse and the discourse of the Creole and the Mestizo [mixed race person].

Yet Black and indigenous social movements have been critical of the *mestizaje* discourse, pointing out how it tends to put the national or Mestizo culture above problems, stories, and situations that might relate to indigenous groups (such as Yukpa or Piora) or might relate to the Blacks from Aragua (who face very specific problems).

However, it's also true that in Venezuela the dynamic of racial interchange and *mestizaje* has been much stronger than in other areas of the continent. That is a reality, and the struggles that have existed are very racially mixed. So it is a bit difficult, a bit unrealistic, to project a Black or indigenous state in Venezuela.

I think what must be put forth is an intercultural state. The struggles have to be directed toward building a state that is fully intercultural, with a view to really understanding, respecting, and valuing other categorical frameworks.

In this moment, there are parallel struggles taking place. The Black movements and communities are leading—and it is a very powerful movement—their own struggles with regard to recognition of

Black culture in the Constitution. With regard to education, there has been a process of incorporating the discourse of blackness, negritude, maroonage, etc., and thought given to how we interpret those terms. It's necessary to make visible such cultural issues and the same goes for themes of indigenous culture.

However, with regard to the project of the state, there must be an effort to bring together all those efforts. There must be a space for everything to come together, a space for sharing and discussing a multiplicity of tendencies.

— May 24, 2019

Notes to Section 6

1. The hard data in this interview comes out of the *Desde Nosotras* report. That document relies on information from different sources, some governmental, some based on field research, and some from international institutions such as the Committee on the Elimination of Discrimination Against Women (CEDAW).
2. Venezuela has a maternal mortality rate of 95 women dead for every 100,000 births, which is well above the continental average of 69 per 100,000 births.
3. Four out of ten households in Venezuela are monoparental (female). These households are far more likely to enter the statistics of extreme poverty.

Index

abortion rights, 321–22; under Article 88, of Bolivarian Constitution, 339–41; *see also* contraceptive and reproductive rights
Abrams, Elliott, 261
Adams, John Quincy, 262
Adeco, 255n1
adjustment extractivism, 134
Admirable Campesino March, 179–80, 222–30, 247–48, 275–77; Bolivarian Campesino Agenda and, 225–28; Chavismo and, 229–30; despotic patrimonialism and, 229–30; El Maizal Commune and, 237; origins of, 222–25; revolutionary bourgeoisie and, 229–30; violence against *campesinos* and, 223–24; working class in, 251–52
Adriani, Alberto, 94
African Diaspora, 346–48
Afro-Venezuelan culture, 342–50; African Diaspora and, 346–48; class struggle and, integration into, 349–50; Creole culture, 343; cultural diversity as revolutionary force, 345–46; improvisation of rituals in, 348–49; on *mestizaje* discourse, 349; oral transmission of, 347;

racialized identities, 343–44; racism of Right movements and, 344–45; in urban communities, 346–48
agency, of citizens: Chavismo and, 21–22; in revolutionary processes, 13–15
agrarian communes: direct democracy in, 53–54; revolution in, 211–13; *see also* El Maizal Commune
agrarian revolution, Bolivarian Process and, 240–41
agriculture: *see* food-agriculture systems
agro-ecological farmers, organization of, 217
Agropatria, 49–52, 223; decentralization of, 225; land reorganization through, 207–8; nationalization of, 51
Alayo, Andrés, 238–48
Alexis Vive Collective, 25
Alexis Vive Patriotic Force: Longa in, 39–47; Marín in, 31; organization of, 40; organization of production in, 33; Panalitos por la Patria and, 33; radicalization of, 44–45; 23 de Enero *barrio* and, 31, 33, 39
Aló Presidente Teórico N° 1

Index

(speech), 65–66, 169; popular power in, 65
Alternative Bolivarian Agenda, 191, 195
Altos de Lídice Commune, 71, 76
Amatina Pioneros Encampment, 85
Antillano, Andrés, 21, 28n2, 297–305
Argentina: Pinochet dictatorship in, 285–86; Urban Revolution in, 79
Asambleas de Barrio (Barrio Assemblies), 79–80, 161–62
assassinations, political: of campesinos, 246; of Chávez, 282, 295–96; of Guevara, 286
autonomy, 175–76

bachaqueros (people who resell goods), 301–2, 314n2
Bandera Roja, 159, 188, 259
Baran, Paul, 294
Barquisimeto, Venezuela, barrios of, 55
Barrío Adentro initiative, 71
barrios, barrio dwellers and: Asambleas de Barrio, 79–80, 161–62; of Barquisimeto, 55; of Caracas, 55; criminalization of, in media, 37–38; Movimiento de Pobladoras y Pobladores and, 77–88; proletarization of, 42, 89n7; of Valencia, 55; see also specific barrios
Basque Country campaign, 76
Basque independentist movement: Bolivarian Process, 41–43; popular power elements during, 41–43
Benjamin, Walter, 24

Betancourt, Carlos, 259; see also Bandera Roja
Betancourt, José Luis, 239
Bettelheim, Charles, 22, 289–90
bio-power, 220–21
Black Marxism (Robinson), 349–50
blackouts, in 23 de Enero barrio, 35–36
Blue Book (Chávez), 17, 65–66, 68, 190–92
Bolívar, Simon, 26, 151–53, 166, 260, 293–94; Communal City project, 212–13; historical legacy of, 152–53, 266–67; as member of oligarchical class, 185; on Meridional America, 262; property rights under, 267; see also Bolivarian Process; Bolivarian Revolution
Bolivar and Zamora Revolutionary Current (CRBZ), 205, 213; campesinos in, 211–13
Bolivarian Campesino Agenda, 225–28; development of, 225
Bolivarian Constitution, 256n15; Article 88, 339–41; oil industry under, 103–9; women's rights in, 317–19
Bolivarian Process, 14–16; agrarian revolution as result of, 240–41; Basque independentist movement and, 41–43; Chavismo and, re-orientation of, 58–61; communes and, 43; crisis of, 192–94; as democratic, 114–15; Dietrich on, 40; economic rights of women as element of, 317–19; European Union intervention in, 75; female participation in, 322–23;

international solidarity with, 74–76, 312–13; Kohan and, 285; land reorganization under, legal framework for, 205–6; leadership of, 281–83; Maduro on, 81; Marxism and, 291; Movimiento de Pobladoras y Pobladores during, 78–81; peasant farmers' movement in, 275–77; people's role in, 9; privatization of industry and production and, 114–15; public debate over, 9; realist reformism in, 281–83; redistribution of land resources, 87–88; Rothe on, 185–86; unity of Latin America as goal of, 186, 201n2; U.S. intervention in, 75, 262; women in, 317–19, 322–23, 338–39

Bolivarian Revolution: alternatives to, 25–27; *campesinos* during, 209–11, 252; Chávez and, 39–40; direct democracy as core of, 65; failures of, 152; indigenous populations and, 129; Land Law and, 238–39; Leftists as leaders in, 171–72; limitations of, 152; multiple origins of, 186; new power structure as result of, 187; participatory democracy as core of, 65; political goals of, 37, 195; privatization of industry and production and, 72, 74; *pueblo* and, historical role of, 69, 74; as response to crisis, 17; Rojas on, 68–70; in rural regions, 207–8; self-government as core of, 65; socialism as goal of, 32; territorial self-government and, 169; Twenty-First Century Socialism and, 184

Bolivarian Socialist Workers Confederation (CBST), 253–54
Bolivarianism, as political ideology, 279; Left movements and, 180–81
Bolivian Circles, 37–38
Bolsonaro, Jair, 263, 270–72
Bourdieu, Pierre, 298
bourgeoisie: *see* revolutionary bourgeoisie
Bravo, Douglas, 161
Brazil: fascism in, 270–72; investment in Venezuela oil industry, 110; Landless Workers Movement in, 264; Real Plan in, 137
Britto García, Luis, 266–69
Brown, John, 156
Budgetary Finance System, 289
Buen Abad, Fernando, 333
Bukharin, Nikolai, 289

Cabello, Diosdado, 247
Caldera, Rafael, 125–26, 139, 159
Calloni, Stella, 285
Campesino Struggle Platform, 238–48
campesinos (rural citizens), 45, 238–48; assassinations of, 246; in Barinas State, 209; in Bolivar and Zamora Revolutionary Current, 211–13; in Bolivarian Revolution, 209–11, 252; combative history of, 206; credit for, 242–45; criminalization of, 73–74, 227–28; Crop to Crop Sowing Plan, 246–47; Development Zones for, 226; Ezequiel Zamora Campesino Front, 240; investment for, 242–45; judicial persecution of,

246; landless, 211; in Landless Workers Movement, 264; in El Maizal Commune, 54–55; Mestizo culture and, 227; militia of, development of, 228–29; murders of, 209–11; National Anti-Kidnapping and Extortion Command and, 50–51; organization of, 209–11; Orinoco Mining Arc and, 129; Peasants Struggle Platform, 252; Plataforma de Lucha Campesina and, 245–48; in Pueblo a Pueblo initiative, 59–60; return of land to, 246; self-organization of, 48–49; as social element in Venezuelan society, 275–76; unity of, 276; violence against, 223–24; as wage workers, 241–42; war against, 206; *see also* Admirable Campesino March; peasant farmers

campo, capitalism in, restoration of, 10

capital: hierarchical logic of, 17; Mészáros on, 17

capitalism: crony, 114; industrial, 104; pro-capitalist tendencies in government, 17; productive, 94; rentier, 87, 94–95, 103, 132; as social formation, 153–54; working class and, 185–86; *see also* neoliberal capitalism

capitalism, restoration of, in *campo*, 10

Capriles, Colette, 220–21

Caracas, Venezuela, *barrios* of, 55

Caracazo insurrection, 158–59, 264–65

CARBONORCA, 255–9

Cargill (food distribution corporation), 220

Caribbean society: Community of Latin American and Caribbean States, 295, 314n3; Economic Commission for Latin America and the Caribbean, 196; feminism in, 329–31

Carosio, Alba, 335–41

Carpentier, Alejo, 198–99

Castro, Fidel, 45, 285; Cuban Missile Crisis and, 261; Guevara and, 261; Russian coup against, 293; Soviet Union and, political alliance with, 293

Castro Soteldo, Wilmar, 68, 115

Central Bank of Venezuela (BCV), 139

Chávez, Hugo, 17, 68, 190–92; *Aló Presidente Teórico N° 1* (speech), 65–66, 169; Alternative Bolivarian Agenda, 191, 195; assassination of, 282, 295–96; Barrio Adentro initiative, 71; Bolivarian Revolution and, 39–40; on centralization of power, 57–58; "Commune or Nothing," 44, 55, 164, 169; communes and, 15, 31–32, 36, 163; on direct democracy, promotion of, 192; economic policy under, 102–3; Enabling Act under, 36; ethics of, as political ideal, 45–46; feminist struggles and, personal connection with, 332–33; *Golpe de Timón*, 16; *Homeland Plan* (2012), 67, 73, 87, 90n18, 169; illness of, 242–45; Land and Agricultural Development Law under, 205, 207; Left movement under, relaunch of, 154–55; Marxism-Leninism and, 164; MBR-200 movement, 188; morals of, as political ideal, 45–46; myths about, as strongman, 19; nationalization of Agropatria under, 51; oil industry under, 99; organization of *campesinos* under, 48; Orinoco Mining Arc under, 125–28; El Panal commune and, 39–40; on participatory democracy, 15, 40, 53–54; Patriotic Circles and, 189, 192; peace initiatives by, 9; Pérez, Edgar, on, 158–67; political coups against, 19, 39, 256n16; political insurrection by, 259; political legacy of, 183–85; on political mechanisms of socialism, 66; popular political movements before, 158–61; on popular power, 57–58; as populist, 21; Prado on, 67–70; on protagonist democracy, 40; public response to, 162–64; reorganization of Venezuelan society under, 9; Revolutionary Armed Forces of Colombia (FARC), peace initiatives with, 19; revolutionary movement created by, 162–64; revolutionary processes promoted by, 15, 183; socialism for, as political philosophy, 15, 21, 26, 171–73; *Strike at the Helm* (speech), 65–67, 70, 72, 169; as symbol of ethics ideal, 45; on territorial socialism, 171–73; "third way", 19; 23 de Enero *barrio* support for, 9; El Valle *barrio* support for, 9; *see also* economic development and policy

The Chávez Hypothesis (Gilbert), 151

Chavismo: abortion rights and, 321–22; Admirable Campesino March and, 229–30; Bolivarian Process and, re-orientation of, 58–61; citizen agency as foundation of, 21–22; class composition of, 189–90; communal councils and, 192; communal production as element of, 21; communes and, 16–17, 58–61; communication between leadership and citizens and, 20; contemporary applications of, 70–71; contradictions of, 74–76; cooperatives and, 58–61; declining participation in, 171–73; direct democracy and, 56–58; diversity of, 190; economic autonomy and, 58; during economic crisis, 303–5; electoral losses for, 305; elements of, 20–21; feminism and, 58–61, 325–26; formations of, 188–89; González Plessman on, 25; Grajales on, 56–61; at grassroots level, 180–81; hegemonic historiography of, 177–78; imperialism and, 194–96; institutional and state power through, 56–58; internal dynamics of, 20–21; Left movements and, 180–81; longterm survival of, as political mechanism, 70–71; in El Maizal Commune, 55; Movimiento de Pobladoras y Pobladores and, 80–83; oil industry and, 99; popular protagonsim as

element of, 56–58; as populist movement, 16; privatization of industry and production and, 71–73, 111–13; Right political movements and, 272; Rojas on, 64–67, 70–71; state-owned factories and, 236–37; territoriality in, 89n5; women in, 219–20; workers councils and, 58–61; Zapatismo compared to, 21
Chavismo Savage (Iturriza), 177–81
Chavistas: *see* Chavismo
children, during economic crisis, 219–20
Chile: Movimiento de Pobladoras y Pobladores in, 78–79; Urban Revolution in, 79
Chiliying Commune, 33, 89n2
China: Chiliying Commune, 33, 89n2; investment in Venezuela oil industry, 110; as model of Marxism, 291–94; neoliberalism in, 127; state-owned factories in, 235–36, 256n13
Chirino, José Leonardo, 260
Christian Democratic Party (COPEI) party, 252n2
citizens: agency of, 12–15, 22; in Chavismo movement, 22; role in revolutionary processes, 14–15
Citizens' Assembly, in El Maizal Commune, 53–55
civil society, materialism of, 154
CLAP, 61–62, 90n17, 170–71, 302–3; communal councils and, 171; food distribution through, 216, 220–21; Maduro support for, 171; women in, 322–23, 332–33

class struggle: Afro-Venezuelan culture and, integration of, 349–50; historical component of, 153; in revolutionary processes, 22–24; in rural regions, 209, 277–78; for working class, 153
class-conscious internationalism, 20
clientelism, 52; in Venezuela, 82, 165
colectivos (grassroots organizations), 37–38; criminalization of, 38
Colombia: demobilization of paramilitaries, 206; National Liberation Army (ELN), 264; in North Atlantic Treaty Organization, 279–81; reactionary Right in, 280; Revolutionary Armed Forces of Colombia (FARC), 280; Venezuela and, international relations with, 280–81
colonialism. colonization and: decolonization, 166–67; indigenous populations and, 129; Non-Aligned Movement and, 307
comedores popular (people's canteen), 34
Comités de Tierra Urbana (CTU), 77–81, 84–85
Communal City project, 212–13
communal councils: Chavismo and, 192. CLAP and, 171; construction of, 9–10; democratic control of production process in, 17; nationwide elections of, 170; organization of, 40; self-liberation as influence on, 164; women in, 322–23, 332–33
communal economy, 195

Communal Federation, 41
Communal Parliament, 53–54
"Commune or Nothing," 44, 55, 164
communes: Altos de Lídice Commune, 71, 76; Bolivarian Process and, 43; Chávez and, 15, 31–32, 36, 163; Chavismo and, 16–17, 58–61; Chiliying Commune, 33, 89n2; Citizens' Assembly in, 53; *comedores popular* in, 34; in Communal Federation, 41; construction of, 9–10; as counter-hegemonic spaces, 32–33; economic reorganization of society through, 31–33; government pigeonholing of, 43–44; as historical subject, 32; Maduro on, 37; El Maizal, 17, 46–55; *see also* El Maizal Commune; Marín on, 31–38; Negro Primero, 46–47; under Organic Law of the Communes, 33, 90n16; El Panal, 17, 33–34, 39–43; Paris Commune, 40; participatory democracy in, 34, 44; political discourse in, 37–38; political reorganization of society through, 31–33; popular power dynamics in, 36–37; privatization of land and, 52–53; protagonist democracy in, 44; Pueblo a Pueblo initiative in, 35; resistance to imperialist aggression in, 34–35; self-defense in, 36–37; self-determination processes in, 36–37, 42; self-government in, 32, 36–37; self-liberation as influence on, 164; separation processes in, 33; socialism and, 16–17; as space of resistance, 31–33; technology transfer in, 43–44; work collectives in, 34; *see also* communal councils; *specific communes*
communication between leadership and citizens: Chavismo and, 20; institutional variants in, 20
Communist Manifesto (Marx and Engels), 306
Communist Party of Venezuela (PCV), 249, 252–53, 256n14
Community of Latin American and Caribbean States (CELAC), 295, 314n3
comuneros (residents of communes), 32
Confederation of Venezuelan Workers (CTV), 256n16
constitutions: *see* Bolivarian Constitution
consumption patterns, 214–16
contraceptive and reproductive rights, for women, 324–25; in Venezuela, 331
Contreras, Juan, 21, 259–65
conuquero, 255n5
cooperatives, Chavismo and, 58–61
Copeyano, 252n2
CORPIVENSA initiative, 234, 255n10
corporate mining: Gold Reserve, 131; Orinoco Mining Arc and, 130–31; Yankuang Group, 131
Correa, Rafael, 332
corruption, 52, 169–71; Rojas on, 68
cosmic race, 183
counter-revolutions, revolutionary processes influenced by, 14

Index

coups, political: against Castro, 293; against Chávez, 19, 39, 256n16; by Guaidó, 17; against Maduro, 268–69
Creole culture, 343
criminalization: of *barrios*, in media, 37–38; of *campesinos*, 73–74
crisis, in Venezuela: Bolivarian Revolution and, 17; causes of, 100–101; daily life during, 197–200; economic, 116–17; Left solutions to, 283–84; macroeconomic solutions to, 105–6; National Constituent Assembly as response to, 17; street protests during, increase of, 199–200
crony capitalism, 114
Crop to Crop Sowing Plan, 246–47
Cruz Villegas Class Conscious Current of Workers, 256n14
cryptocurrency, Petro as, 100–102, 123–24, 141–42
Cuba: class struggle in, 22; currencies in, 102; microfaction in, 293; in Non-Aligned Movement, 293; revolution in, 293; Soviet Union and, political alliance with, 293; U.S. missile crisis in, 261, 293
cultural diversity, 345–46
currency, in Venezuela: anchoring of, 100–102, 250–51; DICOM exchange rate, 138; dollarization of, 143; economic development influenced by, 116; exchange rates, 100–101, 138–39, 142–43; under Illicit Exchange Law, 142; liberalization of exchange market, 123, 141; under Maduro, 100; mining farms for, 146; oil industry production as influence on, 100–102; Orinoco Mining Arc and, 132; Petro cryptocurrency, 100–102, 123–24; under Plan Real, 102; private sector and, 116; scarcity of, economic crisis influenced by, 117–18; Sovereign Bolivar, 100–102, 137–38, 142–44

The Darker Nations (Prashad), 306
decolonization, 166–67; indigenous peoples and, 166
democracy: in Bolivarian Process, 114–15; Rojas on, as integral element of revolution, 68–69; Venezuelan transition to, 156, 240–41; *see also* direct democracy; participatory democracy; protagonist democracy
Democratic Action (AD) party, 255n1
Deng Xiaoping, 289
Desde Nosotras, 317, 338–39, 351n1
despotic patrimonialism, 229–30
developmentalism, Orinoco Mining Arc and, 127
DICOM (currency auction), 138
dictatorships, 201n3–4; Guevara on, 47
Dietrich, Heinz, 40
direct democracy: in agrarian communes, 53–54; Bolivarian Revolution and, 65; Chavismo and, 56–58; in reorganization of society, 10; in *Strike at the Helm* speech, 65–66
Dos Santos, Jessica, 197–200
Dunayevskaya, Raya, 186–87

Duque, Iván, 263, 279–81; Havana agreements and, 280
Dussel, Enrique, 41, 228–29; on decolonization, 166

economic crisis, in Venezuela, 116–24, 297–305; anchoring of currency during, 250–51; *bachaqueros* and, 301–2; Chavismo during, 303–5; children affected during, 219–20; currency scarcity and, 117–18; Economic Recovery Plan and, 118–21, 136–40; emigration and, 249–50; 15 y Ultimo on, 145–46; global economy influenced by, 122; governmental instability as result of, 309–12; healthcare system impacted by, 324–25; induced shortages, 117; inflation during, 249–50; Lácteos Los Andes, 121; liberalization of currency exchange market, 123; under Maduro, 117; national debts and, 117–18; politically-driven causes of, 117–18; socialism as solution to, 123; solutions to, 122–24; women affected by, 219–20, 317–26; women during, 317–26; *see also* women; working class during, 249–50
economic development and policy: anti-inflationary policies, 140; Chavismo and, economic autonomy through, 58; communes and, reorganization of society through, 31–33; currency issues and, 116; cycles of, 103–5; Economic Recovery Plan, 118–21, 136–40; exchange rates, flexibility of, 141; Fifteen Motors Plan, 147; 15 y Ultimo on, 135–36; Gavazut on, 116–24; hyperinflation and, 140; implementation strategies for, 144–45; as informal, 28n2; methodological approach to, 136; monetary lobotomy and, 140–41; under Organic Law for the Development and Promotion of the Communal Economy, 90n16; private investment as element of, 119–21; as reactive, 140–44; regional, 146; in rentier economy, 87, 93–96, 103, 122, 145; sectors for, 28n2; under socialism, 102–3; as solution to social crises, 105–6; tourism development, 144–45; U.S. corporations role in, 122; *see also* capitalism; oil industry; privatization
economic imperialism: through global commodity chains, 308; international solidarity influenced by, 308–9; of U.S., towards Venezuela, 18, 28n2, 308–9
economic independence: Chavismo and, 58; socialism and, 32
Economic Recovery Plan: currency anchoring strategies in, 136–38; electrical infrastructure in, 146–47; hyperinflation and, 136; inflation theory and, 118–19; monetary reconversion and, 136–37; oil industry as focus of, 146–47; Petro and, 137–38; price policies under,

137; private investment incentives under, 119–21; public announcements of, by Maduro, 137–40; Sovereign Bolivar and, 137–38; state-owned factories under, 232
economic rights, for women, 317–19; under Article 88, of Bolivarian Constitution, 339–41
economic sanctions, against Venezuela: financial blockades as, 101; social reproduction influenced by, 337
Ecuador, 133
Eisenhower, Dwight, 294
electrical infrastructure: in Economic Recovery Plan, 146–47; sabotage of, 145
emigration, 249–50
Empresas de Producción Social (Social Production Enterprises), 148n3
Enabling Act, Venezuela, 36
Encuentra de Lucha Popular movement, 188
Engels, Frederick, 23, 83, 306
environmental impact studies, on Orinoco Mining Arc, lack of, 128
Escalante, Anibal, 293
Escalona, Julio, 42, 270–78
Escuela de Cuadros, 151
ethical ideals: Castro as influence on, 45; Chávez as influence on, 45–46; communal construction as, 46–47
European Union, Bolivarian Process and, interventionism in, 75
Eusse, Pedro, 249–54, 256n14; *see also* working class

Exclusive Zones of Communal Production, 89, 89n9
extractivist model: adjustment, 134; Orinoco Mining Arc and, 127, 131–34; Yasuni National Park and, 133
extreme Right political movement: in U.S., 156; in Venezuela, 156, 170
Ezequiel Zamora Campesino Front, 240

farmers: agro-ecological, organization of, 217; *see also* peasant farmers
fascism: in Brazil, 270–72; definition of, 296; in Germany, 271–72; international struggle against, 285–96; in Latin America, resurgence of, 270–72; National Constituent Assembly and, 273–75; in Spanish state, 156; uribismo, 255n4; voluntarist politics and, 156
FEDECAMARAS, 252n3
FEDELAFAS, 252n3
Federal Wars, 206, 342–43
Felicien, Ana, 214–21; Semillas del Pueblo and, 214, 216–18
feminism: in Caribbean societies, 329–31; Chávez and, personal connection with, 332–33; Chavismo and, 58–61, 325–26; Green Tide, 328; imperialism and, 327–29; Left movements and, 327–29; patriarchy, 328–29, 333–34; in post-capitalist society, 327–29; in revolutionary processes, 26; social reproduction and, 335–41; socialism and, 322, 327–34

Fifteen Motors Plan, 147
15 y Ultimo collective, 135–36, 145–46
Fifth Republic Movement (MVR), 188–89
Figueroa, Amilcar, 279–84
Fishing Law, Venezuela, 238–39
FONDAS, 208
food distribution: Agropatria, 49–50; Cargill, 220; through CLAP, 216, 220–21; *comedores popular* and, 34; Polar, 220; Pueblo a Pueblo initiative, 25; Semillas del Pueblo and, 214, 216–18; *see also* food-agriculture systems
food shortages, 28n2; protests over, 199–200
food sovereignty, 207, 219
food-agriculture systems, 214–21; bio-power and, 220–21; consumption patterns and, 214–16; during economic crisis, 214–16; food sovereignty and, 219; public policy and, 219; reconnection to biocultural base, 219; under socialism, 218–19
foreign investment: under Law of Foreign Investment, 108–9, 120; in oil industry, 109–11
4F insurrection, 158
Fourth Republic, 37–38, 68, 297–300
The Fragrance of Guava (García Márquez), 198
France: *gilets jaunes* movement in, 20; Paris Commune, 40
Free from Transgenics campaign, 216–17
Fukuyama, Francis, 154
"Full Oil Sovereignty," 109

Gaddafi, Muammar, 291
Galeano, Eduardo, 166
Gapon, Georgy, 155
Garcés, Marina, 23
García, Kender, 210
García Linera, Álvaro, 36, 42
García Márquez, Gabriel, 198
Gavazut, Luis Enrique, 116–24; on Economic Recovery Plan, 118–21; *see also* economic crisis; economic development and policy
La Gaviota (state-owned fish-processing plant), 233–34
gender diversity issues, 331
gender violence, against women, 319–21
General Agreement on Trade and Tariffs, 309
German Ideology (Marx and Engels), 23
Germany, fascism in, 271–72
Gilbert, Chris, 151–57; on creative political discourse, emergence of, 155–57
gilets jaunes movement, in France, 20
global commodity chains, 308
global Left: criticism of, 20; hypercorrect idealism of, 25–26; materialism of, 25–26
Global North, mining operations in, 131–33
Global South, 83; international solidarity in, 306–7; mining operations in, 131–33; poverty rates in, for women, 323–25
Gold Reserve (mining company), 131
Golpe de Timón, 16
González Plessman, Antonio,

21, 168–76; on Chavismo, 25; on Pink Tide, 174–76; in SurGentes Collective, 56, 168, 173–74
Grajales, Martha Lía, 21, 25, 56–63; on Chavismo, 56–61; on CLAP, 61–62, 90n17; on popular power, 57–58; in Surgentes Collective, 56; on UBCh, 61–62, 90n17; in Unidos San Agustín Convive cooperative, 56, 62–63
Gramsci, Antonio, 292
Gran Misión Vivienda Venezuela (GMVV), 85–88, 168–71; Amatina Pioneros Encampment, 85
Green Tide, 328
Guaicaipuro, 260
Guaidó, Juan, 73, 198; declaration as president, 259–60; political coups, 17
guarimberos (violent right-wing protesters), 245, 252
guerrilla insurgencies, 158–59
Guevara, Che, 42, 285; assassination of, 286; Budgetary Finance System, 289–90; Castro and, 261; on principles of dictatorships, 47; Soviet Union and, political alliance with, 293
Guyanese Mining Arc, 126; *see also* Orinoco Mining Arc

"Hands Off Venezuela," 20
Hegel, Georg W. F., 154
hegemony: in Bolivarian Revolution, 69–70; in *pueblo*, construction of, 69; Rojas on, 73–74; of social property, 72; U.S., 267–68
Hernández, Alejo, 244

hoarding, 143n2
Homeland Plan (2012), 67, 73, 87, 90n18, 169
housing, redistribution of: Gran Misión Vivienda Venezuela and, 85–88; Pink Tide and, 86; for workers, 83; *see also* Movimiento de Pobladoras y Pobladores
housing cooperative movement: in Uruguay, 79; *see also* Movimiento de Inquilinos; Movimiento de Pobladoras y Pobladores
Huberman, Leo, 294
human rights: abortion rights, 321–22; contraceptive and reproductive rights, for women, 324–25; economic rights, for women, 317–19; gender violence against women, 319–21; for women, in Venezuela, 317–19
Hussein, Saddam, 291
Hydrocarbons Law, Venezuela, 238–39
hyperinflation, 17, 101, 140; Economic Recovery Plan and, 136

illegal mining, 130
Illicit Exchange Law, Venezuela, 142
imperialism: appropriation of resources under, 16; Chavismo and, 194–96; economic: *see* economic imperialism; feminism and, 327–29; international solidarity influenced by, 308–9; as patriarchal, 328–29; Pink Tide and, 285–88; resistance to, in

communes, 34–35; revolutionary processes against, 15–16; by the Triad and, 308
income distribution: under Maduro, 272–73; in Venezuela, 194
Independence Wars, 206, 238, 342–43
indigenous populations: Bolivarian Revolution and, 129; colonization as influence on, 129; decolonization and, 166; Orinoco Mining Arc and, 128–30; Yekuana people, 129
Indonesia, Non-Aligned Movement and, 307
industrial capitalism, 104
inflation, 249–50
insurgent movements: *see* guerrilla insurgencies
intellectuals: in Left movements, 175; state power and, 23
International Assembly of the Peoples, 314n1
international law: Orinoco Mining Arc under, 128; *see also* internationalism
international solidarity, 306–13; with Bolivarian Process, 74–76, 312–13; Non-Aligned Movement and, 306–7; South-South solidarity, 306–7; U.S. imperialism and, 308–9
internationalism: class-conscious, 20; New International Economic Order, 307; promotion of, 186–87; Russian Revolution and, 307
interventionist policies: of EU, in Bolivarian Process, 75; of U.S., 75, 260–64, 310–11

Iran-Contra Affair, 261
Iturriza, Reinaldo, 21, 177–81

Japan, 308
Jaua, Elías, 21, 188–96; in Fifth Republic Movement, 188–89
Joint Services Agreements, in oil industry, 108–11, 113
Joint Ventures schemes, 109–10, 148n6

Khrushchev, Nikita, 293
Kissinger, Henry, 286–87
Kohan, Néstor, 285–96; Bolivarian Process and, support of, 285; *see also* Marxism
Kropotkin, Pyotr, 163
Kudlow, Larry, 144

Lácteos Los Andes (state dairy enterprise), 121
Lago, Licino, 239
Land and Agricultural Development Law, Venezuela (2001), 205, 207, 238–41, 255n6
Land Institute (INTI), 208, 223, 238
land ownership: under Bolivarian Process, redistribution mechanisms of, 87–88; Movimiento de Pobladoras y Pobladores and, 77–88; in urban areas, 80
land reorganization: through Agropatria, 207–8; under Bolivarian Process, legal framework for, 205–6; food sovereignty as goal of, 207; under Land and Agricultural Development Law, 205; land tenure, 205–6; Venezuelan Agrarian Federation, 207; *see also campesinos*

Landless Workers Movement (MST), 264
Lara (state), 48, 90n13; see also El Maizal Commune
Latin America: Community of Latin American and Caribbean States, 295, 314n3; Economic Commission for Latin America and the Caribbean, 196; fascism in, resurgence of, 270–72; MERCOSUR, 295, 314n4; Patria Grande and, 186, 201n2; unity of, as goal of Bolivarian Process, 186, 201n2; see also Pink Tide; *specific countries*
Law of Foreign Investment, Venezuela, 108–9, 120
leadership, political: communication with public, 18–20; "third way," 19
Left movements: Bolivarian government and, 180–81; Bolivarian Revolution and, 171–72; Chavismo and, 180–81; feminism and, 327–29; intellectuals in, 175; politics ignored by, 153–54; popular movements and, 164–66, rentier economies and, 169; Venezuela crisis solved through, 283–84; Zapatismo, 21, 154
Left Revolutionary Movement (MIR), 270
Lenin, Vladimir, 155, 163; Marxism-Leninism and, 164, 289, 299; on revolutionary theory, 44; on taking of power, 42
Leninism: see Marxism-Leninism
León, Jesús, 223
León, María, 332
Letelier, Orlando, 286

libertadores, 89n4
Lih, Lars T., 155
Longa, Robert, 21; in Alexis Vive Patriotic Force, 39–47; in El Panal Commune, 39–43; see also El Panal commune
Lukács, Georg, 22
Luxemburg, Rosa, 299

Macri, Mauricio, 139, 263
"Madrugonazo al hampa," 303
Maduro, Nicolás: on Bolivarian Process, 81; on CLAP, as expression of popular power, 171; on communes, 37; communication with citizens and, disconnection in, 19; Communist Party of Venezuela and, 252–53; criminalization of *campesinos* under, 73–74; currency issues under, 100; economic crisis under, 117; Economic Recovery Plan of, 118–21, 136–40, 232; see also Economic Recovery Plan; government stability under, 17; income increases under, 272–73; international criticism of, 266; oil industry and, 93–94; political coup against, 268–69; as political tyrant, 291; presidential address on national crisis, 198; regional economic development strategies, 146; self-organization of *campesinos* under, 49; United Socialist Party of Venezuela and, 51–52, 90n14, 170, 178–79; see also economic development and policy
Magdoff, Harry, 294
El Maizal Commune, 17, 46–55, 90n13, 194; Admirable

Campesino March and, 237; Agropatria and, 49–52; *campesino* initiative in, 54–55; Chavismo in, 55; Citizens' Assembly in, 53–55; communal democracy in, 53–54; Communal Parliament in, 53–54; cultivation of land in, 48; as expression of popular power, 171–73; international influences on, 76; National Anti-Kidnapping and Extortion Command in, 49–52; participatory democracy in, 54–55; populism in, 179–80
Majano, Hugo, 108–15
Mandel, Ernest, 290
Maneiro, Alfredo, 161
Mantovani, Emiliano Teran, 125–34; *see also* Orinoco Mining Arc
Mao Zedong, 24
Mareno, Maikel, 246
Mariátegui, José Carlos, 285
Marín, Anacaona, 21, 25; in Alexis Vive Patriotic Force, 31; on *colectivos*, 37–38; on communes, 31–38; on imperialist aggression, 34–35; on popular power dynamics, 36–37; on Pueblo a Pueblo initiative, 35
market socialism, 289
Maroon settlements, 166
Martí, José, 183
Martínez Heredia, Fernando, 21
Marulanda, Manuel, 285
Marx, Karl, 23, 306; on materialism of civil society, 154; *see also* Marxism-Leninism
Marxism, 285–96; Bolivarian Process and, 291; in Bolshevik Russia, 289; China and, 291–94; as political identity, 290; stages of, 289–90
Marxism-Leninism, 164, 289, 299
materialism, of global Left, 25–26
Mazzeo, Miguel, 58
media: Altos de Lídice Commune in, 71; criminalization of *barrio* citizens in, 37–38
Medina Angarita, Isías, 104
Mella, Julio Antonio, 285
Mendoza, Lorenzo, 44–45, 89n10, 282
Mendoza Potellá, Carlos, 93–99; *see also* oil industry
MERCOSUR, 295, 314n4
Mészáros, István, 17, 85–86
mestizaje discourse, 349
Mestizo culture, 227
methodological approach, to Venezuela political development, 10
military Keynesianism, 294
military-industrial complex, 294
mining operations: corporate, 130–31; in Global North, 131–33; in Global South, 131–33; Gold Reserve, 131; illegal, 130; Yankuang Group, 131; *see also* Orinoco Mining Arc
Miranda, Francisco de, 260
missile crisis: U.S., in Cuba, 261, 293; in Venezuela, 259–65
monetary lobotomy, 140–41
Monroe Doctrine, 262–63
moral ideals: Castro as influence on, 45; Chávez as influence on, 45–46
Morales, Evo, 332
Mota, Gioconda, 317–26
Movimiento de Inquilinos (anti-eviction movement), 78

Movimiento de Ocupantes de Edificios Organizados (vacant building occupiers movement), 78
Movimiento de Pobladoras y Pobladores (Settlers' Movement), 77–88; during Bolivarian Process, 78–81; Chavismo and, 80–83; in Chile, 78–79; Comités de Tierra Urbana and, 77–81, 84–85; as expression of popular power, 171–73; goals of, 82–84; occupation of urban spaces in, 84–86; *Pioneros* and, 84–86; right to the city model and, 83; roots of, 78–81; self-managed initiatives as part of, 81–82; as socialism at local level, 84; Urban Revolution and, 78–83
Movimiento de Trabajadoras Residenciales (Residential Workers Movement), 77

National Anti-Kidnapping and Extortion Command (CONAS), 49–52; *campesinos* and, 50–51
National Constituent Assembly (ANC), 142, 273–75; popular movements and, 168–71
National Constitutional Assembly, 148n4
national debt, economic crisis and, 117–18
National Front of Struggle of the Working Class (FNLCT), 249, 251, 256n14
National Guard, National Anti-Kidnapping and Extortion Command, 49–52

National Liberation Army (ELN), 264
National Liberation Front, El Salvador (FMLN), 279
National Productive Alliance, 211–13
National Security Doctrine: development of, 286–87; goals and purpose of, 287
nationalization of industry, 196; Requeno on, 231–32; *see also* state-owned factories
Negri, Antonio, 41
Negro Primero Commune, 46–47
neo-industrialization, 102–3
neoliberal capitalism, revolutionary processes and, 15
neoliberalism: in China, 127; rejection of, 160; social rebellions as response to, 288; territorialization and, 148n7; in Venezuela, 148n7, 160; working class and, 185–86; Zapatista rebellion and, 288
New International Economic Order, 307
Non-Aligned Movement, 293; colonialism and, 307; Indonesia and, 307; international solidarity and, 306–7
North Atlantic Treaty Organization (NATO), 279–81

oil industry, in Venezuela: under Bolivarian Constitution, 108–9; Brazil investment in, 110; under Chávez, 99; Chavismo and, 99, 111–13; Chinese investment in, 110; corporate model for, 113–14; currency issues influenced by, 100–102; decentralization of,

113; decreases in production, 98, 112; economic cycles influenced by, 103–4; in Economic Recovery Plan, 146–47; exploration and development of, 94–95; foreign investment in, privatization and, 109–11; "Full Oil Sovereignty" and, 109; international oil sales, 96–97; under Joint Services Agreements, 108–11, 113; Joint Ventures schemes and, 109–10; under Law of Foreign Investment, 108–9; legal framework for, 113–14; Maduro on, 93–94; oil reserves, 28n1; Open Oilfield policy and, 108–9; Orinoco Belt, 96–99, 109–10; Petrozamora, 112; privatization of, 97–99, 108–15, 148n5; reinvestment in, 95–96; rentierism and, 93–96; reorganization of society as result of, 94; as resource curse, 93; social programs funded by, 95–96; Southern Procurement Services, 113; Strategic Associations and, 113; "Venezuela effect," 93

Open Oilfield policy, 108–9

Operation Condor, 285–88; assassination of Guevara, 286; contemporary applications of, 288–90; detention centers as part of, 286; Kissinger and, 286–87; National Security Doctrine and, 286–87; as reaction to 1960s social rebellion, 287–88

opportunism, revolutionary processes and, 15

Organic Law for Social Auditing, Venezuela (2010), 90n16

Organic Law for the Development and Promotion of the Communal Economy, Venezuela (2010), 90n16

Organic Law of Popular and Public Planning, Venezuela (2010), 90n16

Organic Law of Popular Power, Venezuela (2010), 53, 90n16

Organic Law of the Communes, Venezuela (2010), 33, 90n16

Organization of Revolutionaries (OR), 270

Orinoco Belt, oil industry and, 96–99, 109–10

Orinoco Mining Arc, 125–35; actors in, 130–31; *campesino* culture and, 129; Chávez and, 125–28; democratic ratification of, 128–30; developmentalism as element of, 127; environmental impact studies on, lack of, 128; extractivist model and, as reformulation of, 127, 131–34; formalization of, 127; hard currency issues with, 132; historical development of, 125–26; indigenous populations and, 128–30; international corporate involvement in, 130–31; international law and, 128; non-mining industries affected by, 133; profit distribution and, 132–33; public information on, access to, 133–34; as regime of exception, 127–28; rentier capitalism and, 132; Special Economic Zones and, 127; taxation and, 132–33; territorialization and, 126–27; Yekuana people and, 129; zoning of, 127–28

Ortega, Arbonia, 222–30; see also Admirable Campesino March
Ortiz, Jean, 90n14

Paddio, Martin, 11
El Panal commune, 17, 25, 33–34, 39–43; Chávez and, 39–40; communal construction as ethical ideal, 46–47; development of, 41; expansion of, 41; as expression of popular power, 171–73; organization of production in, 33; *panalitos*, 41; see also Alexis Vive Collective
Panalitos por la Patria (Beehives for the Homeland), 33
Paris Commune, 40, 186
Parra, Reyes, 224
participatory democracy: Bolivarian Revolution and, 65; Chávez on, 15, 40, 53–54; in communes, 34; in El Maizal Commune, 54–55; Prado on, 53–54; property in, 72; revolutionary processes for, 15
Partido Socialista Unido de Venezuela (United Socialist Party of Venezuela), 9
Party of the Venezuelan Revolution (PRV), 159, 279
Pascual Marquina, Cira, 18, 20, 24
Patria Grande (unity of Latin America), 186, 201n2
patriarchy, feminism and, 328–29, 333–34
patrimonialism: see despotic patrimonialism
Patriotic Circles, 189, 192
patronage, 175–76
PDVSA (state oil company), 289
peasant farmers: Admirable Campesino March and, 179–80; in Bolivarian Process, 275–77
Peasants Struggle Platform, 252
Pedro Camejo (state agricultural company), 225
Pérez, Edgar ('Gordo Edgar"), 158–67, 347
Pérez Arcay, Jacinto, 89n8
Pérez Jimenéz, Marcos, 201n3–4
Pérez-Wilke, Inês, 342–50
Petro (currency): anchoring of, 136–38; as cryptocurrency, 100–102, 123–24, 141–42
Petro, Gustavo, 281
Petrozamora (firm), 112
Pink Tide, in Latin America, 23–24; housing redistribution strategies and, 86; Operation Condor and, 285–88; public analysis of, 174–76; U.S. imperialism and, 285–88
Pinochet, Augusto, 285–86
Pioneros (pioneers), 84–36
Plan de la Patria, 195
Plan Real, 102
Plataforma de Lucha Campesina, 245–48
Polar (food distribution corporation), 220
popular movements: in cities, 158–59; Encuentro de Lucha Popular movement, 188; guerrilla insurgencies, 158–59; Landless Workers Movement, 264; the Left and, 164–66; Movimiento de Inquilinos, 78; Movimiento de Ocupantes de Edificios Organizados, 78; Movimiento de Trabajadoras Residenciales, 77; National Constituent Assembly and, 168–71;

Non-Aligned Movement, 293; social inclusion as goal of, 169; see also Movimiento de Pobladoras y Pobladores
popular power: in Aló Presidente Teórico N° 1, 65; in commune model, 41–42; Grajales on, 57–58; under Organic Law of Popular Power, 53, 90n16; self-defense and, 36–37, 41–43; self-determination and, 36–37, 41–43; self-government and, 32, 36–37, 41–43
popular protagonism, Chavismo and, 56–58
Popular Struggle Committee (CLP), 159
populism: in "backward" countries, 177; in El Maizal Commune, 179–80; in rural areas, 179–80; see also Chavismo
populist movements: Chávez as leader of, 21; see also Chavismo; specific movements
Portugal, Revolutions of the Carnations in, 186
Portuguesa (state), 48, 90n13; see also El Maizal Commune
Posada Carriles, Luis, 286
poverty: in Global South, 323–25; women and, rates for, 323–25, 351n3
power: Lenin on taking of, 42; see also popular power
Prado, Angel, 21, 48–55, 90n14–15; Agropatria and, 49–52; on National Anti-Kidnapping and Extortion Command, 49–52; on participatory democracy, 53–54; on privatization of land, 52–53; on use of Chávez political philosophy, 67–70; see also El Maizal Commune
Prashad, Vijay, 306–12; see also international solidarity
Preobrazhensky, Yevgeni, 289
Primera, Alí, 226
prison population, expansion of, 298–300; "Madrugonazo al hampa" and, 303
prisons, as crime factories, 303
privatization, of industry and production: Bolivarian Process and, 114–15; Bolivarian Revolution and, 72, 74; Chavismo and, 71–73, 111–13; corporate model for, 113–14; justification for, 111–12; legal framework for, 113–14; of oil industry, 97–99, 108–15; as public, 114; socialism and, 62–63, 102–3; in *Strike at the Helm* speech, 72
privatization of land, 52–53; see also land ownership
production process: in communes, 17; Exclusive Zones of Communal Production, 89n9
productive capitalism, 94
Productive Workers' Army, 25, 171–73, 232–33, 236–37
Productive Workers' Councils (CTP), 235, 255n12
profit distribution, with Orinoco Mining Arc, 132–33
proletarization, of *barrios*, 42, 89n7
property: hegemony of, 72; under participatory democracy, 72; see also land ownership; privatization of land
property rights: under Bolívar,

267; under General Agreement on Trade and Tariffs, 309
protagonist democracy, 40; in communes, 44
public health initiatives, Barrio Adentro initiative, 71
pueblo: during Bolivarian Revolution, historical role of, 69, 74; as center of revolutionary process, 301–2; hegemony in, construction of, 69; as political enemy, 301–2
Pueblo a Pueblo food distribution initiative, 25, 194; *campesinos* in, 59–60; in communes, 35; Marín on, 35; in San Agustín del Sur *barrio*, 168; Unidos San Agustín Convive cooperative and, 63
Punto Fijo Pact, 178, 201n3

Quevedo, Manuel, 111

racialized identities, in Afro-Venezuelan culture, 343–44
racism, in Right political movements, 344–45
Ramírez, Kléber, 161
Rangel, Kevin, 205–13; Bolivar and Zamora Revolutionary Current and, 205
Reagan, Ronald, 260
Real Plan, in Brazil, 137
realist reformism, 281–83
recovered farmstead, 255n6
reformism: realist, 281–83; revolutionary processes and, 15
reformist pragmatism, in revolutionary processes, 14–15
rentier capitalism, 87, 94–95, 103; Orinoco Mining Arc and, 132

rentier economy: capitalism in, 87, 94–95, 103; distribution of rents in, 94; Leftist model and, 169; oil industry and, 93–96; Venezuela as, 87, 93–96, 103, 122, 145
rents, distribution of, 94
reorganization, of society: under Chávez, 9; direct democracy in, 10; economic, through communes, 31–33; oil industry development as influence on, 94; political, through communes, 31–33
reproductive rights: *see* contraceptive and reproductive rights
Requeno, Sergio, 25; on state-owned factories, 231–37
resource curse, 93; *see also* "Venezuela effect"
Revolutionary Armed Forces of Colombia (FARC), 280; peace initiatives with, 19
revolutionary bourgeoisie, 73–74, 229–30, 255n7
Revolutionary Organization Party (OR), 159
revolutionary processes: as change of epoch, 23; through class struggle, 22–24; counterrevolutions as influence on, 14; in Cuba, 22; dialectic in, 25; enemies of, 13; feminism in, 26; human agency in, 13–14; against imperialism, 15–16; as internationalist, 186; Lenin on, 44; maintenance of, 24; neoliberal capitalism and, 15; opportunism and, 15; participatory democracy as goal of, 15; Pink Tide, in Latin America,

23–24; reformism and, 15; reformist pragmatism in, 14–15; Russian Revolution, 185; as social rupture, 22; socialism as goal of, 15; societal convergences in, 14–16; in Soviet Union, 22; *see also* Bolivarian Process
Revolution of the Carnations, in Portugal, 186
Ribas, Tomás, 244
Right political movements: Afro-Venezuelan culture and, racism against, 344–45; Chavismo and, 272; Punto Fijo Pact, 178: *see* extreme Right political movement
right to the city model, 83
Robinson, Cedric, 349–50
Rodríguez, Carlos Rafael, 289–90
Rodríguez, Félix, 286
Rodríguez, Indhira Libertad, 327–34; *see also* feminism
Rodríguez, Simón, 152, 166
Rojas, Gerardo: on Bolivarian Revolution, 68–70; on Chavismo, 64–67, 70–71; on corrupt political system, 68; on democracy, as integral element of revolution, 68–69; on hegemonic sectors of government, 73–74; on *Homeland Plan*, 67; on international solidarity with Bolivarian Process, 74–76; on privatization of industry and production, 71–73; on *pueblo*, historical role of, 69, 74; on *Strike at the Helm* speech, 65–67, 70; Voces Urgentes and, 64
Rothe, Eduardo, 182–87; on Bolivarian Process, 185–86; on promotion of internationalism, 186–87
rural regions: class struggles in, 209, 277–78; populism in, 179–80; *see also campesinos*; El Maizal Commune; *specific states*
Russia, as model of Marxism, 291–94
Russian Revolution, 185; internationalism and, 307

Salas, Luis, 21, 100–107, 135–47, 148n2; 15 y Ultimo collective, 135–36, 145–46; *see also* crisis, in Venezuela; economic development and policy
Saleh, Lorent, 46, 89n12
Sandino, César Augusto, 210
San Agustín del Sur *barrio*, 62–63; Pueblo a Pueblo project in, 168
San Martín, José de, 293
Sankara, Thomas, 312
School Alimentation Plan, 234
self-defense, 41–43; in communes, 36–37
self-determination, 41–43; in communes, 36–37, 42
self-government, 41–43; Bolivarian Revolution and, 65; in communes, 32, 36–37
Semillas del Pueblo (People's Seeds), 214; coordination with state institutions, 218; Free from Transgenics campaign, 216–17; goals of, 216
Sieveres, Gerardo, 222–30; *see also* Admirable Campesino March
Simón Planas township, 48–49, 90n14
smuggling goods, 148n2
social economy, 195

Index

social programs, oil industry as source of funding for, 95–96
social reproduction, crisis of: economic sanctions as influence on, 337; feminism and, 335–41; productive country and, 337–38
socialism: Bolivarian Revolution for, 32; Bolivarian Socialist Workers Confederation, 253–54; Chávez and, as political philosophy, 15, 21, 26, 66, 171–73; communes and, 16–17; economic crisis solved through, 123; economic emancipation and, 32; economic policy under, 102–3; feminism and, 322, 327–34; food-agriculture systems under, 218–19; intellectual defense of, 22; market, 289; Movimiento de Pobladoras y Pobladores as, at local level, 84; neo-industrialization and, 102–3; Partido Socialista Unido de Venezuela, 9; political mechanisms of, 66; privatization as alternative to, 62–63, 102–3; revolutionary processes for, 15; self-government and, 32; stagnation in, 22–23; territorial, 171–73; Twenty-First Century Socialism, 42, 45, 288–89; United Socialist Party of Venezuela, 51–52; in U.S., 42; working class and, 249–50; *see also* communal councils; communes
Socialist League, 159, 270
solidarity: *See* international solidarity
Soteldo, Wilmar Castro, 255n7
Southern Procurement Services (SPS), 113

Sovereign Bolívar (currency), 100–102, 137–39; de-Bolívarization, 143–44; devaluation of, 138, 142; exchange rates for, 138–39, 142–43; liquidity of, 142
Soviet Union: Castro alliance with, 293; class struggle in, 22; Guevara and, political alliance with, 293
Spanish state: fascist political parties in, 156; political transition in, 201n1; Venezuela independence from, 182–83
Special Economic Zones, Orinoco Mining Arc and, 127
state violence, 297–305; through police oppression, 297–98
state-owned factories, 231–37; Chavismo and, 236–37; Chinese model for, 235–36, 256n13; under CORPIVENSA initiative, 234, 255n10; under Economic Recovery Plan, 232; La Gaviota, 233–34; Productive Workers' Army and, 232–33, 236; Productive Workers' Councils and, 235, 255n12; recovery of, 233–34
Strategic Associations, oil industry and, 113
Strike at the Helm (speech), 65–67, 70, 72, 169
Sucre, Antonio José de, 260
Sur del Lago (Zulia state), 179–80; violence in, 210
SurGentes Collective, 56, 168, 173–74
Suwandi, Intan, 11
Sweezy, Paul, 294
taxation, taxes and, Orinoco Mining Arc and, 132–33

technology transfer, in communes, 43–44
territorial socialism, 171–73
territorialization: Bolivarian Revolution and, 169; neoliberalism and, 148n7; Orinoco Mining Arc and, 126–27
"third way," 19
The Thought of the Liberator (Britto García), 267
Toledo, Guillermo, 223
tourism, development of, 144–45
trade agreements: through MERCOSUR, 295, 314n4; between Venezuela and U.S., 215
the Triad, 308–9; *see also* European Union; Japan; United States
Trotsky, Leon, 155
Trump, Donald, 260
Turner, Nat, 156
Twenty-First Century Socialism, 42, 45, 288–89; Bolivarian Revolution and, 184
23 de Enero *barrio*: Alexis Vive Patriotic Force and, 31, 33, 39; blackouts in, 35–36; *colectivos* in, 37–38; coup against Chávez and, community response to, 9

UBCh (Bolívar-Chávez Battle Units), 61–62, 90n17
Unidos San Agustín Convive cooperative, 56; female participation in, 62; Pueblo a Pueblo initiative and, 63; remobilization strategies of, 63; repoliticization strategies of, 63
Unitary Framework Agreement, 253

United Nations (UN): Economic Commission for Latin America and the Caribbean (CEPAL), 196; Venezuela recognized by, 82
United Socialist Party of Venezuela (PSUV), 51–52, 90n14, 170, 178–79, 213, 253; Chavismo and, 179
United States (U.S.): Bolivarian Process and, interventionism in, 75, 262; corporate role in, 122; economic imperialism of, 18; economic sanctions against Venezuela, 337; economic warfare by, 17–18; extreme Right in, 156; hegemonic policies of, 267–68; interventionist policies of, 75, 260–64, 310–11; Iran-Contra Affair, 261; Monroe Doctrine, 262–63; National Security Doctrine and, 286–87; Operation Condor, 285–88; seizure of Venezuelan resources, 294–96; trade agreements with Venezuela, 215; 21st Century socialism in, 42; white supremacism in, 156
Urban Land Committee, 168–71
Urban Revolution, 78–83; in Argentina, 79; in Chile, 79; in Venezuela, 78–81
uribismo, 255n4
Uruguay, housing co-ops in, 79
Uslar Pietri, Arturo, 95, 104, 110

Valencia, Venezuela, *barrios* of, 55
El Valle *barrio*, coup against Chávez and, community response to, 9
Vargas, Hernan: ALBA Movement and, 77; Comités de Tierra

Urbana and, 77–78; Movimiento de Pobladoras y Pobladores and, 77–88; *see also* Movimiento de Pobladoras y Pobladores; Movimiento de Trabajadoras Residenciales and, 77
La Vega *barrio*, 158
Venezuela: active borders for, 276; Afro-Venezuelan culture, 342–50; brain drain from, 105–6; class struggle in, 153; clientelist practices in, 82, 165; Colombia and, international relations with, 280–81; communication between leadership and people in, 18–20; corruption in, 52, 169–71; creative discourse in, emergence of, 155–57; currency: *see* currency; democracy in, transition to, 156, 240–41; economic imperialism towards, by U.S., 18, 28n2; *see also* economic imperialism; imperialism; Enabling Act, 36; extreme Right political movement in, 156, 170; Federal Wars, 206, 342–43; Fishing Law, 238–39; Fourth Republic, 37–38, 68, 297–300; gender diversity issues in, 331; "Hands Off Venezuela," 20; human rights in, for women, 317; Hydrocarbons Law, 238–39; Illicit Exchange Law, 142; income distribution in, 194; independence from Spanish rule, 182–83; Independence Wars, 206, 238, 342–43; institutions in, 165; Land and Agricultural Development Law, 205, 207, 238–41, 235n6; Law of Foreign Investment, 108–9, 120; malaria incidence rates in, 130; oil industry in: *see* oil industry; Organic Law for Social Auditing, 90n16; Organic Law for the Development and Promotion of the Communal Economy, Venezuela, 90n16; Organic Law of Popular and Public Planning, 90n16; Organic Law of Popular Power, 53, 90n16; Organic Law of the Communes, 90n16; political development in, methodological approach to, 10; prison population in, growth of, 298–99; productive capitalism in, 94; as rentier economy, 87, 93–96, 103, 122, 145; reorganization of society in, 9, 94; reproductive rights in, 331; revolutionary history of, 151–53, 158–61, 182–83; sovereignty of, 20; trade agreements with U.S., 215; UN recognition of, 82; U.S. and: *see* United States; U.S. economic imperialism and, 18, 28n2, 308–9; U.S seizure of resources, 294–96; *see also* Bolivarian Process; Bolivarian Revolution; Chávez, Hugo; crisis; economic development and policy; Maduro, Nicolás
"Venezuela effect," 93
Venezuelan Agrarian Federation, 207
Vicente Gómez, Juan, 131
voluntarist politics, fascism and, 156
Walter Benjamin in Venezuela (Gilbert), 151
white supremacism, in U.S., 156

women: abortion rights, 321–22; in Bolivarian Process, 317–19, 322–23, 338–39; in Chavismo movement, 219–20; in CLAP, 322–23, 332–33; in communal councils, 322–23, 332–33; contraceptive and reproductive rights for, 324–25; in Desde Nosotras, 317, 338–39, 351n1; during economic crisis, 219–20, 317–26; economic rights for, 317–19, 339–41; gender violence against, 319–21; human rights issues for, 317; poverty rates for, 323–25, 351n3; right to violence-free life for, 317–19; in Unidos San Agustín Convive cooperative, 62; *see also* feminism
work collectives, in communes, 34
workers councils, Chavismo and, 58–61
working class: Admirable Campesino March and, 251–52; Bolivarian Socialist Workers Confederation, 253–54; capitalism and, 185–86; Cruz Villegas Class Conscious Current of Workers, 256n14; development and rise of, 249–54; during economic crisis, 249–50; formation of, 153; National Front of Struggle of the Working Class, 249, 251, 256n14; neoliberalism and, 185–86; social protest by, 251–52; socialism and, 249–50
World Health Organization, 130
Wuytack, Francisco, 159

Yankuang Group (mining company), 131
Yasuni National Park (Ecuador), 133
Yates, Michael, 11
Yekuana people, 129

Zamora, Ezequiel, 151–52, 206, 238, 240, 260
Zamora Takes Caracas March, 223
Zapatismo: Chavismo compared to, 21; rejection of state politics and, 154
Zapatista rebellion, 288, 295